Everything You Must Know When
BUILDING YOUR
COUNTRY HOME

By Homer Emery, Ph.D.

HOME PLANNERS
TUCSON, ARIZONA

728.37
EME

International Standard Book Number: 1-881955-71-0
Library of Congress Catalog Card Number: 00-134178
Home Planners, LLC,
wholly owned by Hanley-Wood, LLC
Tucson, Arizona 85741

10 9 8 7 6 5 4 3 2 1

Book design by Paul Fitzgerald
Cover photo by Tim Becker, Creative Images
For a similar house plan, see page 162

Acknowledgments and Dedication

Without the help and encouragement of my wife, Florence and our three sons, completing this project would not have been possible. Their patience and understanding in putting up with a "Sanitarian-in-the-House" for more than thirty years is greatly appreciated.

Without the help of the Home Planners editorial staff this publication would have been just another book on the shelf. The talents and skills of Paul Fitzgerald in layout and visual design are apparent on every page. A special thanks goes to Paulette Mulvin, Editor, for her editing skills, timely reminders and helpful suggestions.

This book is dedicated to Rurel Warren, Glen Early, Rex Netherton and other Professional Sanitarians who advised countless rural homeowners on the construction of safe water supplies and on-site sewage disposal systems long before there was an EPA and the environmental movement of the 1970s.

TABLE OF CONTENTS

1 CHAPTER 1: INTRODUCTION
   A brief overview of the history of the migration from city to country life.

13 CHAPTER 2: NIGHTMARES TO AVOID
   A photo essay of rural dream homes that turned into nightmares.

25 CHAPTER 3: PICTURE PERFECT
   A photo essay of rural homes that turned out right.

35 CHAPTER 4: YOUR NEXT STEP
   Finding the right site and contractor.

73 CHAPTER 5: WATER SUPPLY SYSTEMS FOR RURAL SITES
   How to choose and install water wells.

123 CHAPTER 6: ON-SITE SEWAGE DISPOSAL FOR RURAL SITES
   How to choose and install on-site sewage disposal systems.

153 CHAPTER 7: COUNTRY HOMES YOU CAN BUILD
   A gallery of homes with blueprints available separately to build in the country.

192 APPENDIX ONE
197 APPENDIX TWO
203 APPENDIX THREE
215 APPENDIX FOUR
221 GLOSSARY

INTRODUCTION

If you are planning on building or purchasing a home in the country, *Building Your Country Home* is intended to help you to avoid some real headaches. It has been written specifically to help those who are planning to move to the country and build the dream home of their choice. No matter how scenic and peaceful a site may be, a contaminated water well or an overflowing sewage system can turn any dream home into a virtual nightmare.

Focus of this Book

The major focus of *Building Your Country Home* is on the planning, construction and maintenance of on-site water and sewage disposal systems. *Building Your Country Home* also provides information on other environmental subjects such as radon, pesticides and endangered species, to name just a few. When neglected in the initial planning stages, these environmental concerns may become a major problem for the rural homeowner.

Who Can Use this Book?

Individuals planning to buy an existing home will be able to use *Building Your Country Home* in an evaluation of water well systems, on-site sewage disposal units and other potential environmental concerns. Current rural homeowners will also find *Building Your Country Home* a handy reference for the care and maintenance of their existing water and sewage disposal systems. Technical terms such as MCL, mg/L and aerobic are explained in nontechnical language.

Key Questions

Building Your Country Home provides key questions to ask prior to making decisions related to site selection and choosing a building contractor, water well contractor or septic tank installer. By asking the right question at the right time, you may be able to avoid buying an abandoned waste dump or having water that is unfit to drink.

Case Histories

Case histories are presented in *Building Your Country Home* to provide lessons learned from other homeowners' experiences in building a home in a rural location. These lessons learned may be valuable in helping you to avoid the same mistakes. The case histories presented are based on actual situations encountered by the author while working in county health departments and as an on-site sewage system design consultant.

Checklists

Checklists are provided in Appendix One to help in making the final decision on selecting a building site. You will also find key questions to ask about environmental site assessments and property history.

Regulations

Regulations for building and constructing on-site water supplies and sewage disposal systems vary widely from state to state. Regulations even vary from county to county within the same state. A sample of regulations related to on-site sewage disposal systems is provided in Appendix Three; however, take the time to check the regulations in your own state and county. Appendix Two provides a discription of sewage disposal systems.

Additional Information

Since it is impossible to provide an answer to every conceivable question about building a home in the country, readers are provided with numerous sources for finding additional information. Instructions for obtaining information on environmental site conditions from the U.S.

You may find these publications helpful in finding the right design for your home in the country.

Environmental Protection Agency (EPA) and state and local agencies are included.

Sources for Plans

If you haven't yet made a decision on the type of home to build, the designs in Chapter 7 will help you in your search. You may also want to check Home Planners design series publications: *Country Houses; Homes Filled with Natural Light; Waterfront Homes;* and *Vacation and Second Homes.*

Rural Migrations

Since early settlers first landed on North American shores, the desire to build in the wide-open spaces has been a dream pursued by many Americans. The lure of free or low-cost land for building new homes and raising families in the "ideal environment" attracted millions of immigrants to the new world.

At the end of the American Revolution, many of the returning soldiers were offered free land to settle new territories in the Appalachian Mountains and beyond. North Carolina offered veterans of the Continental Army free land in what was known as the Military District (North Central Tennessee). The rank and time of service of the veteran determined the amount of free land awarded. A soldier with the rank of private and two years of service could claim up to 228 acres. An officer with seven years of service and the rank of brigadier general was awarded up to 12,000 acres.

In Georgia, free land was distributed on a "headright" system. The head of a household was entitled to up to 200 acres of free land and 50 additional acres for each family member. While the maximum amount of a headright was set at 1,000 acres, several Georgia governors approved larger rights.

Both the North Carolina and Georgia free-land deals experienced their share of fraud. Georgia Governor George Mathews is reported to have approved one headright of more than one million acres. In North Carolina, free Tennessee land was awarded to individuals who had not served in the American Revolution.

A few unscrupulous individuals staked claims to free land only for reselling to other settlers. Advertisements describing land as "rich in timber and flowing streams" lured many settlers into buying sight unseen. Many times the "rich in timber and flowing streams" turned out to be pine barrens or swamp land.

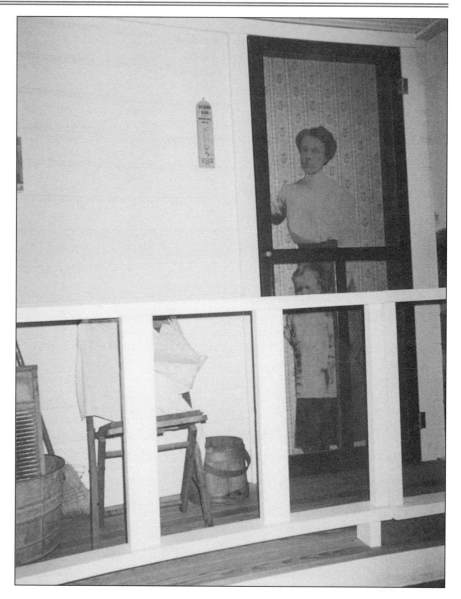

Early settlers faced an almost impossible task in building even the simplest of rural homes. This little house on the prairie may have been simple, but it was a dream home for the family who lived here. Taken at the Cherokee Strip Museum in Perry, Oklahoma.

Challenges

If you think building a home in the country is difficult now, the challenges faced by these early Americans must have seemed impossible. Trails and roadways for wagons didn't exist. Husbands often had to leave their families with friends and relatives while crossing the mountains to stake claim to free land.

Brothers and other relatives would often make the journey into the wilderness together. Supply loads had to be light when travelling on horseback. Supplies normally included a wooden bucket containing a pound of nails, an ax and other primitive tools for building a cabin. After clearing the land, planting a corn crop and constructing a crude shelter, the young settler would then return to accompany his wife and children to their new home in the wilderness.

From the end of the American Revolution to the mid-1800s, this scenario was re-enacted time and time again. In some areas the population was doubling every ten years. In 1795, when Tennessee became a state, the population count was 75,000. By 1830, this number had grown to 600,000, and by 1850, Tennessee had a population of more than a million. With new immigrants arriving daily on eastern shores, wave after wave of settlers began moving west. The Age of the Pioneer had begun.

Pioneer families had to face countless hardships and problems in taming the land and building their new homes. Without the advantage of modern power tools, the land had to be cleared with an ax. Water wells and outdoor privies (outhouses) had to be dug by hand. The sacrifices that had to be made by all members of the pioneer family to settle beyond the eastern cities were too numerous to count.

Statue of the Pioneer Woman in Ponca City, Oklahoma. A tribute to the countless women pioneers who helped settle the West.

It took hard work by all members of the pioneer family to make rural life possible. These are just a few of the photographs on display at the Cherokee Strip Museum in Perry, Oklahoma, depicting the hardships faced by pioneer families.

The pioneers of the 1800s had to contend with some of the same problems faced by early settlers. Relying on the promises of unscrupulous land developers and eastern newspaper advertisements, describing lush valleys with spring-fed streams, eager pioneers would often purchase land, sight unseen. Many arrived at their dream site to find that their valley was lush only in the spring after the streams had flooded. During the summer, with no rain, the springs and streams were dry, and in winter the valley was full of snow. Hard-sell land developers even provided free train trips for settlers to inspect ten-dollar-an-acre land before buying. By offering these free trips at the right time of year, swampland would be dry and deserts would be green from spring rains.

During these early rural migrations, agriculture was the main motivation for the movement west. Pioneer families moving west did so to establish self-sustaining farms and ranches. Their full-time job was the upkeep and maintenance of their rural way of life. Commuting from a rural paradise to a job in the city was not a consideration.

The Changing Urban Areas

As early settlers moved west, clearing the forest and plowing the land for farming, cities and towns were also changing. By the 19th century, major cities were developing further inland to support the wave of immigrants moving west.

With the beginning of the Industrial Revolution in the 1800s, things began to change. Driven by the offer of plentiful jobs, more immigrants coming to America began to settle in the industrial cities along the eastern coast. With rapid industrial development, cities were transformed nearly overnight into overcrowded and polluted "megalopolis" complexes.

Following the Civil War, agriculture in the South was in a state of confusion and undergoing reconstruction. Many southerners migrated to northern cities in search of new jobs and opportunities. At the same time, jobs fueled by the Industrial Revolution continued to attract new foreign immigrants. The megalopolis was becoming American's new frontier.

Though, up to the late 1800s America could still be described as a nation of farmers, the Oklahoma land rush in the early 1900s, offering free land to those willing to stake claims and build homes, signaled the beginning of the end of American's great westward movement. During the Great Depression, many farm families, ruined by Dust

Even without the convenience of electric or gas appliances the pioneers established their homes and tamed the West.

The Oklahoma land rushes of the early 1900s signaled the end of the pioneer movement west. Photo taken at the Cherokee Strip Museum in Perry, Oklahoma.

Bowl droughts, floods and wildfires, seeking a new and better life, left their farms behind for work in the cities.

As the number of available jobs in the cities continued to grow, a reverse rural migration began to take place. America could no longer be described as a nation of farmers; it was a nation of factory workers.

Current Trends in Rural Home Building

With a reverse rural migration taking place, major American cities once described, as "Melting Pots" became "Boiling Pots." Supporting high-density populations with deteriorating social and physical infra-structures, the inner core of American cities began to feel the stress.

Following World War II and with the help of the automobile, workers with higher paying jobs were able to afford to move outside the inner city. Tract housing developments with $10,000 ranches and Cape Cods emerged seemingly overnight to satisfy the flight from crowded and deteriorating inner-city neighborhoods.

The urban patterns that developed were similar in many cities. Rings of new home developments began to encompass the deteriorating hub of factories and older houses. In the early 1980s, as housing developments in the outer rings became crowded, an increased demand for rural building sites beyond the city limits began to take place.

Today's Rural Migration

Today, with more and more families building new homes and purchasing existing homes, the demand for rural building sites is greater than ever. In a recent consumer survey, when asked about preference for building sites, more than 32% of those surveyed said they desired a rural location. In the same survey, about 25% indicated a preference for a suburb closer to the city. Applied to current homebuilding statistics, these percentages take on some significance. In just three years, between 1994 and 1997, the number of homeowners grew by four million, increasing the homeownership rate to an all-time high of 65.7 percent. During the first six months of 1998, homebuilders reported a record number of 586,549 new starts for single-family housing units. This represents an increase of 11% over 1997. In some areas of the U.S. this rate was more than doubled. Even more surprising is the number of new homes being built in the country. More than 30% of the homes built in 1998 were being built in rural areas.

Rural counties in close proximity to large cities are experiencing what could be described as the "land rush" of the 1990s. In recent years, rural counties around Dallas, Texas have experienced population increases as high as 52% in just a four-year period. At the same time, the city of Dallas only experienced a population increase of about 9%.

As more families have sought to build in rural areas, many of our major cities and adjacent rural areas have been transformed into giant Metroplexes. With improved highway systems, rural pioneers of today are able to live in the country while commuting 40 to 60 miles to work in the city.

Impacts of the Current Trends

The impact of this new rural migration is being felt everywhere. In the Atlanta Metroplex, new-home building in surrounding rural counties has been phenomenal. To meet the demand for improved commuter transportation, major highways are being expanded from eight to ten traffic lanes.

Nearly 200,000 new housing starts were reported in the Atlanta area between 1990 and 1995. Rural Georgia counties, such as Cobb, DeKalb and Clayton, have formed a suburban circle surrounding Atlanta. Families now trying to find that perfect country site have to search in rural areas outside this suburban circle, such as Cherokee, Fayette and Henry counties.

The move to the country has increased competition for farmland near major urban areas. In some areas this competition has led to land use and water conflicts between farmers and rural homeowners.

Not only are more new homes being built, but the size of new homes is also increasing. In 1997 the average-sized new home was reported to be 2,250 square feet. Nearly 15% of the units built in 1997 were larger than 3,000 square feet.

In some areas of the country, new housing demands have exceeded the ability of local builders to keep pace. Shortages in building supplies and building sites have also been reported.

The 1990s rural migration has created some new and unique problems. Many rural counties experiencing rapid growth have experienced fiscal problems attempting to meet the demand for higher levels of road maintenance, solid waste disposal, health care, fire protection and other essential services.

Furthermore, the new rural migration has resulted in a significant loss of existing farmland. Established farms have been carved up into five-acre country estates and ranchettes. This has led to some areas placing limits on the pace of developing existing farmland.

Finding the Ideal Site

Everyone planning to build in the country wants to find the "ideal" building site. The "ideal" building site is one with a great view, large size, low cost, lots of good quality water, suitable soil for a low-cost sewage disposal system and lack of environmental problems.

With the rural land rush of the 1990s, the ideal rural building site is getting harder to find in many parts of the country. Some individuals have had to settle for a site with a great view on a small lot and a two-hour-a-day commute.

A few unfortunate individuals have found that the site they purchased had environmental problems ranging from contaminated water supplies and polluted streams to elevated levels of radon. When these environmental conditions are considered in early planning most can be easily mitigated with good engineering and construction practices. When neglected or overlooked they may be major problems later on.

That ideal building site can be found for your new home in the country. By asking the right questions concerning water, on-site sewage and other environmental factors before you buy, you can avoid headaches later on.

NIGHTMARES TO AVOID

This isn't a Love Canal, but roadside dumps can be a real headache. Ask local officials if illegal dumps are a problem in your area.

When site limitations or environmental considerations are overlooked or neglected, results can be a real nightmare for the homeowner. Problems can range from a pool of toxic waste in the backyard to poor water quality.

Fortunately, the homeowner nightmares described in this chapter are the exception and not the rule. The majority of those who have built in the country have had enjoyable experiences. However, some problems can be expected to occur as rural areas undergo rapid development. Here are a few examples of nightmares and other problems that could have been avoided if the right questions had been asked before buying.

Enter at Your Own Risk

Building a home near or over an old waste dump may not be a health hazard, but it can bring property prices down when trying to resell. Love Canal in Niagara Falls, New York is probably the best known example of a homeowner nightmare due to toxic waste.

13

A sure sign of past industrial activity is finding 55-gallon drums with unlabeled "stuff." The "stuff" could be hazardous material or toxic waste.

What started as a program with good intentions turned into one of the most notorious examples of what can happen when environmental conditions are neglected. In the mid-1950s, the City of Niagara Falls wanted to provide more medium-priced building sites in its suburbs. City officials supported the development of the Love Canal property for housing. The story actually began in the 1890s when William T. Love dug a canal to divert waters from Niagara Falls to produce low-cost electrical power. In 1942, a chemical company purchased the canal to use as a disposal site for chemical wastes. Chemicals were simply dumped into the canal inside 55-gallon drums and buried. This method of chemical dumping was a common industrial practice at the time.

After filling the canal with more than 20,000 tons of chemicals, the company sold the Love property to the City of Niagara for $1.00. In 1955 a new elementary school was built adjacent to the canal. The new school and low-cost building sites attracted several hundred unsuspecting, new homeowners to the suburbs.

Homeowners at Love Canal were unaware of any problems until heavy rains in 1975 and 1976. Higher than normal rainfall raised groundwater levels and pushed chemical waste and 55-gallon drums to the ground surface. By 1978 the New York State Health Commissioner had declared the Love Canal area as a threat to human health. Twenty years and $100 million dollars later, the U.S. Environmental Protection Agency announced that Love Canal had been cleaned up.

Today, thanks to the EPA's Superfund law brought about by the Love Canal incident, it is possible for a prospective buyer to obtain information on environmental conditions about a site before deciding to buy. In Chapter 4 of *Building Your Country Home*, step-by-step procedures for obtaining environmental information on a site is provided. Key questions to ask land owners, developers and builders about potential environmental problems are also provided.

Building Code Blues

If your reason for building in the country is to escape the hassles of having to obtain city permits and adhere to those strict municipal building and zoning codes, think again. You may find that developments advertised as "no building restrictions" may turn out to be more than you bargained for.

Without some type of restrictions on the type and size of homes to be built, your Green Acres may turn into a real nightmare. Outside the

Without some type of restrictions your next door neighbor can do just about anything.

Figure 2-1
Example of "Architectural" Committee Controls

No building shall be erected, placed or altered on any lot until construction plans and specifications have been approved by the Architectural Control Committee.

(1) No fence shall be erected and placed on any lot nearer to any street than a line parallel with the rear of the dwelling, and on side no nearer than minimum setback line.

(2) Decorative fences shall only be permitted upon approval of the Architectural Control Committee.

(3) No satellite dish or other receiving instruments shall be erected and placed on any lot nearer than a line parallel with the rear of the dwelling, and on side no nearer than minimum set back line. All plans, including location, are to be approved by the Architectural Control Committee prior to installation.

(4) The principal dwelling constructed on any lot, exclusive of open porches and garages, shall not be less than 3,000 square feet.

(5) No building shall be located on any lot nearer to the front lot line or nearer to the side street line than the minimum building setback lines shown on the recorded plat. In any event, no building shall be located on any lot nearer than 50 feet to the front lot line, or nearer than 50 feet to any side street line.

(6) No building shall be located nearer than 10 feet to an interior lot line. Carports or roofed porches shall be considered as part of the building and the overhang shall not extend beyond or over the minimum 10 feet setback on side lot line or 35 feet setback from front lot line, as shown on the map of record referred to above, unless approved by the Architectural Control Committee.

(7) No dwelling shall be erected or placed on any lot having less than 75 feet at the minimum building setback line.

(8) Easements: 15 feet in width are reserved along all property lines for installation and maintenance of utilities and drainage facilities Within these easements, no structure, trees or other material shall be placed or permitted. The easement area of each lot shall be maintained continuously by the owner of the lot, except for those improvements for which public authority or utility company is responsible.

city limits of southwest border cities from California to Texas, sites sold with no building restrictions have turned into what are frequently called Colonias.

More than 1,300 of these Colonias have developed as virtual shantytowns along the border area. With the promise that community water and sewage disposal systems would be available as more sites were sold, developers sold the land, but broke their promise. More than a

Your new rural neighbors may be anything from pigs and chickens to cows. Some may produce that distinctive country-air odor.

few northern residents have purchased Colonia sites without first inspecting the property. What they thought were low-cost ranchette sites with no building restrictions, soon turned out to be Colonias.

At the same time, planned developments in rural areas may have more building restrictions than city building and zoning codes. Some housing developments have "Architectural Committees" to approve all property improvements. Examples of building restrictions established by architectural committees are shown in Figure 2-1.

The majority of these types of building restrictions help to maintain and improve property values. When purchasing property just be sure that you know and fully understand all building restrictions to which you agreed.

Keep in mind that outside the city limits zoning codes may not exist. Without some type of zoning requirements your new rural "neighbors" may be anything from pigs and chickens to cattle. This may be more than you bargained for.

Water Worries

When planning for vacation travel you will sometimes hear the advice, "Have fun—but don't drink the water." This may be good advice for traveling in some third-world countries. For rural home-owners, a warning of "don't drink the water" could be a major prob-lem and the start of a real nightmare.

It has been estimated that about 95% of rural residents in the U.S. use groundwater supplies. When it comes to drinking water, the two most important considerations are quantity and quality. Poor quality water can usually be improved with treatment, but it's hard to make up for not having enough water. Some home lenders specify that a well should be able to produce at least five gallons per minute (GPM) for up to four continuous hours of pumping.

Water quality includes both health and aesthetic concerns. Crystal clear water may harbor disease-causing pathogens (viruses, bacteria, protozoans). At the same time, murky, rust colored water may be per-fectly "safe" from a public health standpoint.

Chapter 5 of *Building Your Country Home* provides in-depth informa-tion on water quality and development of groundwater resources for rural homeowners. If considered in preplanning, most groundwater contamination problems can be resolved with some type of treatment. When groundwater problems are neglected, homeowners may face some of the headaches described below.

Contaminated groundwater supplies have been found from Maine to California. Probably the best known example of groundwater contam-ination occurred in Woburn, Massachusetts. This event was portrayed in the movie, *A Civil Action,* staring John Travolta.

In 1979, Woburn residents, alarmed about increased numbers of childhood leukemia deaths and other problems, pressed health offi-cials to investigate. After 16 years of study the Massachusetts Department of Public Health blamed contaminated well water as the source of the problem. Well water in Woburn was found to be con-taminated by a number of industrial chemicals including a solvent known as trichloroethylene (TCE).

In the Midwest, the EPA has reported groundwater contamination from agriculture chemicals. A study conducted by the University of Iowa showed that up to 45% of home wells tested in that state exceed EPA maximum contaminant levels (MCL) for bacteria. The

Water Nightmares in the News

PERSISTENT DROUGHT IN U.S. THREATENS SOUTH, MIDWEST

Lingering drought gripping parts of the United States will intensify this spring, according to the federal government's annual spring drought forecast.

GOV. RIDGE LIFTS DROUGHT EMERGENCY

Gov. Tom Ridge has lifted drought-emergency water-use restrictions for Somerset County, the last remaining county under mandatory water-use restrictions.

DEP OFFERS DROUGHT INFORMATION TO WELL OWNERS

Department of Environmental Protection (DEP) officials advise private well owners to arm themselves with knowledge and conservation measures to get through the current drought emergency.

DEPARTMENT OF HEALTH ISSUES STUDY RESULTS

The Department of Health (DH) has issued preliminary findings of an on-going survey of people with illness who reside in the Rural Water District (RWD). The survey is being done to determine a possible connection between a July 14 sewage spill at a city sewage pumping station and illnesses reported among users of the RWD. Preliminary results show that those who drank water supplied from the RWD in the days immediately following the sewage spill were at significantly higher risk of illness. Residents whose drinking water was supplied by the RWD were five times more likely to be ill than residents whose water was supplied by the city.

Just a few of the water worries that have made the headlines. With conservation and other planning homeowners can avoid these types of worries.

same study showed that as many as 15-20% of the wells tested exceeded MCLs for nitrate-nitrogen.

Groundwater supplies in Oregon have been reported with levels of TCE over 15,000 parts per billion (ppb). California groundwater supplies have been reported containing farm chemicals used to kill parasitic worms.

In other parts of the country, homeowners have faced a water shortage from over-pumped groundwater supplies. During South Texas droughts homeowners have had to ration water. Landscaped lawns and shrubs have dried up and died.

Some rural developments advertise state-approved community water systems. Most of the time this is a benefit for homeowners. However, when operation and maintenance of a community water system is neglected, serious problems may and do occur. A number of disease outbreaks have been reported from community rural water systems, which were poorly operated.

You don't need to build in a floodplain to have standing water in your backyard after a heavy rain. Building sites with little slope and poor drainage may become a backyard lake when it rains.

It is common practice for homeowner associations to be responsible for their own community water systems, once all sites in the development have been sold. Be sure to ask about homeowner responsibilities for financing future operation and maintenance of community water systems, if you purchase in such a community.

Use the information in Chapter 5 to check the water situation before you buy and keep in mind the old axiom, "You don't miss the water till its gone."

A lake in the backyard can be great when a home is on the shores of an actual lake. But when a lake is created from heavy rainfall, it's just not the same. Even if your site is outside an established flood zone, excessive rains may still create problems. When farmlands undergo rapid development with fields being paved for roads and parking lots, more rainwater is allowed to runoff. Filling in low-lying areas and wetlands to increase the number of building sites can also lead to more runoff. Adding to the potential flooding problem is the amount of rain shed from home roofs and other buildings.

One homeowner in Florida described his situation in the *Pensacola News Journal* as follows: "If we hear a thunderstorm coming, we break into a cold sweat. We live in fear. It's still our home, but it's a nightmare home, not a dream home."

Just because a site is high and dry when you visit doesn't mean it isn't subject to flooding during heavy rains. More than one new homeowner has found water in his den after the first heavy rain. If you can, try to visit potential sites after a heavy rain.

Road Rage

If you are planning to commute from your rural home to work in a nearby urban area, take the time to evaluate traffic and road conditions during rush hour before you make a final decision. Unpaved roads can be a major headache during peak traffic times and inclement weather. The dust from unpaved roads may also make respiratory problems, such as asthma, a problem for younger children.

Two lane country roads may be picturesque, but can become major traffic snarls during rush hour. Try to imagine that country lane with 20 to 30 drivers all trying to get to work at the same time. If roads in the area are poorly maintained, you can expect increased auto maintenance and repairs.

This peaceful country lane may become a commuter's nightmare during rush hour traffic. As more homes are built in this area, roadways will soon become bottlenecks.

You can avoid having sewage flowing in your backyard by using the advice in Chapter 6 in selecting your best option for on-site sewage disposal.

Automobile accidents related to rural and expressway driving have become such a problem that the National Safety Council has included an entire chapter on this subject in its Defensive Driving Course. Railway crossings are of special concern on rural roads since many are not equipped with lighted warning signals. Meeting a train on the commute home to your country hideaway is one nightmare you want to be sure to avoid.

Other hazards you will see more often on rural roads range from wild animals jumping in front of your car to slow-moving farm vehicles. You are also likely to encounter more school buses on rural roads.

Sewage in Yard

When it comes to sewage, all rural homeowners will agree—this is one subject best left out of sight and out of mind. But, when on-site sewage disposal systems are improperly designed or the homeowner uses too much water and overloads the disposal system, backyards may be full of sewage. If the soil is sandy, septic tank effluent may not be seen but may contaminate groundwater supplies.

To be kept out of sight and out of mind, the on-site sewage disposal system must be properly planned, installed and maintained.

Chapter 6 provides in-depth information on the planning, installation and maintenance of on-site sewage disposal systems.

In Boulder, Colorado, suburban and rural neighborhood associations were asked to identify homeowner problems and concerns. Traffic was the concern mentioned most often, followed by drinking water contamination, sewage disposal and noise. While it may not be possible to avoid all of these problems, it is possible to reduce the impact by selecting the right contractor and taking time to check the site before you buy.

PICTURE PERFECT

The Dominion luxury home development, a virtual recycled water oasis, is home to the rich and famous including NBA pro-basketball player, David Robinson and country singing star, George Strait.

Building a family home, vacation hideaway or retirement retreat in a rural location can be a rich and rewarding experience. However, things can be unpleasant when water and sewage disposal or other environmental considerations are neglected or just not thought about.

In Chapter 4 of *Building Your Country Home,* you will be provided with an overview of environmental conditions from A to Z which should be considered in selecting a rural building site. Chapters 5 and 6 provide in-depth information for planning on-site water and sewage disposal systems.

With the demand for rural building sites at an all time high, finding a "perfect" site may be impossible in some areas of the country. Just about any site will have some limitations, which should be considered prior to purchase and construction. Even when building on a site with environmental limitations, the end results can still be picture perfect. Just take a look at some of the following examples.

Recycled Water Oasis

Building a major development in an environmentally sensitive area can be a challenge for any builder. To conserve limited water resources the developers of the Dominion, a luxury home development in the Texas Hill Country, elected to recycle waste water. Instead of homeowners having to install and maintain individual on-site sewage disposal systems, a centralized wastewater treatment plant "recycles" water to irrigate a 260-acre 18-hole championship golf course. The developers of the Holmes Harbor Golf Club and Yacht Club Subdivision on Whidbey Island in Puget Sound faced a limited groundwater supply and poor soils for on-site septic tanks. With innovative planning and sound engineering practices these limitations were turned into sites for building picture perfect homes.

*The Dominion's central-
ized sewage treatment
system was designed to
conserve limited water
resources by "recycling"
treated wastewater for
golf course irrigation.
Aeration units were
installed in storage
ponds to provide addi-
tional oxygen and main-
tain the quality of recy-
cled water.*

Working with state and local environmental regulatory agencies, Holmes Harbor developers were able to design and construct a water reclamation system. By using treated wastewater (effluent) from septic tanks on each site, recycled water was available to irrigate the community golf course. Effluent from homeowner septic tanks is pumped under pressure to a central treatment unit for additional "polishing" prior to golf course irrigation.

To ensure that recycled water is used wisely, weather stations such as the one shown here are installed at key locations. Temperature, humidity, wind speed and other environmental factors are monitored daily to determine golf course water needs.

A lakeside vacation or retirement home can be a rewarding experience when planning helps to avoid the nightmares described in Chapter 2.

All wastewater is utilized for golf course irrigation; none is discharged into the environmentally sensitive Puget Sound. This septic tank effluent pressure (STEP) system helps to conserve water, allowing homeowners to build on sites with poor soils.

*Another lakeside picture
perfect retreat.*

Lakeside Dream Homes

Building the picture perfect home on the shores of a lake can be challenge for any builder. But imagine trying to build a home in one of the most environmentally sensitive lake areas in the U.S. Described as, "one of the crown jewels, unique among them all. A national treasure that must be protected and preserved," by President Bill Clinton, Lake Tahoe can be a real challenge.

Named the "Big Water" by the Washoe Indians, Lake Tahoe has enough water to cover all of California more than one foot deep. The crystal clear waters of the lake form a mountain lake 22 miles long and 12 miles wide with depths up to 1,645 feet. To keep waters crystal clear, wastewater from homes built around the more than 71 miles of Lake Tahoe shoreline is pumped to treatment facilities outside the lake's drainage basin.

Regional Water Quality Control Boards play a major role in monitoring homeowner sewage disposal system construction and maintenance. In addition to the water quality control boards, the Tahoe Conservancy was established by the State of California in 1983. As an independent state agency the Conservancy purchases undeveloped lands to preserve wildlife habitat and maintain scenic beauty.

On The Farm

During the 1990s the demand for rural building locations has been so intense in some areas that established farms are disappearing at a rapid rate. In many areas strip malls have replaced farming lands in a sprawl of unplanned and inefficient rural development. A number of rural counties have enacted regulations to restrict farmlands from being subdivided for new home sites.

When developers and builders work to balance growth while preserving farmlands, the results can be surprising. Following are a few examples of new rural housing developments designed to meet new housing demands with minimal impact on existing farming lands.

In Alabama, the Elk River Development Agency's Elkmont Rural Village, is another example of how the need for new rural building sites can be met while maintaining a balance with existing farmland. The Elkmont Rural Village is a 1,500-acre development providing rural building sites with nature trails for hiking and horseback riding and waterways for fishing and boating.

Planned as an alternative to strip-mall type development, Elkmont Village offers homeowners a rural site without urban sprawl. Located

This rural development offers homeowners a mini-farm large enough for horses and other animals.

29

Air-park rural developments can provide homeowners a private hanger and landing strip for their airplane.

about 35 miles northwest of Huntsville, Alabama, it provides a unique option for homeowners wishing to live in the country.

The Farmcolony in Standardsville, Virginia, is a unique 300-acre farm community development with 49 residential sites and a 150-acre working farm. The farm is owned and managed by the homeowners association. The farm includes cropland, pastures and fishing lakes. The main farmhouse also serves as the community clubhouse.

Protecting the Aquifer

In South Texas, the Edwards Aquifer is the only source of drinking water for more than one million people. The aquifer is fed by rainwater infiltrating a vast recharge zone over 100 miles long and, in some locations, up to two miles wide. The karst geology of this recharge zone makes it possible for rainwater to rapidly enter the aquifer through numerous cracks, crevices and sinkholes.

This rapid recharge makes it possible to keep the aquifer full when it rains, but it also makes it easy for surface pollutants to contaminate this underground water supply. Most of the Edwards Recharge Zone (RZ) is located in rural areas with prime building sites.

In areas undergoing rapid development, protection of sensitive underground drinking water aquifers has become a major concern.

Local and state agencies have established best management practices (BMPs) for builders to follow during construction on the Edwards Aquifer RZ. By following these BMPs and other site restrictions, picture perfect homes are able to be built over the RZ without polluting the aquifer.

In Harmony with Nature

Living in harmony with nature can be a challenge when you build on a site that is home to an endangered species. But, when preplanning is accomplished early in the development phase, it is possible to build your home and still be in harmony with rare and endangered plants and animals. Chapter 4 of *Building Your Country Home* provides more information on protecting endangered species when building in rural areas.

Lakeway, near Austin, Texas, is a planned housing development consisting of more than 5,000 acres. Located on Lake Travis in the environmentally sensitive Texas Hill Country, the area is home to several endangered species. Building homes in this natural scenic beauty and protecting these species has been a challenge for builders.

Here's how one developer met the challenge. Prior to developing the 304-acre Lakeway Rough Hollow located in the Lakeway property, a Habitat Conservation Plan was prepared to help protect the Golden-cheeked Warbler, an endangered bird. One of more than 200 species of threatened or endangered migratory birds, the Golden-cheeked Warbler spends the summer months in North America. During the winter it heads to the tropical rain forests of South America.

Portions of the Lakeway property were found to be a critical nesting area for the Warbler. To allow the building of new homes, a Habitat Conservation Plan was developed permitting homeowners to build while protecting nesting areas. By following the conservation plan builders were able to construct picture perfect homes in harmony with nature.

Homeowners at this site found they needed a permit from the U.S. Fish and Wildlife Service to protect the Golden-Cheeked Warbler, an endangered bird.

You can also find examples of picture perfect success stories in your own backyard. The next time you go on a drive in the country take time to stop and ask new homeowners about their lessons learned. Most new homeowners will be happy to share their stories with you.

When homeowners, developers and environmental agencies work together the results can be picture perfect, even in environmentally sensitive areas.

YOUR NEXT STEP

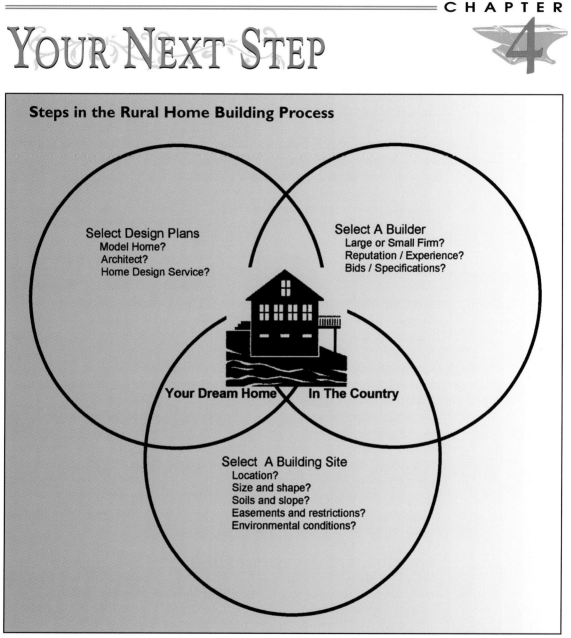

Steps in the Rural Home Building Process

Select Design Plans
Model Home?
Architect?
Home Design Service?

Select A Builder
Large or Small Firm?
Reputation / Experience?
Bids / Specifications?

Your Dream Home   In The Country

Select A Building Site
Location?
Size and shape?
Soils and slope?
Easements and restrictions?
Environmental conditions?

Figure 4-1 No matter which step in the home building process you may take first, asking the right questions will help make your dream home in the country a reality

If you have decided to follow in the footsteps of earlier pioneers and build a home in the country the next steps you take may be the difference between realizing your dream or finding you're living one of the nightmare situations described in Chapter 2. The decisions you make during each step will be important.

What the Experts Recommend

Experts tend to disagree on the exact sequence for taking the next step in the rural homebuilding process. Ask a real estate agent and you might hear that the first step in the process is to decide on a building site. Your real estate agent may also know of existing rural homes built just for you. If you do consider buying an existing home in the country, *Building Your Country Home* will be a big help in evaluating environmental factors, especially water and sewage disposal systems. A few real estate firms may be able to offer construction management services and assist with the entire building process.

Builders tend to recommend that the first step is to select a builder. Larger, and even some smaller building firms, will be able to provide a turnkey job. This will include providing the site, providing building plans, providing interior designs, and, of course, managing the construction phase.

Most architects would rather have you first select a site and then design a house to fit the site. If you are considering more than one site, an architect can aid you by doing concept drawings for each site. An architect will also be able to provide insight on orientation, approach and technical aspects of construction.

Follow Your Instincts

So, what should the next step be now that you've decided to build in the country? The simple answer is that there is no exact sequence of steps that is best for everyone. If your dream has always been to live in a home with a particular style and design, then find the plans to meet that dream first. If you have always wanted to live on a hill surrounded by pine trees, then find that site first. Having a builder or real estate firm to manage the entire process may be your best option, especially if you don't have a lot of time.

Just keep in mind that each step in the process is likely to influence the other steps (see Figure 4-1). For example, some plans and designs may have certain site requirements. If those dream plans are for a hillside home then you need to find a site with a hill. Some building sites may also limit the design of the home you build. Building a basement in solid rock may be difficult. Most builders will have certain types of construction in which they specialize. If your dream home is a castle be sure your builder has successfully built a few castles. Some families moving to the country may decide to combine the design and construction phases and have a "systems-built" home erected or moved to their site.

Kit homes will be one of the many options for building your country home.

In reality, the exact sequence of steps you take doesn't make a lot of difference. If you already own property, it will be best to match your design with the size and layout of the site. No matter what sequence of steps you take, information provided in this section will be helpful in making the many decisions that will need to be made.

Systems-built Option

The "systems-built" home option combines the design and construction steps. These units, ranging from kit and modular or mobile homes to log homes, are popular for vacation and weekend retreats. Younger families are finding the systems-built option a way to meet their budget and still move to the country. A major advantage of the systems-built approach is a shorter time required for move in.

"Kit-homes" provide lumber and other materials already pre-cut at the factory. Materials are shipped to the building site for final assembly. Depending on the price and specifications, the kit may include windows and doors and even mechanical, electrical and plumbing systems. When assembly is do-it-yourself, construction labor costs can be minimized. Pre-cut log homes are another popular version of this option.

No longer just a "mobile home," modular or sectional homes are now available in a number of designs and configurations. Modular units typically come in 12, 14 or 18-foot-wide sections. Some can even be stacked in two-story configurations. Electrical, mechanical and plumbing systems are often pre-installed at the factory. Other factory options include carpeting, cabinets, paint, interior trim, furniture and even appliances. All you have to do is move in.

Modular and kit units still require the same amount of detail when it comes to site selection. Before a systems-built home is selected, make sure that the site you choose will allow this option. Building restrictions and zoning in some areas may not permit modular units. Information in *Building Your Country Home* on environmental factors and on-site water and sewage disposal systems will also apply for systems-built homes.

Decisions about Design and Plans

Model Homes

Selecting the design and layout of a model home already built and on display will take less time and effort when dealing with larger builders and developers. Exterior and interior finishes and colors are likely to be the only customizing options you will have. The finished product may have the appearance of a "cookie cutter" design.

Architects or Designers

For those who want a truly unique home, the services of a professional architect or interior designer may be best. Unfortunately, the average homebuilder's budget may not include the cost of professional architectural services.

Stock Plan Option

If you don't want to take the "cookie-cutter" approach and just can't afford an architect, you may want to consider using plans from a home design service, such as Home Planners. This option makes it possible to obtain a semi-custom design from an experienced architect or designer at an affordable cost. Depending on size, style and the number of plan sets required, the cost of this option can range from $400 to $1,300.

Home Planners will not only provide building plans, but for many of their designs will also be able to provide a cost estimate based on the zip code in which you plan to build. Other services provided by Home Planners include a specification outline, construction detail sheets for plumbing and mechanical systems, a materials list and a Plan-A-Home© kit.

Using the services provided by a home planning firm might save you both time and money. One customer of a home design firm commented, *"Our home is a fine example of the results one can achieve by purchasing and following the plans which you offer… Everyone who has seen it has assured us that it belongs in a 'picture book.' I truly mean it when I say that my home is a DREAM HOUSE."* Additional information and examples of home design plans, which can be provided by Home Planners, can be found in Chapter 7 of *Building Your Country Home.*

Finding the Right Builder

When it comes to selecting a builder the best advice is to take your time. One real estate expert advises, "Shop for your builder as carefully as you shop for your home."

Whether your house plans are for a weekend cabin on the lake, a retirement condo in a planned development, or a custom home along a country lane, a quality, reputable builder is a must. You may not know you selected the wrong builder until the backyard floods, the foundation cracks or the deck railing falls off.

Finding that the roof leaks on your new home isn't a picnic; but imagine finding that part of your new home has been built on the property next door. This has actually happened to a few unfortunate new homeowners. Many builders have a professional engineering or surveying firm verify the location of the foundation, setbacks and easements before any concrete is poured. The contractor with the lowest bid may not always provide this service.

You may hear a builder claim, " I've been building homes for people in this area for 20 years. My word is my bond, and a handshake is my guarantee." Just because a builder has 20 to 30 years of experience doesn't mean that he is the right one for your project.

One builder with more than 30 years of experience in one state had to apply for a contractor's license under a newly enacted state regulation. A review of the builder's application showed that the firm had court ordered judgments totaling more than $300,000 still pending. The firm also had a large file at the local Better Business Bureau. This builder certainly had a reputation, but it was a bad one.

Size of Building Firm

Building firms come in all sizes. Firms starting 25 or fewer units a year are generally considered small-volume builders. Those with 100 or more starts a year are considered large builders. Small-volume builders typically account for about 14 percent of annual housing starts while large builders account for about 70 percent.

Large builders may be limited to larger developments and planned communities to achieve economies of scale, though some large builders will be able to provide custom building services on individual sites in rural areas.

Small- and medium-sized builders may be easier to find in rural counties. Many small volume builders limit their new starts to only six a year. They cite the benefit of being able to provide individual service to each customer.

Financial Profile

Financial profile is another factor to consider when selecting a builder. No matter how large or small a builder may be, one having financial problems can create headaches for you later on. Be sure to ask for a written release of liens before making final payments.

One indicator of financial strength is approval by the Farm Home Administration (FHA) and Veterans Administration (VA). The FHA and VA require builders to build the home on the builder's money with payments at the end of the project. Builders who refuse to take on FHA and VA projects may be experiencing financial problems.

Finding a builder is as easy as looking through the yellow pages. The real estate section of your local newspaper is another good place to start. Ask friends and relatives who have recently built homes to share their experiences in selecting a builder.

The Better Business Bureau's Role

Once you have a list of five or six potential firms, contact the Better Business Bureau (BBB) in your community. Don't be surprised if a complaint has been filed about a builder on your list. Ask for details about the complaint. The important issue is how was the complaint resolved. If a single homeowner has complained that it took nearly four hours to respond to a squeaking door, you may not want to eliminate the builder at this point. To be fair, ask builders about complaints filed with the BBB.

Builder References

A good builder should be willing to provide the names of their last five customers. Ask past customers how the builder responded to requests for repair work after move-in. Find out how the builder responded to any emergency situations. If it took the threat of legal action for a builder to respond, you may want to place this firm at the bottom of your list.

You may also want to contact county and city building inspection agencies. A good reputation with building inspectors can be a good sign. You may find that a builder you are considering is well known by inspectors for trying to cut corners or using low-grade or unapproved materials.

Licensing
Prior to contacting builders in your area, check on state and local licensing laws. Most states have enacted legislation to protect homebuyers from unethical builders and defective workmanship. State licensing laws may require general contractors to pass a written examination, provide references and document building experience. License renewal often involves continuing education requirements. Many states have also established a record-keeping system for tracking complaints about licensed builders

Insurance
States such as Minnesota also require builders to provide a certificate of liability insurance and workers' compensation insurance when applying for a license. Minnesota also has enacted a licensing law for residential roofers and manufactured (mobile) home installers.

A preliminary phone call may eliminate a name or two on your list. If a state builder's license is required, you can eliminate those who are not licensed. Be sure to ask if the builder is a member of a local or national homebuilder's association.

Warranty and Guarantee
Another important factor to consider in selecting a builder is the warranty and guarantee provided with the new home. Typically, builder warranties are for a one-year period after move-in, though a few firms may offer warranties beyond a one-year period. A builder may provide a warranty backed by an insurance carrier. Other builders will back their own warranty on materials and workmanship. No matter which type of warranty is provided or how long the warranty is in effect make sure it is in writing. Most important, take the time to read and understand just what the builder has agreed upon. A ten-year warranty which covers only manufacturing defects may not be as good as a one-year warranty covering all workmanship.

Components of mechanical systems such as air conditioning and plumbing fixtures will likely come with manufacturer warranties and guarantees. Your builder should provide a copy of these during your final walk-through inspection. Keep all of these documents in a file for future reference.

EXAMPLE OF SPECIFICATIONS

ENERGY-SAVING CONSTRUCTION SPECIFICATIONS

INSULATION: Ceiling: R-30; walls-frame: R-15; masonry walls more than 50% or more below grade: R-5 to two (2') feet below grade. Floors-frame: R-19; concrete slab edge less than two (2') feet below grade: R-5 for 24 inches. Water heaters: if electric, R-7. Access panels: Insulated same as adjacent area and weather-stripped.

VAPOR BARRIERS: Required on living side of wall and floor insulation and under concrete slab.

INFILTRATION: Windows and Doors: caulked around frames.

MEASURES: Sill plates: sealed.

VENTILATION: Attic and crawl spaces: ventilate to HUD minimum property standards.

WINDOWS & DOORS: Windows: double glazed, with low infiltration rate. Doors: insulated with low infiltration rate. Glass area: not to exceed 10% of heated floor area.

FIREPLACE: Controlled or outdoor combustion air, tight dampers and firebox doors.

HEATING & AIR CONDITIONING: Ducts in unconditioned spaces insulated with 2" wrap or 1" lined with vapor seal. Refrigerant piping: ½" foam rubber insulation. Heat pump, if electrically heated and cooled, selected and sized for energy efficiency.

Figure 4-2 Construction specifications need to provide sufficient detail to avoid any confusion as to what the builder is responsible for doing. Beware of the builder who doesn't need or refuses to provide written specifications. Home Planners and other design service firms can provide professional construction specifications acceptable industry-wide.

Project Estimates

After you narrow your list to three or four builders it will be time to ask for project estimates. If you already have professionally prepared plans and a material list from a home planning service it will be easier to compare cost estimates from different builders. Most experts agree that when reputable and competent builders provide bids on the same set of detailed plans and specifications, the bids will be very similar. An example of construction specifications for energy conservation measures is provided in Figure 4-2.

If the builder provides plans and specifications, insist that every detail be included. Specifications need to identify not only what the builder will provide, but also what the builder will not provide. Beware of specifications consisting of only two or three pages. One expert cautions prospective homeowners about written specifications less than 20 pages long. In most cases the lowest bid will be from the builder providing the minimal specifications or none at all.

Questions to Ask when Selecting a Builder

✓ Is the builder willing to provide names and phone numbers of past customers?

✓ Are past customers willing to recommend this builder?

✓ Did the builder respond to customer complaints in a timely manner?

✓ Have complaints been filed with Better Business Bureau?

✓ What is the builder's reputation with area building inspection agencies?

✓ Is the builder experienced with building your particular design?

✓ Does the builder have experience in the county where your site is located?

✓ Will the builder assume responsibility for any subcontractors used?

✓ Does the builder verify the location of the foundation in relation to property lines, setbacks and easement?

✓ Will a professional engineer design the foundation based on a soil report?

✓ Does the builder have a history of finishing projects on time?

✓ Has the builder filed for bankruptcy?

✓ Is the builder a member of local and national homebuilders' associations?

✓ Does the builder provide a written warranty (typical warranty is one year, some builders provide a paid 10 year Home Protection Plan)?

Figure 4-3 No matter which step in the home building process you may take first, asking the right questions will help make your dream home in the country a reality.

Be sure that costs for site improvements, utility connections, roads and permit fees are included in the bid as a firm price instead of an allowance. Development and permit fees may be as high as $10,000 to $12,000. For example, the cost for site preparation and improvements will be a lot higher in rocky soil than in other types of soil conditions. Also be sure to have all costs related to foundation preparation, grading and fill included in the bid.

Permit fees for on-site water and sewage disposal systems vary widely. Installation costs will also vary. It is a good practice to have the cost for on-site water wells and sewage disposal systems as a firm bid price. A builder willing to provide a firm price bid for these items will be sure to thoroughly evaluate your building site. Chapters 5 and 6 of *Building Your Country Home* provide detailed information on planning on-site water and sewage disposal systems.

After Move In

Keep a written list of all minor items that need attention after you move in. Most builders will schedule return calls a month or two after closing. This will be a good time to check your list and have these minor problems corrected. A month or two before your written warranty expires, take the time to check all major items covered.

Builders to Avoid   Figure 4-4

✓ Has a large file at the Better Business Bureau.
✓ Has an out-of-state address that's only a Post Office Box number.
✓ Never heard of the National Home Builder's Association.
✓ Can't find the address and phone number of past customers.
✓ Can only give you a verbal estimate or verbal guarantee.
✓ Construction specifications are one page long.
✓ Doesn't need to bother with surveys to site the foundation.
✓ Tells you not to worry about all those rules and regulations for on-site sewage disposal systems.
✓ Tells you that the "rotten egg" odor of local groundwater supplies can be treated easily.
✓ Tells you not to worry about those rumors of dwindling local groundwater supplies.
✓ Guarantees that your great view of rolling hills and open space will not be disturbed by future housing developments.

Selecting your builder is definitely one of the most important decisions you will make. Compare builders and ask questions, the more the better. Questions you may want to ask are provided in Figure 4-3 on page 43. Be sure to call or visit recent customers before you make your final decision. Most will be happy to share their homebuilding experience with you.

Builders to Avoid
There are a few builders you want to be sure to avoid. The chart above lists examples of the builders to avoid.

Selecting A Site
Even with the demand for rural building sites at an all-time high, it won't be hard to find rural property for sale. It seems that just about everyone knows someone wanting to sell a great site at a bargain price. Be sure to do your homework on property deals that sound too good to be true, you may avoid buying someone else's problem.

All you need to do to find rural property for sale is to look in the real estate section of your local newspaper. Full-color real estate books can also be found at newsstands. Most of these real estate books are free of charge. You can also find rural property listings on the Internet. Here are just a few examples of rural property listings you might find:

Two acres—corner lot. Near Smith Junior College. Only 15 miles to downtown. Hillside side retreat, perfect for building. No need to see this one, just call to close the deal.

2½ acres near Pensacola, Fl. Adjacent to small fishing lake. First $1,500 offer takes this steal.

Four-acre ranchette. In the middle of farm country. With flowing stream. Close to major highway. A real deal at $2,000.

Each one of the sites described in the above real estate advertisements may seem to be a good buy at first glance. But, by asking the right questions, you may find the site isn't exactly what was advertised. The rest of the story on the properties described above can be found in Figure 4-5.

Buying property sight unseen is definitely not recommended. Try to avoid the "rush to buy this weekend" syndrome. Start out by first

Figure 4-5 By taking time to inspect each property and asking the right questions you will be able to avoid these so-called real estate deals.

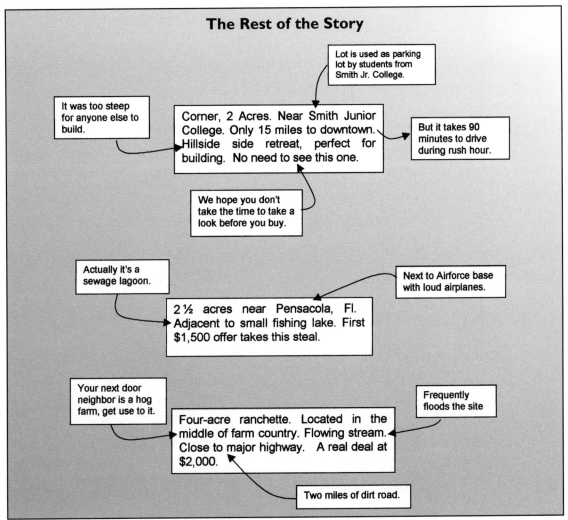

The Rest of the Story

Lot is used as parking lot by students from Smith Jr. College.

It was too steep for anyone else to build.

Corner, 2 Acres. Near Smith Junior College. Only 15 miles to downtown. Hillside side retreat, perfect for building. No need to see this one.

But it takes 90 minutes to drive during rush hour.

We hope you don't take the time to take a look before you buy.

Actually it's a sewage lagoon.

Next to Airforce base with loud airplanes.

2 ½ acres near Pensacola, Fl. Adjacent to small fishing lake. First $1,500 offer takes this steal.

Your next door neighbor is a hog farm, get use to it.

Frequently floods the site

Four-acre ranchette. Located in the middle of farm country. Flowing stream. Close to major highway. A real deal at $2,000.

Two miles of dirt road.

Try to imagine that two-lane country road during rush hour traffic.

making a list of personal and family factors to consider. Here are a few examples of those factors to consider in selecting a site:

Price: Is the price within your budget? Even if the asking price of the property is outside your budget range, go ahead and collect other information about the site. You may be able to find information to use as a bargaining tool in purchasing the site at a reduced cost.

Location: Do you prefer an isolated area or a site in a large development? If this is to be your permanent residence, how far and how long are you willing to commute back and forth to work? In general, land prices and construction costs tend to drop as the distance from urban centers increases. You may want to check rush hour traffic in and around different sites before making a final decision. That two-lane country road may look different with bumper to bumper cars.

Schools, Parks and Recreational Services: If you have children and this is to be a primary residence, how long will your children have to ride a school bus before reaching school? In some rural areas an hour bus ride to and from school is common. Will you be able to get your kids to little league practice and soccer games?

Emergency Services: What types of emergency services are provided in the area? In some cases you may find that emergency medical services (EMS) and fire services are not available at all. In many rural areas EMS and fire department services are provided on a volunteer basis. Volunteer EMS and fire response may be paid for with subscriber fees from area residents. Non-subscribers may not be eligible for services in the event of an actual emergency. Don't wait for a fire or medical crisis to find out that you're not a paid subscriber and therefore not eligible for emergency services. If you do have emergency services available be sure to ask about correct telephone numbers to call; 911 systems may not be used in all rural areas.

General Factors to Consider

It will pay to obtain as much information as you can about each site. The more information you have in evaluating different properties, the better decision you will be able to make. General site factors to consider in your selection include size and shape, easements, slope, zoning and general types of soil.

Size and Shape: State or local regulations may establish the minimum size of a rural building site. Installing both a water well and sewage disposal system on a site smaller than one acre may not be allowed. In some states or jurisdictions a site of at least one and a half acres is required when on-site water and sewage disposal must be

911 call systems and other emergency services may not be available in the country. "Support your local fire department" may take on new meaning if you have an opportunity to serve as a member of a local volunteer fire department.

provided. Check your state and local regulations related to minimum lot size.

Easements and Setbacks: An easement is a right-of-way authorizing a person or company access to part of your site. A ten-foot electrical utility easement along property lines is common. When repairs or other work needs to be done, the utility company will be able to dig or trench within the easement. The setback is the distance from the ends or sides of a lot beyond which buildings cannot extend. Setback or buffer zones for components of the on-site sewage disposal system have been established in many jurisdictions. Easement and setback distances will vary and may be found in subdivision restrictions, deeds or zoning codes. After you apply easements and setback distances you may find that your one-acre site has shrunk to a smaller size (see The Shrinking Acre Figure 4-6).

Encumbrances and Encroachments: An encumbrance is a legal right to certain portions or use of a property. Encroachments are buildings or parts of buildings or other structures extending beyond property lines. Both may restrict your use of certain portions of your property and diminish future value.

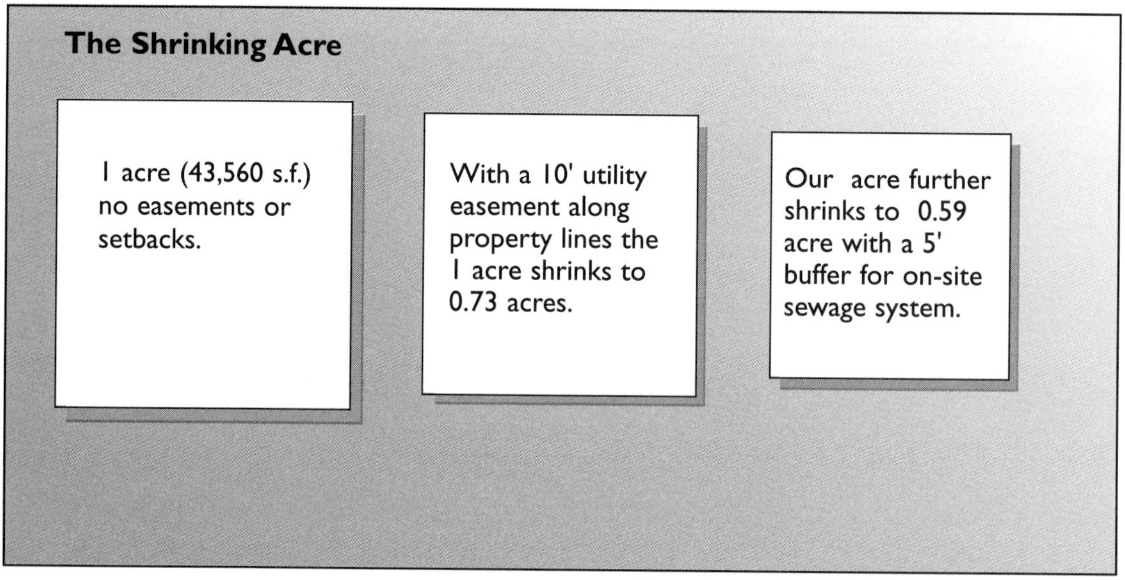

Figure 4-6 A one-acre site may sound big, but with easements, setbacks and buffers, your acre will begin to shrink. In some locations the minimum size for a building site with both on-site water and sewage will be greater than one acre.

Slope and Grade: A flat site with little or no slope may be prone to temporary flooding during heavy rains. Sites with a slope greater than

The Shrinking Acre

I acre (43,560 s.f.) no easements or setbacks.

With a 10' utility easement along property lines the I acre shrinks to 0.73 acres.

Our acre further shrinks to 0.59 acre with a 5' buffer for on-site sewage system.

30% may require special attention when it comes to design and installation of sewage disposal systems (see Chapter 6).

Soil: Soil types and characteristics can vary a great deal both horizontally and vertically. A well-drained soil, such as a sandy loam or loam with a minimal amount of clay, having a depth of at least 48 inches, could be described as an "ideal" soil. Unfortunately, such ideal soils are now hard to find. The amount of clay, silt and sand along with the depth to seasonal groundwater and depth to rock will have an influence on the cost associated with developing a specific site.

The design, installation cost and future maintenance cost of your sewage disposal system will depend on the soil characteristics of the site. See Chapter 6 for a detailed discussion of soil evaluations for planning sewage disposal systems.

Be sure to check building restrictions of homeowners associations. In some cases, these restrictions may be more of a problem than city zoning codes.

Zoning and Building Codes: If you want to maintain horses or other animals make sure there are no restrictions. On the other hand, if you don't want to live next to a hog farm, be sure that hog farms and other animal feeding operations are restricted. If the hog farm

Beware the Bargain Lot

If price is your only consideration, you may wind up buying an abandoned waste dump at a bargain price. You may even find that you will be responsible for paying to clean up the site. In one case, a family purchased a 20-acre site considerably below market value. The site was covered with a dense growth of brush and scrub trees making it impossible to thoroughly inspect the property. After buying the site, the new owner began clearing it. During the clearing, several piles of rumble and building waste were found that had been dumped years earlier. This was the first sign that the bargain price may not have been such a great deal.

The new owner obtained a burn permit from the county environmental office and began to burn cleared brush and wooden construction waste that had been dumped. The burning went fine until thick black smoke started pouring from the fire. Over 200 buried tires had caught fire. Unable to extinguish the burning tires, the new owner was fined for violating the burn permit.

Investigation by the state environmental agency showed that several illegal dumpsites were located on the property. One area with high levels of lead and cadmium had to be cleaned up at the owner's expense. This was a costly lesson in buying property.

was there first, you may have to get accustomed to the "country atmosphere." It is better to find out before you buy how other properties in the area are used. Trying to obtain zoning restrictions against a farming practice that has been conducted for many years may be difficult if not impossible to do. In fact, new zoning laws may grandfather existing operations. That hog farm may be your neighbor for a long time.

A to Z Environmental Factors to Consider

When it comes to environmental factors, no site will be perfect, but it is better to know about environmental conditions prior to purchase. Except for Love Canal situations, experienced builders and developers should be able to correct many environmentally limiting conditions. Following is a description of environmental factors from A to Z to consider in selecting your site.

Abandoned Wells: If abandoned water wells or oil and gas wells are located on the property make sure they have been properly plugged. Without being plugged, abandoned wells can be an easy route for surface contamination to enter groundwater supplies. Abandoned wells may also present a potential safety hazard for young children. If you purchase property, and then later find an abandoned well, you may be responsible for proper plugging and paying for the cost of any environmental damages.

It is better to know that you have a rock quarry as a neighbor before you buy. Take time to check adjacent properties to avoid being blasted out of bed some morning.

Adjoining Properties: The property next door may seem to be just another tree-lined site. Without checking you may find it has been used as toxic waste dump or is being used as a sewage sludge disposal site. If your site is next to farmland, take time to ask the owner about future plans, or you may wake up one morning and find a pig farm as your next door neighbor. Unless there are subdivision restrictions or zoning laws, other landowners will be able to use adjoining properties just about any way they choose.

You may also want to check to see what lies beyond the trees. Finding that your ideal site is only a few hundred yards from a rock quarry can be an earthshaking experience, especially if dynamite is used to blast rock. Don't wait until a train whistle awakens you at 4 a.m. to find that you've built your home close to a railroad track.

Asbestos: Once known as the "miracle fiber" for its fire protection and insulation properties, asbestos was widely used in building products including pipe insulation and heating duct joints. Asbestos became a major environmental health issue during the 1970s and '80s when elevated rates of asbestosis, lung cancer and mesothelioma (a rare but normally fatal disease) were identified among asbestos workers. While asbestos is no longer used in building products in the

51

U.S., older buildings such as barns and garages may contain asbestos. Sites where old farm buildings containing asbestos materials have been demolished without proper environmental protective measures being taken may have elevated levels of this material.

Coastal Barrier Resource: Coastal barrier resources are unique landforms that provide protection for diverse aquatic habitats and serve as the mainland's first line of defense against the impacts of coastal storms and erosion. In 1982 Congress recognized the vulnerability of coastal barriers and passed the Coastal Barrier Resources Act (CBRA).

The CBRA designates undeveloped coastal barrier islands for inclusion in the Coastal Barrier Resources System. Areas so designated are ineligible for direct or indirect Federal financial assistance that might support development, including flood insurance. Specific maps available from the U.S. Fish and Wildlife Service depict these areas.

Even the U.S. portion of the Great Lakes shoreline is subject to the CBRA. The State of Michigan has passed a Sand Dune Protection and Management Act, which prohibits certain building activity and regulates commercial and residential development. Other states may have similar rules and regulations related to development around inland lakes. Before you purchase a coastal or lakeside building site, determine what restrictions might apply.

Earthquakes and Landslides: The potential for an earthquake to occur in California is well known. Not well known is that other portions of the U.S. have also experienced large earthquakes in the past. The New Madrid earthquake occurring near St. Louis, Missouri, in 1811, was powerful enough to change the course of the Mississippi River. The New Madrid quake was one of the largest seismic events ever recorded in North America.

A hilltop site may provide a great view, but if the area is prone to landslides, you may find your hilltop home slip sliding away. Fortunately, only a few areas in the U.S. are prone to large-scale landslides. These areas may be a geologist's dream but are a homeowner's worst nightmare.

Nearly every state in the U.S. has experienced some amount of earthquake activity and will have areas prone to landslides. In high hazard risk zones, builders can use seismic designs to reduce the damage to buildings from earthquake activities. Studies have indicated that when seismic designs are used, building damage may be reduced by more than half. The Federal Emergency Management Agency

(FEMA) has published guidelines for building homes in areas prone to earthquake activity.

Electromagnetic Fields (EMF): Sources of electromagnetic fields (EMF) are easy to find. Just about any type of electrical appliance, from electric blankets and TVs to coffee makers and vacuum cleaners, can produce weak EMF. Electrical lines, especially high-voltage transmission lines, also produce EMF.

Several studies in the 1980s linked EMF to an increased risk of childhood leukemia. These early studies energized the public utility industry to conduct extensive research and investigations concerning the health risks of EMF. After several years of research many scientists came to the conclusion that there was "insufficient scientific evidence to conclude that EMF is harmful to human health."

Some citizen groups still regard EMF as a very real environmental concern. In 1995, the California Supreme Court reviewed the EMF controversy and concluded that based on existing scientific research, "there is no risk that low frequency power lines cause cancer."

While high-voltage transmission lines have been cleared for causing increased health risk, they may be a source of "visual pollution." A steel tower next to your dream home in the country can sure spoil your view of the countryside.

Endangered Species: Congress passed the Endangered Species Act (ESA) to save national wildlife treasures such as the Bald Eagle and

Electrical transmission lines are not only an eye sore, but may cause concerns about the health effects of electromagnetic fields (EMF), which may lower property values.

Whooping Crane. Few Americans would argue about the need to protect and preserve critical habitats used by these species to live and
breed. Some individuals though might question the need for the same
level of effort to protect and preserve critical habitat for a fruit fly or
cave spider.

Imagine finding out you had to *"contribute"* several thousand dollars
to a semi-private governmental wildlife conservation organization to
obtain a permit to build on your property. If your rural building site is
located in an area that the U.S. Fish and Wildlife Service (USFWS)
has designated as critical habitat for an endangered species you may
need to obtain a federal permit.

It is better to find out if the site is located in an area that has been
designated as critical habitat for an endangered species before you
buy. This will allow you to plan for extra costs that may be required
for biological studies and obtaining a "take-permit" from the USFWS.

Before you purchase a site, contact the regional USFWS field office
and ask about areas designated as critical habitat for endangered
species. Also ask about any proposed listings of species that may
impact your property in the future.

Floods: Floods are the most common type of natural disaster. In the
U.S. the price tag from floods is about $2 billion in property damage
each year. It's important to keep in mind that floods occur not only
when streams overflow their banks, but may also occur from rapid
runoff during a heavy rain. As rural areas are developed with more
paved surfaces and roof space, the amount of runoff from rains can
drastically increase. Areas not prone to flooding in the past may
become subject to flooding as a result of rural housing development.
The 100-year floodplain is used as the basis for flood insurance
requirements. Check floodplain maps to determine if prospective sites
are located within known floodplains. Evaluate the grade and slope of
surrounding properties to see if they will drain across your site.

Formaldehyde: This chemical is not a site selection concern, but can
be a problem in some types of building and home furnishing materials. Formaldehyde was used for many years as a preservative in products ranging from pressed wood and foam insulation to embalming
fluids. Formaldehyde has also been used in fabrics to bind color pig-
ments and as a fire retardant. Some readers may recall having to dis-
sect frogs pickled in formaldehyde during high school biology class.
Formaldehyde can be found at low levels, normally less than 0.03
ppm, in both outdoor and indoor air. Exposure to formaldehyde may
cause allergy-type reactions. If you have experienced eye irritation

Development of rural property may increase water runoff and temporary flooding of properties. During heavy rains this channel becomes a raging river.

while visiting fabric shops, low levels of formaldehyde may have been the cause. Infants, the elderly and persons with chemical sensitivities may be especially vulnerable to low levels.

Polychlorinated Biphenyls (PCB): Chemical compounds with excellent insulating and fire-retardant properties, PCBs were widely used in various industrial applications including the manufacture of products such as plastic, adhesives, paints, fluorescent light ballasts and electrical transformers. It has been estimated that between 1929 and 1977, more than one billion pounds of PCBs were produced in the United States.

Two well-known poisoning episodes in Japan and Taiwan were linked to rice contaminated with PCBs. Studies have also linked PCBs to cancer in laboratory animals. Due to public concerns, the commercial production of PCBs in the United States was discontinued in 1979. PCB compounds degrade very slowly and can persist in soil and water for many years. They also build up in the food chain. A small amount released to a stream may result in levels of concern in fish tissue.

Even though production of PCBs has ceased in the U.S., these compounds can still be found in soil and stream sediments due to past disposal practices. Property with a past history of commercial waste disposal activity or the storage and maintenance of electrical transformers should be suspect.

Pesticides: If you are considering a building site that has been actively farmed in the last few years, check on the type and amount of chemicals used for pest and weed control. Information on the use of pesticides in the area may be obtained from local county extension agents. Depending on the type of farming, past pesticide usage may range from the aerial spraying of pesticides of crops to the use of herbicides for weed control. The EPA has undertaken a National Pesticide Survey of groundwater. The survey has indicated pesticide contamination of groundwater aquifers in rural areas.

Ask about the location of any underground pipelines on or adjacent to proposed building sites. Contact the owner of the pipeline and ask about the type of hazardous materials transported and what is being done to prevent accidental spills and leaks. Ask about what to do in the event of a pipeline failure.

Pipelines: More than 1.8 million miles of pipelines transport a wide range of hazardous materials across the U.S. ranging from natural gas and crude oil to liquid butane. Experts at the National Transportation Safety Board (NTSB) have stated, "The potential threat to public safety has become more severe in recent years, as the rate of residential and commercial development adjacent to all types of pipelines has increased." A summary from the Office of Pipeline Safety shows that from 1985 to 1999 a total of 2,777 pipeline accidents resulting in 229 injuries and 35 fatalities were reported. At this time, the state and federal agencies responsible for pipeline safety do not have a comprehensive system for inspecting and testing pipelines.

There is nothing wrong in having a pipeline as a neighbor as long as the owner routinely inspects and maintains the system. Unfortunately, in some cases, a company's pipeline inspection and maintenance system may consist of "Call us if you smell anything" and "Don't fix it unless it's leaking."

Before you buy, ask about the location of pipelines within a half-mile radius of potential sites. Ask the pipeline owner about products transported, inspection and maintenance programs beyond the minimum required by regulations, and the past accident history of the company.

Radon: Radon is a radioactive gas released from the decay of uranium naturally present in the ground. It may enter a home by rising through cracks and holes in a home's foundation. Homes with basements and having little outside ventilation are of special concern. As radon decays, it emits small radioactive particles, which may become airborne. These small particles can damage the lungs when inhaled

---

Pipeline Leaks

Gasoline leaking from a corroded pipe in St. Helena Parish, Louisiana, allowed more than 400,000 gallons of gasoline to contaminate groundwater supplies. The company's accident prevention program included "flying over the pipeline to check for dead vegetation!"

Pipeline leaks can have tragic consequences. A liquid butane leak near Lively, Texas, in 1996, ignited when two nearby residents drove through a vapor cloud. The explosion and fire resulted in the evacuation of 25 homes and two deaths. The NTSB investigation report recommended an improved inspection program for the pipeline owner. The NTSB report also recommended that the pipeline owner develop a public education program to assist residents near the pipeline in recognizing the hazards and responding to a leak.

In 1999, a gasoline leak from a pipeline resulted in the deaths of two 10-year-old boys. A pipeline near their home had been leaking gasoline into a dry creek bed for several days. As the boys played along the creek, more than 88,000 gallons of gasoline ignited in a giant fireball, killing the boys and another resident. Most of the homeowners living in the area were not even aware that the pipeline was there. It was ironic that many homeowners had moved to this area to escape the hazards of the city.

and have been linked to an increased risk of lung cancer. Radon cannot be seen, smelled or tasted. Commercial devices may be used to detect and measure radon levels inside a home. Radon can also enter groundwater supplies. Ask local health deptartments about radon levels in the area where you plan to build.

Underground Storage Tank (UST): If the proposed building site is located near a former rural residence you may want to ask about past storage of heating fuel in underground storage tanks (USTs) or aboveground storage tanks (ASTs). It was a common practice for leaking USTs to simply be abandoned and left in place while a new tank was installed. Past fuel spills or leakage from storage tanks can be a potential source of groundwater contamination. New property owners may be financially liable for cleaning up past problems.

Water and Riparian Rights: Riparian rights are legal rights of property owners with land bordering a lake, stream or other body of water. Just because you have a stream passing through your property doesn't mean you have an endless supply of water. Riparian rights may grant property owners certain use of lands between high and low water marks of a stream. In most states you will need an authorization to pump or otherwise take water from the stream. In some states and regions you may also need an authorization to pump groundwater from your own well.

These authorizations are typically referred to as a "water right" and will require that a written application be submitted to the appropriate agency. Your authorization will limit the amount of water that can be pumped and will likely limit or prohibit pumping during a drought.

Wind: Experiencing a summer breeze without the smog and air pollution of the city is one reason many families choose to move to the country. The musical, *Oklahoma*, described it best, as "The waving wheat can sure smell sweet, when the wind comes right behind the rain." But, when the wind behind the rain turns out to be a tornado, be prepared to take cover! The same advice applies to hurricanes.

Although tornadoes occur throughout the world, the U.S. has the distinction of being the capital. This is especially true for the famed Tornado Alley stretching from Texas and Oklahoma through the plains to the Dakotas. More than 1,000 tornadoes are recorded in the U.S. each year with the majority occurring in Tornado Alley.

The actual risk of a tornado or hurricane striking a particular area is extremely small. But, if you plan to build in Tornado Alley or in a coastal hurricane-susceptible region, it may be wise to include wind-

To encourage homeowners to conserve limited water supplies, xeriscape demonstration plots have been established by many cities. This is a xeriscape education center in Lompoc, California.

resistant construction and a storm shelter in your building plans.

Wildfire: Tree-covered building sites are great, except when a wildfire, fanned by strong winds, is rapidly approaching. Every year one to two million acres of forest and grasslands burn in the U.S. The price tag for wildfires is enormous. In 1996, federal agencies alone spent more than $100 million battling wildfires. In Southwestern states more than 400 homes were destroyed by recent wildfires in forested areas. The best time to think about reducing the risk of wildfires to your home is prior to building. Ask local fire authorities about past wildfire areas and history related to prospective building sites.

Xeriscape Landscaping: Xeriscape comes from the Greek word Xeros, meaning dry. If you think xeriscaping is cactus and rock gardens, think again. Xeriscape landscaping incorporates landscape planning and design; soil analysis and improvement; appropriate plant selection; practical turf areas; efficient irrigation; use of mulches; and appropriate maintenance which can significantly reduce water requirements. If you will be using groundwater, plan on xeriscaping instead of high-water-demand grasses like St. Augustine.

Zoonosis: These are infectious diseases transmissible from animals

Animal control can be a major problem in some rural areas.

(deer, raccoons, skunks, bats, dogs, cats, etc.) to humans. That wild raccoon that seems to be friendly may just be experiencing the first stages of rabies. When wild animals first contact this dreaded disease, some seem to lose their fear of humans. During this stage, animals normally seen only at night may be seen wandering around during daylight. In later stages, the same animal may become excitable, exhibiting the familiar "mad dog" symptoms. In final stages, paralysis occurs making it difficult or impossible for the animal to swallow, with excessive drooling and "foaming" at the mouth. No matter where you live, country or city, be sure to have all pets vaccinated against rabies on an annual basis.

Small deer may be cute, but may also be responsible for helping to transmit Lyme disease. Cases of this disease, transmitted by infective Ixodes ticks, have been reported in 48 states. In 1997, health authorities reported more than 12,500 cases of Lyme disease in the U.S., with most occurring in rural areas.

The Bubonic Plague of Medieval European, while rare today, is still being reported in Western states. Rural areas in California and New Mexico with populations of ground squirrels and Prairie Dogs have been reporting several cases of plague on an annual basis. In recent years, health alerts have been issued in some rural areas for diseases

Disease	Potential Sources and Description
Rabies	Raccoons, skunks, wolves, foxes and bats are common carriers. Wild animals appearing to have no fear or abnormal behavior should be avoided. Usually fatal if not promptly treated. All household pets in rural areas should be vaccinated for rabies. Seek immediate medical attention for any animal bite or scratch.
Lyme Disease	Transmitted by the bite of an infected "deer" tick. More common in rural areas with high deer populations. Ask local health departments about occurrence. Use insect repellents in outdoor areas.
Salmonellosis	Both pet and wild reptiles (esp. turtles & lizards) are common source. Caused by Salmonella bacteria found in feces and on the skin. After handling these creatures of the wild thoroughly wash hands. Can cause severe illness in younger children.
Tularemia	Known as rabbit fever. Can also be transmitted by muskrats, beavers and some domestic animals. Caused by exposure to bacteria when dressing infected animal. Can also be caused by consuming undercooked wild rabbit meat.
Plague	Caused by infected rodent fleas. Has been a problem in some western states with large populations of prairie dogs and ground squirrels.
Giardiasis and Cryptosporidiosis	Also known as "hikers diarrhea." Caused by parasites in feces from wild animals (beavers, raccoons, bears, deer, other) from drinking water from a stream without disinfection. Assume all water in a stream is contaminated no matter how clear it may appear.

Figure 4-7

such as rabies, Lyme disease, and even plague. See Figure 4-7 for more information on these and other zoonotic diseases.

Finding Environmental Information

Information concerning environmental conditions of different properties can be obtained from a number of sources. Inspecting the property yourself is a must. Asking the owner and land developer about past environmental conditions is also valuable.

Local or Regional Sources

Local or regional environmental agencies or public health departments will be one of your best sources of information for obtaining environmental information. The county extension agent with the local U.S. Department of Agriculture office will also be able to answer questions about environmental issues. In many instances, local, county and regional agencies will have more influence on your building project than state or federal agencies. It will pay to become acquainted with these local officials.

Self-inspect

Take time to carefully inspect each site you are considering. Walk the property yourself. Finding abandoned 55-gallon drums may be an indication of past chemical dumping. Discolored soils may be signs of past chemical spills. Old garages and farm machine shops may have surrounding soils contaminated with waste oil and other petroleum products. At one time it was common practice to dispose of waste chemicals by simply pouring them onto the ground outside.

Check to see what's beyond the treeline and over the hill. Try to drive at least a half-mile radius around the site. If this is not possible, obtain an aerial photo. If you find a rock quarry or other type of industrial operation, check into its current use and future plans. If you find a train track near a proposed building site, you may want to ask other residents about noise especially early morning train whistles.

Online Sources

Thanks to the electronic age it is possible for buyers to obtain a great deal of information about a site and surrounding properties prior to making a final decision. The EPA and other organizations now provide information over the Internet that can assist you in finding environmental information about potential building sites. For example, by using the EPA ENVIROFACTS Web site, it was possible to determine that the main source of water for the "flowing stream" described in Figure 4-5 was treated wastewater from a poultry-processing plant.

Even if you don't have a personal computer you may still be able to use this resource. Local libraries are likely to provide computer resources for the general public to use in accessing information on the Internet. Some will even be able to assist you in conducting your search. Figure 4-8 provides a summary of some of the current Web sites you may find useful in obtaining environmental information about the sites on your list.

The EPA has several Internet sites providing environmental information. The ENVIROFACTS Warehouse is a good starting point. The Warehouse is a collection of a variety of EPA databases. All you have to do is enter information such as the address or ZIP code of the site, or the city or county in which the property is located.

The ENVIROFACTS Warehouse search can provide information on chemical disposal sites, chemical releases, wastewater discharge points and hazardous waste processing facilities which may be located near the property. You may find that a rock quarry or chemical processing plant is just over the hill. An example of information available from this Web site is provided in Figure 4-9 on page 64.

Web Site	Description
Surf Your Watershed http://www.epa.gov/surf/	Provides information on the quality of water in local streams and lakes. You can literally Surf Your Watershed and find information on water quality, water quality related to recreational use, suitability for fish and potential pollution sources. You can even print a map of the watershed.
Groundwater Quality http://water.usgs.gov/wrd002.html	The US Geologic Service (USGS) maintains this Web site. Links are provided to state and regional USGS offices with detailed reports on major aquifers. Some provide results of groundwater studies that can be downloaded.
Questions About Drinking Water http://www.epa.gov/OGWDW	If your building site will be connected to a public water system, you can obtain information on chemical pollutants. Recent test results for your community water supply can also be provided.
Drinking Water Pollutants http://www.epa.gov/ogwdw/dwh/health.html	Both technical and non-technical information on how different drinking water pollutants affect health can be found at this EPA Web site. Drinking-water health advisories can be downloaded for future reference.
Sources of Potential Pollution http://www.epa.gov/enviro/zipcode.html	By typing in the zipcode for prospective building sites you can find information on nearby industrial polluters. If your site is within a mile of a chemical industry ask local officials about emergency plans.
EnviroMapper Web Site http://www.epa.gov/enviro/html/em/index.html	This site can provide maps showing potential problems related to drinking water, toxic chemical releases, hazardous waste, water discharge permits and Superfund sites. EnviroMapper also links to full text reports, providing even more information.
Contact State Environmental Agencies http://www.epa.gov/epapages/statelocal/envrolst.htm	Find Web sites for state environmental agencies. State regulations for on-site sewage and water systems can be directly downloaded from many of these sites. **Figure 4-8**

Environment Maps

It is even possible to obtain an environmental map of the area in which you are interested. EPA's ENVIROMAPPER site can provide several different map scales—from an area view down to a street

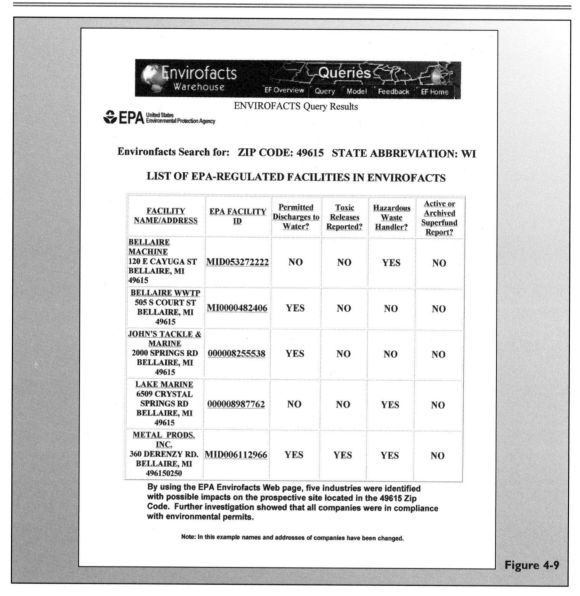

ENVIROFACTS Query Results

Environfacts Search for: ZIP CODE: 49615 STATE ABBREVIATION: WI

LIST OF EPA-REGULATED FACILITIES IN ENVIROFACTS

FACILITY NAME/ADDRESS	EPA FACILITY ID	Permitted Discharges to Water?	Toxic Releases Reported?	Hazardous Waste Handler?	Active or Archived Superfund Report?
BELLAIRE MACHINE 120 E CAYUGA ST BELLAIRE, MI 49615	MID053272222	NO	NO	YES	NO
BELLAIRE WWTP 505 S COURT ST BELLAIRE, MI 49615	MI0000482406	YES	NO	NO	NO
JOHN'S TACKLE & MARINE 2000 SPRINGS RD BELLAIRE, MI 49615	000008255538	YES	NO	NO	NO
LAKE MARINE 6509 CRYSTAL SPRINGS RD BELLAIRE, MI 49615	000008987762	NO	NO	YES	NO
METAL PRODS. INC. 360 DERENZY RD. BELLAIRE, MI 496150250	MID006112966	YES	YES	YES	NO

By using the EPA Envirofacts Web page, five industries were identified with possible impacts on the prospective site located in the 49615 Zip Code. Further investigation showed that all companies were in compliance with environmental permits.

Note: In this example names and addresses of companies have been changed.

Figure 4-9

view. The ENVIROMAPPER can be used to show the location of industrial facilities, railroads, rivers, military installations, airports and other items of environmental interest. Using the ENVIROFACTS Web site you can also obtain an "environmental scorecard" for areas in which you are considering building sites. An example of such a "scorecard" is provided in Figure 4-10.

Surf Your Watershed

Before buying that lakeshore property or the site with a spring-fed stream, take a few minutes to SURF YOUR WATERSHED on the EPA water quality Web site. This site provides information on lakes and streams impaired by contamination from farm and urban stormwater runoff and discharges from city owned or industrial wastewater treatment facilities.

Lakes and streams once designated for swimming and fishing may no longer be able to support these recreational uses. Using the "Surf Your

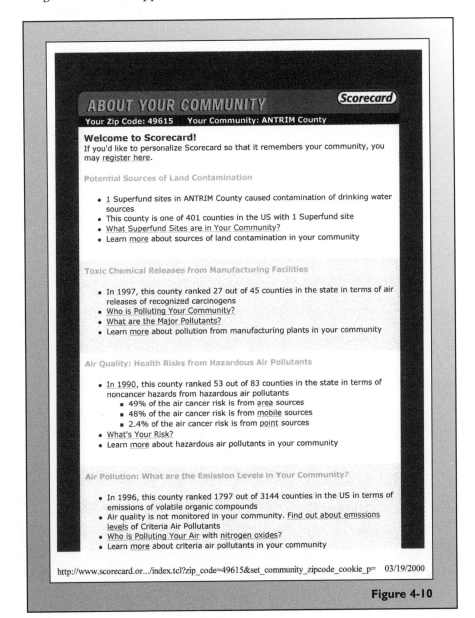

Figure 4-10

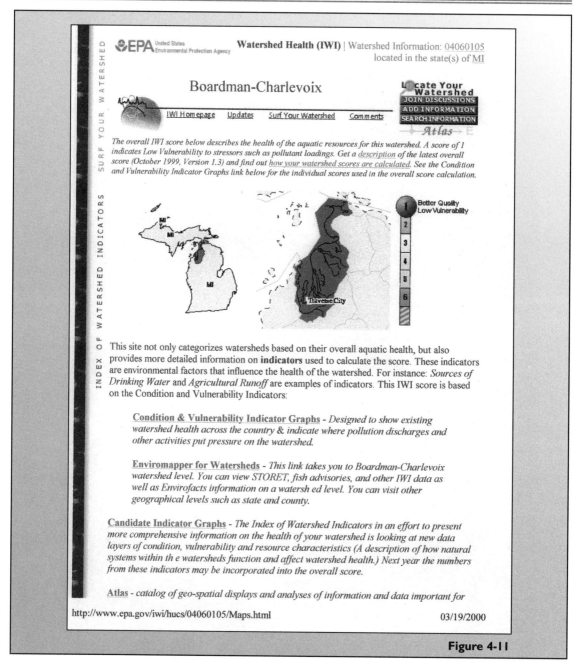

Watershed Health (IWI) | Watershed Information: 04060105
located in the state(s) of MI

Boardman-Charlevoix

IWI Homepage   Updates   Surf Your Watershed   Comments

Locate Your Watershed
JOIN DISCUSSIONS
ADD INFORMATION
SEARCH INFORMATION
Atlas

The overall IWI score below describes the health of the aquatic resources for this watershed. A score of 1 indicates Low Vulnerability to stressors such as pollutant loadings. Get a description of the latest overall score (October 1999, Version 1.3) and find out how your watershed scores are calculated. See the Condition and Vulnerability Indicator Graphs link below for the individual scores used in the overall score calculation.

This site not only categorizes watersheds based on their overall aquatic health, but also provides more detailed information on **indicators** used to calculate the score. These indicators are environmental factors that influence the health of the watershed. For instance: *Sources of Drinking Water* and *Agricultural Runoff* are examples of indicators. This IWI score is based on the Condition and Vulnerability Indicators:

Condition & Vulnerability Indicator Graphs - *Designed to show existing watershed health across the country & indicate where pollution discharges and other activities put pressure on the watershed.*

Enviromapper for Watersheds - *This link takes you to Boardman-Charlevoix watershed level. You can view STORET, fish advisories, and other IWI data as well as Envirofacts information on a watershed level. You can visit other geographical levels such as state and county.*

Candidate Indicator Graphs - *The Index of Watershed Indicators in an effort to present more comprehensive information on the health of your watershed is looking at new data layers of condition, vulnerability and resource characteristics (A description of how natural systems within the watersheds function and affect watershed health.) Next year the numbers from these indicators may be incorporated into the overall score.*

Atlas - *catalog of geo-spatial displays and analyses of information and data important for*

http://www.epa.gov/iwi/hucs/04060105/Maps.html   03/19/2000

Figure 4-11

Watershed" Web site, you may find that a health alert has been issued against eating certain types of fish caught from nearby warterways.

Acid rain, caused by air pollution, combined with the discharge of wastewater from certain industries has resulted in health advisories

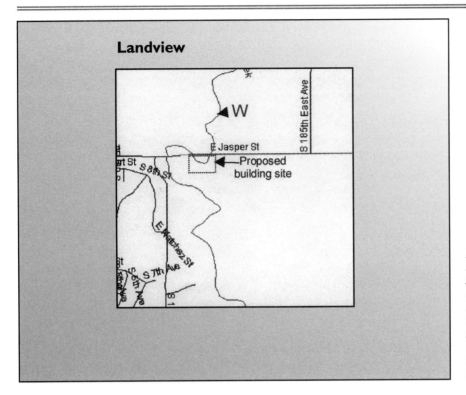

Landview

Figure 4-12 With the help of LandView III, a sewage treatment plant (W) was identified as the major source of water for the stream crossing this site. The prospective buyer also found that the site is located in the 100-year flood plain.

being issued for many waterbodies in the far Northeast. In some states, fish consumption health advisories have been issued for nearly every lake in the state due to elevated levels of mercury in fish tissue. Other fish consumption health advisories have been issued due to contamination from pesticides, PCB, cadmium and other pollutants.

If you find the lake or stream in which you have an interest has been identified with pollution concerns, consult regional and local environmental authorities. Find out what is being done to restore impaired streams. You may be able to take part in clean-up efforts as an interested stakeholder. An example of information you may be able to find while surfing your watershed is shown in Figure 4-11.

LandView III

LandView III is an available software tool that can be used to find information related to potential building sites. LandView III is a Windows-based, software-mapping program developed by the U.S. Bureau of the Census and the EPA. This program must be downloaded and installed on your personnel computer. Environmental data from the EPA and statistics from the latest census for a given region can be accessed by the user. LandView III can help identify waste treatment facilities, airports, roads and highways, railroads, schools, hospitals and other major features. This tool can also be used to obtain census data concerning the number of people living within a prescribed distance of your site. An example of a LandView III map is shown in Figure 4-12 on page 67.

Other Environmental Web Sites

Internet environmental Web sites are also maintained by a number of concerned citizen groups and industrial groups. In many cases, citizen groups may exaggerate the risk or hazard associated with existing conditions. At the same time, industrial groups may tend to under-state the problem.

A good example is the controversy related to EMF. Some citizen groups claim that any exposure to EMF is a health hazard and should not be allowed. Electrical power companies will state that there are no health problems related to EMF exposure. When faced with con-flicting health hazard information, you may want to consult with your health care provider or local public health professionals.

Other Sources of Information

Developers and property owners are another source of information related to environmental conditions of potential building sites. At a minimum, ask the seller to complete some type of property transac-tion screen questionnaire or checklist. The American Society for Testing and Materials (ASTM) has developed a standard format (E 1528) and procedures to use for the property transaction screen. A copy of this transaction screen questionnaire can be purchased from the ASTM at the following address: Headquarters, 1916 Race Street, Philadelphia, PA 19103.

Other organizations have developed similar questionnaires and check-lists for the property transaction screen. A typical checklist is shown as Figure 4-13. Some states have real estate transaction laws, which require the seller to disclose certain information about the property to prospective buyers.

For example, in Hawaii, the seller must inform buyers in writing about any defect or condition related to the property, regardless of whether it has been corrected or repaired. Information that the seller must disclose to the buyer in Hawaii includes land slides, asbestos, flood plain location, soil contamination, termites, wood rot, murders on the property and even reputations of haunting. Your real estate agent should be able to provide information on state disclosure laws and assist you in having sellers complete a disclosure form.

ENVIRONMENTAL CHECK LIST	Figure 4-13	
AREAS OF POTENTIAL IMPACT	YES	NO
1. Subsurface conditions (soils, underground water, seismic).	❏	❏
2. Land formations (low areas, steep slopes, floodplains, wetlands).	❏	❏
3. Vegetation and wildlife (endangered species).	❏	❏
4. Existing land use and zoning (compatibility with building plans).	❏	❏
5. Community water supply available/ water quality & quantity.	❏	❏
6. Community sewage system/ if not, is site suitable for on-site system?	❏	❏
7. Solid waste disposal service available.	❏	❏
8. Underground or above-ground storage tanks.	❏	❏
9. Past industrial activity / farm machine shop / pesticide use?	❏	❏
10. Noise sources (airports, railway, highway).	❏	❏
11. Pipelines cross property?	❏	❏
12. Is site located in a known radon area?	❏	❏
13. Adjoining property land use.	❏	❏
14. Stained or discolored soils observed?	❏	❏
15. Has site been used for public or private dumps?	❏	❏
16. Abandoned wells on property?	❏	❏

For property transactions involving large tracts of land or commercial use of a property, most lenders will require that a formal environmental site assessment (ESA) be performed. The ESA may be limited to a questionnaire transaction screen completed by the seller. For commercial properties, the lender will normally require the buyer to have a qualified environmental professional conduct a Phase I ESA .

Phase I and Phase II ESA
A Phase I ESA consists of a visual inspection of the property to observe and report signs of surface or subsurface contamination. The Phase I also includes a review of historical records, insurance records and aerial photos to identify past industrial activities. A search of EPA

Figure 4-13 This is not a complete listing of all possible environmental concerns. If a formal environmental site assessment (ESA) has been performed in the past, ask the seller for a copy of the executive summary. The majority of potential environmental problems can be overcome. When problems are found, ask the seller for a reduced price to help cover the cost of any remediation.

databases for reports of chemical spills and other conditions in close proximity to the property is also performed during the Phase I ESA.

Information found during the Phase I is summarized in a written report for the buyer and lending agency. If information from a Phase I ESA indicates potential contamination problems, a Phase II ESA may be planned to collect and analyze soil and water samples from the site. Samples collected from the site are analyzed to characterize the extent of contamination that may be present. This information will be useful in estimating the cost of site clean up.

With the results of a Phase II ESA, a site clean up or Phase III ESA can be planned. The purpose of a Phase III ESA is to clean up a contaminated site for its intended future use. If a contaminated site is cleaned up for use as a parking lot, but the site is later sold for use as homebuilding sites, problems may still exist.

The cost of having a formal ESA conducted can range from $2,000 to more than $4,000 for a Phase I, with the cost of a Phase III clean-up easily reaching $100,000 to $500,000. While you are not likely to have a formal ESA conducted for residential property, you should ask property owners and developers if such studies have been performed in the past.

Figure 4-14 You may decide to not purchase this property based on the information provided in this Phase One ESA Report.

Example of Phase One Executive Summary
ESA Phase One Executive Summary

A Phase One Environmental Site Assessment (ESA) was conducted by Insight Environmental Professionals on August 23, 1996. During the site visit it was noted that a pipeline crosses the south end of the property. The owner/operator of the pipeline was contacted and confirmed recent notices of safety violations.

Visible signs of possible chemical leaks or spills were observed along the south boundary of the property. Historical records indicate that the adjacent property was once used for a farm machine repair shop and has been listed as a state Superfund site. The north end of the property is located within the Muddy River flood plain. An industrial wastewater treatment plant located one-half mile up stream is currently under an EPA Administrative Order for permit violations.

A large residential dump was observed on the southeast end of the property. Five fifty-gallon drums label "cynaide" were observed at this dumpsite. A search of EPA Risk Management Program (RMP) databases showed the site is located within 1 mile of five chemical companies. Accidental chemical releases from these companies will require evacuation of the area.

Useful EPA 800 Numbers For Locating Environmental Information

Safe Drinking Water Hotline
1-800-426-4791 (information on pollutants
reported in drinking water)

National Small Flows Clearinghouse Hotline
1-800-624-8301 (information on on-site sewage
disposal systems)

Community Right-To-Know Act (EPCRA)
1-800-424-9346 (information on chemicals used
and stored by local industries)

Indoor Air Quality Information Clearinghouse
1-800-438-4318 (information on indoor air pollutants from building materials)

National Radon Hotline
1-800-767-7236 (information on how to reduce
exposure to naturally occurring radon)

Acid Rain Hotline
1-202-564-9620

Air Risk Information Center Hotline (Air RISC)
1-919-541-0888

Asbestos Abatement/Management Ombudsman
1-800-368-5888

National Lead Information Center
1-800-424-LEAD [1-800-424-5323]

National Pesticide Network
1-800-858-7378

Ozone Protection Hotline
1-800-296-1996

Superfund and EPCRA Hotline
1-800-424-9346 (information on hazardous
waste disposal sites similar to "Love Canal")

Toxic Release Inventory - Community Right To
Know - 1-800-535-0202 (information on toxic
air pollutants from local industries)

Toxic Substances Control Act (TSCA) Hotline
1-202-554-1404

Wetlands Information Hotline
1-800-832-7828

Hazardous Waste Ombudsman
1-800-262-7937

Climate Wise Wise-Line
1-800-459-WISE (1-800-459-9473)

Figure 4-15 These numbers will be useful in obtaining additional information on a number of environmental concerns. Local environmental and public health agencies are also excellent sources of information.

The executive summary of a Phase I report will only be a page or two long, but can provide a great deal of information about the past history and existing environmental conditions of the site. An example of a Phase I Executive Summary Report is provided as Figure 4-14. From information provided in the example, the prospective buyer was able to determine that the fishing lake described in the brochure is actually a sewage treatment lagoon for a nearby community.

Environmental Information Hotlines

If your investigations do not indicate major environmental concerns and the site is to be used for residential purposes, you can probably proceed with comparing properties and making a final decision. If your search indicates potential problem areas or concerns, ask for guidance from your local environmental agency, public health department or county extension agent. You may also want to call the

Environmental Information Hotlines maintained by the EPA. A summary of current EPA Hotlines is provided in Figure 4-15 on page 71.

Working with Your Builder

Voice any concerns about environmental conditions of the property to your builder. You may want to have any corrective measures that need to be taken included in written specifications and bids. Ask the seller to reduce the price to offset any work your builder may need to do to reduce or correct environmental-related problems.

Before making your final site selection decision, take time to read and become familiar with the information provided in Chapters 5 and 6 on rural water supplies and sewage disposal systems. This information will be valuable in making your final decision and in caring for and maintaining these systems later on.

WATER SUPPLY SYSTEMS FOR RURAL SITES

Groundwater Questions to Ask Local Officials

✓ What is the main underground water supply aquifer in the area I plan to build (If aquifer has a name, write it down for future reference).

✓ Are there known groundwater contamination problems in this aquifer?

✓ What is the typical hardness level of water from this aquifer?

✓ Where can I find water quality information about this aquifer?

✓ Is this aquifer subject to surface runoff and other sources of contamination?

✓ Do people using water in this area often complain about taste and odor problems?

✓ Have users of this aquifer been on mandatory conservation during previous droughts?

✓ Do any regulatory agencies control the amount of water withdrawn from this aquifer?

✓ Do any endangered species depend on springs flowing from this aquifer?

Figure 5-1

Water Basics

When you ask most kids, "Where does your water come from?" most will reply, "Why, from the water faucet, of course." If you ask adults the same question, you tend to get the same type of answer. In fact, most people don't know where their water comes from, how it is treated or how it is actually delivered to their home.

When visiting potential building sites, ask about the water supply. Examples of questions to ask are provided in Figure 5-1. The source of your water will be either from a community water supply system or from your own private water system.

If water will be provided from a community system, ask if the home-owners association is responsible for operation and maintenance. A few unscrupulous developers advertise a worry-free community water supply and then rely on the homeowners association to pay costly operational and maintenance bills. These high costs will be passed on to homeowners. When the operation and maintenance of small community water systems are neglected, rural homeowners can face serious consequences. See the case history "Tragedy in Walkerton" in Appendix Four.

Smaller community water supply systems may not be able to comply with new EPA safe drinking water regulations. The costs to upgrade these systems will be paid by users. Some rural areas experiencing rapid growth are having groundwater aquifers literally "sucked dry," creating problems for both community systems and private water well owners. That old saying that, "You don't miss the water 'til the well runs dry" is as true today as ever. If you wait until the well runs dry to learn about your rural water supply, it may be too late.

The homeowners association responsible for this aging system will have to increase water rates to replace and maintain failing and rusted components. Some small community water systems may need to drastically increase water rates to comply with new EPA drinking water rules.

Some Water History

Early man recognized the importance of a reliable water supply. Entire civilizations sprang up around natural water sources from which nearby crops could be irrigated. As early as 5,000 years ago, irrigation ditches were being used in Pakistan to carry water to crops. Cities in Pakistan were known to be using clay water pipes in 2700 BC. Metal water pipes were in use in Egypt around 2450 BC, and on Crete by 2000 BC. In 400 BC, China's Grand Canal was in use with more than 1,500 miles of waterways.

First constructed in 312 BC, the Roman aqueducts may be the best known example of man's early efforts to develop water supplies. The first Roman aqueduct, now known as the Aqua Appia, was about eight miles long. Constructed during the reign of Appius Claudius, the Aqua Appia was able to bring water to Rome from the Sabine Hills outside the city.

Aqueducts later constructed by the Romans were up to 40 miles long and capable of delivering 300 gallons per person per day. Water from the aqueducts was used not only for drinking purposes, but also for irrigation and supplying fountains and public baths. Lead was commonly used by the Romans for pipes to distribute water from the aqueducts. Some historians attribute the leaching of toxic amounts of lead as one cause of the decline and fall of the Roman Empire.

Early man also knew the importance of sewage disposal. Ancient cities in Iran had toilets with drainage systems nearly 6,000 years ago. Some experts credit the Romans with inventing the first flush toilets and public sewage collection systems. The Cloaca Maxima, constructed in the 2nd century BC, was one of the largest collection systems constructed by the Romans.

Even though early man did see a need for water distribution and sewer collection systems, little was known about how diseases were spread by contaminated water and sewage. Many of the early toilets were simply flushed into the neighboring streets with little or no attention paid to nearby water cisterns and wells. It wasn't until the mid-1800s that water's role in disease transmission became known.

Anton van Leeuwenhoek's invention of the microscope in 1676 made it possible to see the tiny microbes present in water. For the first time it was possible for scientists to theorize that a connection existed between polluted water and certain diseases. During an 1854 cholera epidemic in England, Dr. John Snow was able to demonstrate that contaminated water could transmit disease. By charting the number of cholera cases, Snow showed that over 500 people living within a

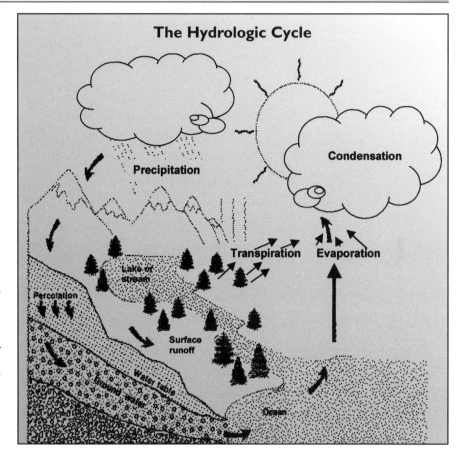

The Hydrologic Cycle

Precipitation

Condensation

Transpiration **Evaporation**

Lake or stream

Percolation

Surface runoff

Water table

Ocean

Figure 5-2 There is no such thing as "naturally pure" water. Throughout the hydrologic cycle, water is subject to chemical, biological and physical contaminants. Poor quality water can usually be treated. For the rural homeowner, water quantity may be more important than water quality.

couple of blocks of London's Broad Street had died. He was able to pin point the source of the disease outbreak to a public well on Broad Street, and by removing the pump handle, stopped the deadly epidemic in its tracks.

Until 1993, when more than 400,000 people became ill from drinking water in Milwaukee, Wisconsin, most people took a plentiful and safe water supply for granted. However, for those planning to build in the country, it is a serious issue. Before making a final decision on your building site, obtain as much information as possible about what you can expect in terms of water quality and quantity.

The Hydrologic Cycle

While early man knew the importance of having a convenient and plentiful water supply, he didn't have a complete understanding of where water comes from or where it goes. Today we know that water continually cycles through the environment in several different forms and by different natural processes. Natural processes involved in the water cycle include: (1) condensation, (2) precipitation, (3) infiltration, (4) runoff and (5) evaporation. These processes take place in a continuous hydrologic cycle. The hydrologic cycle is depicted in Figure 5-2.

Condensation

Condensation occurs as warm moist air begins to cool. If the moist air continues to cool, tiny droplets are formed that cling to dust particles in the air forming clouds or fog. These droplets increase in size and gain weight until they begin to fall as precipitation (rain, snow, hail or sleet, depending upon temperature conditions). Precipitation varies in amounts and in intensity from one season to another and from one geographic region to another.

Precipitation, Infiltration and Runoff

When precipitation reaches the Earth's surface, it can do one of three things: (1) enter the ground (infiltration); (2) flow into surface streams and lakes (runoff); or (3) return to the atmosphere as water vapor (evaporation). Runoff and infiltration are interrelated and are influenced by the form of precipitation (snow, sleet or rain), the type and amount of vegetation and type of soil in a given area.

Grass and other vegetation tend to reduce the amount of water running off the ground surface during the initial stages of a rainstorm. If surface soils become saturated, increased amounts of stormwater runoff occur, finally entering streams or lakes as surface water. Paved surfaces, roofs of building and other developments can significantly increase the amount of runoff occurring.

Water infiltrating the ground passes through several different soil zones. The depth of these soil zones may vary a great deal even on the same building site. When water first infiltrates the soil, it enters the root zone. In the root zone, plant roots absorb small amounts of water. Soils having a high percentage of sand do not readily retain water in the root zone, but allow water to quickly infiltrate (percolate) downward until reaching the zone of saturation.

In the zone of saturation, pores in the soil or rocks are full of water. Water in the zone of saturation is referred to as groundwater with the top of the zone known as the water table. Groundwater continues percolating downward and horizontally through cracks, cervices and pores in soil and rock formations until a restrictive layer is reached. Water that moves horizontally underground may eventually emerge into a stream or lake as surface water.

Groundwater exists everywhere below the water table but may not be available in useable amounts. A geologic formation in which groundwater occurs in a useable amount is known as an aquifer. Aquifers come in all shapes and sizes and include different types of soil and rock formations. They may be small and located in isolated gravel or sand deposits left by glaciers during the ice age. Or, they may be very large, stretching across several states. Portions of the Ogallala aquifer extend from Nebraska through the Great Plains states to Texas.

Groundwater movement is very slow, moving only a few inches per month, or even per year, through clay soils and shale. Groundwater movement through aquifers composed of cracked and caved limestone will be somewhat faster. In comparison, water movement in surface streams is very fast and is measured in cubic feet per second (cfs). Smaller brooks and streams may have average flows of only 1-5 cfs while the average flow in larger rivers can easily exceed 1,000 cfs.

Aquifers close to the ground surface having the water table or a porous formation as their upper surface are referred to as unconfined aquifers. While unconfined aquifers may be close to the surface and require less drilling, they may be prone to more contamination problems than deeper aquifers. These deeper confined aquifers have a restrictive rock formation or tight soil layer, such as clay, as their upper surface.

Groundwater in confined aquifers may be subject to sufficient pressure that causes the water level to rise above the confining layer within a tightly cased well. These are known as "artesian aquifers." If the pressure in a confined aquifer is great enough, water in the well casing will rise to the surface as a free-flowing artesian well. Naturally occurring springs also result from this same process.

Evaporation and Transpiration

Evaporation and transpiration are two other important processes in the hydrologic cycle. As surface water in lakes and streams is heated by the sun, water is changed into its gaseous form, water vapor, and enters the atmosphere by evaporation. Water vapor is also released from tree and plant leaves through a similar process know as transpiration.

Water Quantity

Water quantity concerns the amount of water needed by the rural homeowner and the amount that can be provided. When it comes to water quantity, the first word is **conservation**. Tips on water conservation are provided in Figure 5-3.

Just because your home in the country may be connected to a community water supply system doesn't mean you will have an endless supply of water. Public water supply systems in some rural areas have to implement water-rationing restrictions every summer. Typical water rationing may include no landscape watering, no filling of swimming pools and even being without water during periods of peak

Water Conservation Tips for the Rural Homeowner

Outdoor Water Use

✓ Check for leaks in outdoor faucets, pipes and hoses. Even slight drips can add up to many gallons of wasted water.

✓ Plant drought-resistant trees, plants, and lawn grass. Consider xeriscape.

✓ Water your lawn only when it needs it. A good way to see if your lawn needs watering is to step on the grass. If it springs back up when you move, it doesn't need water. If it stays flat, it needs water.

✓ Avoid watering on windy days. Wind will carry water away from its intended area. Water during the coolest part of the day, generally early morning, to avoid excess evaporation and to help prevent the growth of fungus.

✓ Deep-soak your lawn when you do water. Give the grass ample moisture to penetrate down to the roots where it will do the most good.

✓ Put a layer of mulch around trees and plants. Mulch will slow the evaporation of moisture and discourage weed growth.

✓ Do not use a constant stream of water when washing the car. Wash from a bucket of soapy water, using the hose only to rinse. Wash less frequently during dry, hot weather.

✓ Use a broom, not a hose, to clean driveways and sidewalks.

Kitchen and Laundry Water Use

✓ Use your automatic dishwasher and automatic washing machine only for full loads, never for just a few items.

✓ If you wash dishes by hand, don't leave the water running continuously for rinsing. Fill one side of the sink with clean water for rinsing, or put the washed dishes in a rack and rinse them all at once with a spray attachment or a pan of hot water.

✓ Check faucets and pipes for leaks. Even a small leak can waste thousands of gallons in a month.

✓ Reduce the use of the garbage disposal, which requires a great deal of water for operation. Dispose of food scraps and peelings in the trash container or use food waste in a garden compost pile.

✓ Install water conservation flow restrictors in faucets.

✓ Keep faucet washers in good shape or use washerless faucets.

Bathroom Water Use

✓ Check the toilet for leaks. Put a few drops of food coloring in your toilet tank. If, without flushing, the color begins to appear in the bowl, you know you have a leak that needs to be repaired.

✓ Specify low water flush toilets and showerheads in your building plans. Low-flow plumbing fixtures will also reduce operation and maintenance problems with your septic tank system.

✓ Limit the length of showers to two or three minutes. Consider turning the shower off while you soap up and turn it on again only to rinse.

✓ Turn off the tap while brushing your teeth. Use only enough water to wet the brush and rinse your mouth.

✓ Teach children to turn faucets off tightly after use.

✓ Check faucets and pipes for leaks. Even a small leak can waste thousands of gallons per month. Keep faucet washers in good shape or use washerless faucets.

Figure 5-3

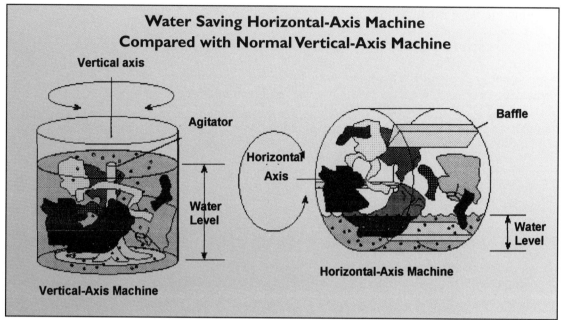

**Water Saving Horizontal-Axis Machine
Compared with Normal Vertical-Axis Machine**

Figure 5-4 Newer horizontal-axis washing machines use about half the water required in a normal top-loading machine. Homeowners will also save in the amount of detergent and other cleaning products used in washing clothes. Studies show that the horizontal unit removes more water from clothing during the spin cycle and that clothes are just as clean. Use of these water-saving washing machines will also mean that less water is going to your on-site sewage disposal system.

demand. If you will obtain water from a community water supply system, ask about past water rationing.

For properties without a public water supply, a private well will be necessary. Before buying a building site, find out as much as possible about what to expect when it comes to water quantity. Your first step should be to determine just how much water you think you will need for your home in the country. If you are planning on extensive landscape irrigation or growing certain plants and crops, your water needs may be a lot different than that of the average family.

Household Uses

Most experts estimate that, when all household uses (drinking, bathing, flushing toilets, washing machines) are added up, each person in the U.S. needs about 75 to 100 gallons of water per day. For a family of four, household water needs may be as much as 400 to 500 gallons per day. Don't forget about overnight guests. A few rural homeowners have to actually ration showers when friends and relatives spend the night.

Automatic washing machines account for more than 20% of a family's water use. A newer designed horizontal-axis washing machine can save up to 50% of water use on laundry days. A horizontal-axis washing machine is compared to a normal washing machine in Figure 5-4. Estimates of water use for other types of household appliances and use are provided in Figure 5-5.

Landscaping

Depending on the type of landscaping you choose, your summer water use may be more than triple water use during winter months. If summer droughts are common in your area, avoid high water-demand turf grasses such as St. Augustine. Talk to your builder about xeriscape landscaping (see Chapter 4). The photo on page 82 shows examples of grasses and shrubs with low water requirements.

Estimating Use

After you have identified all potential uses of water, estimate your maximum daily water needs by using Figure 5-5. Next, compare your estimated daily need with the amount of water that is expected to be available. Obtain as much information as possible about local aquifers. Information about the type and depth of soils and rocks in local aquifers will be useful. It may be better to drill 300 feet to a limestone aquifer than to drill to only 100 feet in a clay and shale aquifer.

Estimates of Domestic Water Use		
Water Use	**Daily Need**	**Peak Demand**
Per person per day	75 to 100 gpd	5 gpm
Clothes Washer, standard	30 to 50 gals/load	5 to 10 gpm
Clothes Washer, horizontal	20 to 30 gals/load	4 to 5 gpm
Garbage Disposal	4 to 6 gpd	2 gpm
Toilet, standard	5 to 7 gals a flush	3 gpm
Toilet, low-flow design	1.6 to 3 gals a flush	1 gpm
Shower, standard design	23 gals / 5 min	5 gpm
Shower, low-flow design	14 gals/ 5 min	3 gpm
Tub bath	30-40 gals	7 to 8 gpm
Pool filter backwash	100 to 200 gals	8 to 10 gpm
Softener regeneration	50 to 100 gals	5 to 8 gpm

Figure 5-5 Plan for the highest water use situation, such as a weekend with overnight guests. If your system can not provide sufficient water to meet peak demands, a water storage tank may help alleviate the problem (gpd= gallons per day) (gpm= gallons per minute)

Ask local county extension agents about landscaping to reduce water demand. Most extension offices will have a number of useful booklets and guides for the rural homeowner.

Underground formations such as fractured limestone may be able to yield large amounts of groundwater. A farmer's well located in the Edwards Aquifer of SW Texas was able to produce more than twenty million gallons of water a day. Unfortunately, for the farmer, the well had to be capped, due to pumping restrictions required to protect endangered species of fish living in springs located more than 30 miles from the property. Aquifers located in clay and shale formations produce less water than limestone and gravel formations.

Yield Test

After a well is constructed, most drillers conduct a yield test. This may be required by water well regulations in some states. A yield test is performed by pumping water for a specified length of time, and then measuring the maximum rate of sustained water delivery in gallons per minute (gpm).

Other Use Considerations

Keep in mind that your demand for water will not be the same throughout the day. During the morning when family members are getting ready for work and school and in the evening when everyone is home, water demand will be high. In theory, a well with a maximum pumping rate of 1.5 gallons per minute (gpm) will be able to produce 2,160 gallons of water per day, but may not be able to meet a family's peak demand. Most mortgage lending agencies call for a private water system to be able to yield a minimum of 5 gpm. Some authorities recommend a minimum pumping yield of at least 8 gpm to meet peak demands.

When a well is drilled there is no guarantee that the amount of water found will support sustained pumping. If you find you have a low-yield well (less than 5 gpm), ask your builder or plumber about the installation of a storage tank to help meet peak demands. A storage system may cost an additional $2,000 to $3,000, but will help to provide water to meet your peak demands.

In addition to being the first word, the last word in any discussion of water quantity is conservation. Many rural areas undergoing rapid development are literally running out of water as aquifers are being over pumped. Even if your rural home will be supplied water from a community system, conservation measures need to be followed.

With water-saving plumbing fixtures specified in your building plans, you will be able to reduce your family's water needs by as much as 25%. Following the "Tips on Water Conservation" described in Figure 5-3 on page 79 can further reduce water consumption. For rural homeowners, water conservation must become a part of everyday life for every member of the family.

Primer on Water Quality

When it comes to water quality, most homeowners simply want to know, "Is it safe to drink?" and "Does it taste good?" Water that is safe to drink is referred as being "potable." While potable water may be safe to drink, it may not be very palatable or pleasing to taste.

By asking the right questions and doing your homework, it will be possible to have a rural water supply that is potable and also tastes great. To do this you will need a basic understanding of the physical, biological, chemical and radiological factors that can be used to describe drinking water quality.

Pollutants

In nature, water is not pure. The notion of pristine water from clear mountain streams is a myth. In fact, water from clear mountain streams may harbor microscopic organisms that can cause severe illness. Every year, hikers and other outdoor enthusiasts get sick from drinking water from so-called pristine mountain steams.

Throughout the hydrologic cycle, water quality is constantly changing due to both natural and man-made substances. Any substance, which results in an undesirable change in water quality, may be referred to as a "pollutant." When this occurs, water may be described as being polluted. As mountain streams make their journey across farmlands and through industrialized urban areas, there are many opportunities for pollutants to change water quality.

Precipitation is subject to small amounts of pollutants in the air. Though natural rainfall is somewhat acidic, when falling rain is exposed to industrial air pollutants such as nitrous oxides or sulfur dioxide, it may become more acidic and fall as "acid rain" (see Glossary for more details).

Stormwater runoff is able to pick up pollutants from a wide variety of "non-point sources." Examples of agricultural non-point-source pollutants include pesticides sprayed on croplands and nutrients from animal waste. Oils and grease and even metals such as lead have been found in stormwater runoff from roads and highways. In some rural areas, poorly designed and poorly operated on-site sewage disposal systems have been found to be major sources of non-point pollution.

Water quality in streams and lakes is subject to pollution from "point sources" including the discharge of municipal and industrial wastewater treatment plants. These treatment facilities are designed to reduce pollutants to an acceptable level. In some cases the quality of the treated wastewater being discharged is better than the water already in the stream.

As groundwater percolates through soil and rock formations naturally occurring minerals are dissolved. Pesticides and other farm chemicals may also dissolve and pollute groundwater. Chemical spills on the surface and from underground storage tanks (UST) can be another source of groundwater pollution.

The challenge for the rural homeowner is to find the best quality of water available. The "Primer on Water Quality" provides a basic understanding of the physical, chemical, radiological and biological factors to consider for ensuring that your rural water supply is both potable and palatable. Information provided in the "Primer" also helps the rural homeowner in deciding the type and frequency of water quality testing to perform.

How Small Is Small?

Improvements in laboratory methods during the last 50 years have made it possible for scientists to detect smaller and smaller amounts of chemical substances in the environment. A well-equipped water laboratory in the 1950s was able to detect with some degree of reliability chemicals at one part per million (ppm or mg/L). Anything below 1mg/L was considered as undetectable. By the 1970s, detection at one part per billion (ppb or ug/L) was possible. Some laboratories today are able to detect some substances at the one part per trillion (ppt) level! A pesticide that was undetectable in 1955 could now be reported as being present in your water supply at 500 ppb.

Water Quality Standards

The EPA has established water quality standards for public drinking water systems for both health-related and aesthetic factors. While these standards are not enforceable for private water systems they can be useful in evaluating water quality by the rural homeowner.

Maximum contamination levels (MCLs) have been developed for about 54 chemical substances having known adverse health effects. The MCL is the maximum allowable amount, which may be present in drinking water provided to a customer of a public water system. In addition, secondary maximum contamination levels (SMCLs) have been established for physical and general chemistry factors that affect aesthetic qualities of drinking water.

If you plan on using your rural water supply for a business operation such as a restaurant, it may be considered as a "public drinking water system." As a public water system you will be required to meet all EPA and state health department requirements.

Physical Factors

Color, taste and odor are examples of physical factors related to water quality. The apparent color of water may be influenced by fine suspended particles know as turbidity. High levels of turbidity may make it more difficult to destroy disease-causing organisms. After particles causing turbidity have been removed, the true color of water can be measured. The true color of water is measured in "color units" (CU) based on a standard platinum-cobalt color scale. Most individuals would not be able to detect any color in water at 10-15 CUs. At 90-100 CUs, water may have the appearance of tea. EPA recommends no more than 15 CUs for public water supplies.

A sudden change in the color of water may be an indicator of a change in other water quality concerns. Plumbing cross-connections may cause water to change color due to contamination from antifreeze used in fire sprinkler systems. Chromate, a toxic chemical used in cooling towers and air conditioning systems, may turn drinking water yellowish-green when back-flow conditions occur.

Small amounts of iron or manganese in a groundwater supply are sufficient to cause a color problem. Hydrogen sulfide, which imparts a very offensive rotten-egg like odor can also be a groundwater problem. The majority of color, taste and odor problems can be minimized or eliminated with home water treatment units.

Any sudden color change in a water supply should be investigated. Local health department officials can be asked to evaluate the problem. It would be prudent to use bottled water or another water source until the questionable supply is given a clean bill of health.

General Chemistry Factors

General chemistry concerns that rural homeowners need to know about include pH, hardness, total dissolved solids (TDS) and chloride. These factors are related more to taste and palatability than to public health concerns.

Generally, pH can be defined as a measure of how acidic or alkaline a substance is. A scale from 0 (very acidic) to 14 (very alkaline) is used to describe pH. A pH of 7.0 would be considered as neutral. Normal rain is slightly acid, having a pH of about 5.6. Acid rain caused by industrial air pollutants may have a pH as low as 4.4.

As rainwater percolates through soil and rocks, various minerals may be dissolved. In limestone rock, percolating rainwater is able to dissolve calcium, magnesium and other minerals creating small voids and crevices in the rock formation. Given sufficient time (several thousand years), these small voids may become huge caves. As groundwater continues its underground journey additional minerals and chemical compounds dissolve, changing water quality.

Hardness represents the amount of calcium, magnesium and other minerals dissolved in water. Calcium and magnesium are normally the only significant minerals contributing to hardness. As water hardness increases, more soap will be required to produce foam and lather. Increased hardness is also responsible for producing scale in hot water pipes, boilers and heaters. This is the same scale you see forming in dishwashers and other appliances.

In the U.S., water hardness is reported as calcium carbonate in terms of milligrams per liter (mg/L). Water hardness may range from being "soft" (0 to 50 mg/L) to "very hard" (300 + mg/L). Another term used for measuring hardness is "grains per gallon." About 17.1 mg/L is equal to one grain per gallon of hardness. See Figure 5-6 for a comparison of these various terms used to describe hardness.

Description of Water Hardness		
Water Hardness		
mg/L (a)	Grains per gallon	Description
0 to 50	0 to 3	Soft
50 to 150	3 to 9	Moderate
150 to 300	9 to 17.5	Hard
300+	17.5+	Very Hard

Figure 5-6 As water hardness increases more soap will be required to produce lather. Increased scale in hot water tanks, water pipes and spots on dishes will also be experienced. Some individuals choose to use a commercial water softener when hardness is above 100 to 200 mg/L. Many families have used hard water for many years without any treatment. (a) Reported as calcium carbonate.

Hardness is probably the single biggest reason most homeowners install water treatment units. As water hardness approaches or exceeds 150 to 200 mg/L (8.7 to 11.7 grains per gallon), many homeowners elect to treat their water. Hard water can be "softened" using several different treatment methods. Water softening and other types of treatment are discussed later in this chapter.

Total dissolved solids (TDS) is simply a measure of all dissolved minerals. High levels of TDS may be responsible for sediments, cloudiness or stain problems. A salty or bitter taste may be a problem in some areas having high TDS levels.

The EPA has established the secondary maximum contaminant level (SMCL) for TDS as 500 mg/L based on physiological concerns. Groundwater in many parts of the country will exceed the EPA's 500 mg/L SMCL. It should be noted that the World Health Organization (WHO) and other health agencies use 1,000 mg/L as the recommended limit for TDS. If the TDS level in your water supply exceeds 1,000 mg/L, ask for advice from your local health department.

Chlorides by themselves are not a significant public health problem. The chloride level in many groundwater supplies will be low (10 mg/L) unless introduced from natural mineral deposits, geological processes or other sources. Sudden changes in chloride levels may be an indication of pollution from septic tanks or agriculture activities. At levels above 500 mg/L, water may have a somewhat salty taste. The EPA's SMCL for chloride is set at 250 mg/L.

Groundwater with a chloride level below 1,000 mg/L is generally referred to as "fresh water" compared to brackish water with a chloride level of 1,000 to 4,000 mg/L. Typical chloride levels in seawater are around 19,000 mg/L. Aquifers near the coast may have chloride levels above 1,000 mg/L. Deeper groundwater aquifers influenced by natural mineral deposits may produce brine water with chloride levels exceeding 150,000 mg/L. Fortunately, high levels of chloride and TDS can be reduced by several different treatment methods, such as ultra filters or reverse osmosis (see a complete description of these systems later in this chapter).

Toxic Chemicals

There are literally thousands of chemical compounds that exist today. Most of these chemical compounds are rarely, if ever, detected in water supplies and are not routinely tested for in drinking water supplies. As already mentioned, the EPA has so far established maximum contaminant levels (MCLs) for more than 50 chemical substances based on concerns for adverse health effects.

The MCL for some of these substances is based on acute or immediate health effects. Acute health effects such as diarrhea, vomiting, nausea or stomach cramps may occur within several minutes to several hours after consuming the contaminated water. To prevent acute health effects, the EPA sets the MCL well below the level that would result in any adverse health effects.

The MCL for other chemical substances regulated by the EPA is based on chronic or long-term health effects. Chronic health effects such as cancer, birth defects, miscarriages, nervous system disorders and organ damage may take years or even decades to appear.

For toxic chemicals that do not cause cancer, the EPA uses information from animal studies to establish a reference dose. The *reference dose* is the amount of the substance that an individual can consume daily over a 70-year life span without any adverse health effects.

In developing standards for chemical substances known to cause cancer, the EPA assumes the only concentration that is safe is zero. Since it is not always possible to detect or treat these chemicals at extremely low levels, a maximum contaminant limit goal (MCLG) may be established. The MCLG is only a target for public water systems and not a regulatory limit.

The EPA uses a risk estimate approach to establish enforceable MCLs for cancer-causing contaminants. In developing an MCL risk estimate, the EPA assumes the average adult drinks two liters of water each day over a 70-year life span. MCLs are then established to reduce the risk of cancer to between 1 in 10,000 and 1 in 1,000,000 for the individual drinking 2 liters for an entire 70-year life span.

Figure 5-7, shown on pages 91-94, provides a summary of chemical contaminants regulated by the EPA. See Chapter 4 "Environmental Factors A to Z" for additional information on groundwater contaminants most often encountered by rural homeowners.

Radiological Concerns
A variety of radiation particles are emitted by radioactive materials (radionuclides) during the natural decay of uranium in rocks and may be found in groundwater. Possible chronic health effects from excessive exposure to these radiation particles include cancer, bone and kidney damage and birth defects. The EPA has regulated several radionuclides for more than 20 years. New EPA water quality standards for radon and uranium are pending.

Radon in drinking water increases the health risk both from the inhalation of radon when showering and from ingestion of water. The EPA recommends that "individual homeowners with private wells should test their indoor air radon levels" (see Chapter 4 "Environmental Factors A to Z").

Some aquifers may be more prone to radiological contaminants than others due to natural geological conditions. A few areas of the country have experienced radiological contamination of groundwater from military bases and Department of Energy facilities. Rural homeowners with questions about radiological contamination of groundwater in a particular area should contact their local health department for advice. Information on radiological contamination and other water quality concerns can also be obtained from the EPA's Drinking Water Hotline (800-426-4791).

Biological Concerns
Biological organisms important in water quality include viruses, bacteria and protozoans. When it comes to size, viruses are the smallest and can only be seen with high-powered microscopes. Bacteria are next on the size list ranging from about 0.1 microns to more than 30 microns. Protozoans range in size from 3 microns to those able to be seen by the naked eye. A size comparison chart is provided in Figure 5-8 on page 90.

The importance of biological organisms in drinking water was clearly demonstrated by Dr. John Snow, in 1854, when he traced 500 cholera deaths to contaminated water from London's Broad Street

Size Comparison of Biological Contaminants

(one micron equals about 0.00004 inches)

- Viruses are the smallest biological contaminants about 0.003 to 0.05 microns in size. Can only be seen with very powerful electronic microscopes. Includes Hepatitis and Polio viruses.
- Bacteria are somewhat larger, ranging in size from 1 to 40 microns.
- Protozoan are larger, ranging in size from 0.5 to more than 100 microns. This group includes several parasites harmful to man, including Cryptosporidium, the "bug that made Milwaukee sick."

note: Dust particles in air can be seen at about 40 to 50 microns in size. Rain droplets range in size from 600 to 10,000 microns.)

Figure 5-8 Unseen biological contaminants in drinking water can be a real problem. Recently, more than 500 persons attending a county fair became ill as a result of drinking well water contaminated with the toxin-producing E. Coli strain of bacteria. In Walkerton, Canada as many as 20 deaths were linked to drinking water contaminated with this rare strain of E. Coli (see Appendix 4 for more information on the Walkerton outbreak).

well. Biological organisms capable of causing human illness are referred to as pathogens. Currently, there are more than thirty pathogenic organisms capable of being transmitted by contaminated drinking water. Examples of pathogenic organisms are shown in Figure5-9 on page 95.

Because it is not practical to check for the presence of every disease-causing microorganism, health authorities use coliform bacteria as an indicator of contamination. Coliform bacteria are commonly found in the environment and are not themselves generally harmful. If a preliminary test is positive for total coliform bacteria, additional laboratory testing may be done to check for the presence of fecal coliform bacteria. Fecal coliform bacteria may indicate the presence of sewage or animal waste. A typical laboratory report is shown as Figure 5-10 on page 96.

After the construction of a new water well or repair work on an existing well, it is common practice to use a chlorine solution to disinfect. Recommended disinfection procedures are shown in Figure 5-11 on page 97. If coliform bacteria are found after a well has been disinfected recommendations from your local health authority should be followed. Most health authorities recommend having rural water

EPA Drinking Water Standards for
Inorganic Chemical Contaminants

(Units are in milligrams per Liter (mg/L) unless otherwise noted.)

Contaminant	MCLG	MCL	Potential Health Effect
Arsenic	none	0.05	Skin damage; circulatory system problems; increased risk of cancer
Asbestos (fiber >10 micrometers)	7 million fibers per Liter	7 MFL	Increased risk of developing benign intestinal polyps
Barium	2	2	Increase in blood pressure
Beryllium	0.004	0.004	Intestinal lesions
Cadmium	0.005	0.005	Kidney damage
Chromium (total)	0.1	0.1	Some people could experience allergic dermatitis after several years of exposure.
Copper	1.3	Action Level=1.3	Short term exposure: Gastrointestinal distress.
Cyanide (as free cyanide)	0.2	0.2	Long term exposure: Liver or kidney damage. Nerve damage or thyroid problems
Fluoride	4.0	4.0	Bone disease (pain and tenderness of the bones); Children may get mottled teeth.
Lead	zero	Action Level =0.015	Infants and children: Delays in physical or mental development. Adults: Kidney problems; high blood pressure
Inorganic Mercury	0.002	0.002	Kidney damage
Nitrate (measured) as Nitrogen)	10	10	"Blue baby syndrome" in infants under six months—immediate medical attention. Symptoms: Infant looks blue and has short ness of breath.
Nitrate (measured) as Nitrogen)	1	1	"Blue baby syndrome" in infants under six months—immediate medical attention. Symptoms: Infant looks blue and has short ness of breath.
Selenium	0.05	0.05	Hair or fingernail loss; numbness in fingers or toes; circulatory problems
Thallium	0.0005	0.002	Hair loss; changes in blood; kidney, intestine, or liver problems

Figure 5-7

EPA Drinking Water Standards for
Organic and Pesticide Chemical Contaminants

(Units are in milligrams per Liter (mg/L) unless otherwise noted.)

Contaminant	MCLG	MCL	Potential Health Effect
Acrylamide	zero	TT	Nervous system or blood problems; increased risk of cancer
Alachlor	zero	0.002	Eye, liver, kidney or spleen problems; anemia; increased risk of cancer
Atrazine	0.003	0.003	Cardiovascular system problems; reproductive difficulties
Benzene	zero	0.005	Anemia; decrease in blood platelets; increased risk of cancer
Benzo(a)pyrene	zero	0.0002	Reproductive difficulties; increased risk of cancer
Carbofuran	0.04	0.04	Problems with blood or nervous system; reproductive difficulties.
; Carbon tetrachloride	zero	.005	Liver problems; increased risk of cancer
; Chlordane	zero	0.002	Liver or nervous system problems; increased risk of cancer
Chlorobenzene	0.1	0.1	Liver or kidney problems
2,4-D	0.07	0.07	Kidney, liver or adrenal gland problems
Dalapon	0.2	0.2	Minor kidney changes
1,2-Dibromo-3-chloropropane (DBCP)	zero	0.0002	Reproductive difficulties; increased risk of cancer
o-Dichlorobenzene	0.6	0.6	Liver, kidney, or circulatory system problems
p-Dichlorobenzene	0.075	0.075	Anemia; liver, kidney or spleen damage; changes in blood
1,2-Dichloroethane	zero	0.005	Increased risk of cancer
1-1-Dichloroethylene	0.007	0.007	Liver problems
cis-1, 2-Dichloroethylene	0.07	0.07	Liver problems
trans-1,2-Dichloroethylene	0.1	0.1	Liver problems
Dichloromethane	zero	0.005	Liver problems; increased risk of cancer

Figure 5-7

MCLG= Maximum contaminant level goals are not enforceable standards but provide the water industry guidelines for selecting the best water supply source and treatment technology.
MCL= Maximum contaminant level is the maximum permissible level of a contaminant allowed for a public water supply.
Instead of testing your on-site water supply for all of these contaminants ask local health officials about the quality of groundwater in your area. Shallow groundwater aquifers will be more likely to be contaminated with these contaminants. Building sites near military bases and industrial areas will be more prone to contamination problems.

Organic and Pesticide Chemical Contaminants *Continued*

Contaminant	MCLG	MCL	Potential Health Effect
1-2-Dichloropropane	zero	0.005	Increased risk of cancer
Di(2-ethylhexyl)adipate	0.4	0.4	General toxic effects or reproductive difficulties
Di(2-ethylhexyl)phthalate	zero	0.006	Reproductive difficulties; liver problems; increased risk of cancer
Dinoseb	0.007	0.007	Reproductive difficulties
Dioxin (2,3,7,8-TCDD)	zero	0.00000003	Reproductive difficulties; increased risk of cancer
Diquat	0.02	0.02	Cataracts
Endothall	0.1	0.1	Stomach and intestinal problems
Endrin	0.002	0.002	Nervous system effects
Epichlorohydrin	zero	TT	Stomach problems; reproductive difficulties; increased risk of cancer
Ethylbenzene	0.7	0.7	Liver or kidney problems
Ethelyne dibromide	zero	0.00005	Stomach problems; reproductive difficulties; increased risk of cancer
Glyphosate	0.7	0.7	Kidney problems; reproductive difficulties
Heptachlor	zero	0.0004	Liver damage; increased risk of cancer
Heptachlor epoxide	zero	0.0002	Liver damage; increased risk of cancer
Hexachlorobenzene	zero	0.001	Liver or kidney problems; reproductive difficulties; increased risk of cancer
Hexachlorocyclopent-diene	0.05	0.05	Kidney or stomach problems
Lindane	0.0002	0.0002	Liver or kidney problems
Methoxychlor	0.04	0.04	Reproductive difficulties
Oxamyl (Vydate)	0.2	0.2	Slight nervous system effects
Polychlorinated	zero	0.0005	Skin changes; thymus gland problems; immune deficiencies; reproductive or nervous system difficulties; increased risk of cancer

Figure 5-7

Your local health department or family physician will be your best source of information on the health effects of drinking water contaminants. If one of the contaminants listed is found to be presence in your drinking water ask about its source and what is being done to routinely test for the substance. Some chemical contaminants may be naturally occurring, others may be from industrial spills and leaks. Over time low level contaminants may increase or even disappear as the substance travels through the groundwater supply.

Organic and Pesticide Chemical Contaminants *Continued*

Contaminant	MCLG	MCL	Potential Health Effect
Pentachlorophenol	zero	0.001	Liver or kidney problems; increased risk of cancer
Picloram	0.5	0.5	Liver problems
Simazine	0.004	0.004	Problems with blood
Styrene	0.1	0.1	Liver, kidney and circulatory problems
Tetrachloroethylene	zero	0.005	Liver problems; increased risk of cancer
Toluene	1	1	Nervous system, kidney or liver problems
Total Trihalomethanes (TTHMs)	none	0.10	Liver, kidney or central nervous system problems; increased risk of cancer
Toxaphene	zero	0.003	Kidney, liver or thyroid problems; increased risk of cancer
2,4,5-TP (Silvex)	0.05	0.05	Liver problems
1,2,4-Trichlorobenzene	0.07	0.07	Changes in adrenal glands
1,1,1-Trichloroethane	0.20	0.2	Liver, nervous system or circulatory problems
1,1,2-Trichloroethane	0.003	0.005	Liver, kidney or immune system problems
Trichloroethylene	zero	0.005	Liver problems; increased risk of cancer
Vinyl chloride	zero	0.002	Increased risk of cancer
Xylenes (total)	10	10	Nervous system damage

Figure 5-7

EPA Secondary Drinking Water Standards

Contaminant	Secondary Standard
Aluminum	0.05 to 0.2 mg/L
Chloride	250 mg/L
Color	15 (color units)
Copper	1.0 mg/L
Corrosivity	noncorrosive
Fluoride	2.0 mg/L
Foaming Agents	0.5 mg/L
Iron	0.3 mg/L
Manganese	0.05 mg/L
Odor	3 threshold odor number
pH	6.5-8.5
Silver	0.10 mg/L
Sulfate	250 mg/L
Total Dissolved Solids (TDS)	500 mg/L
Zinc	5 mg/L

Figure 5-7

EPA secondary standards are non-enforceable guidelines regulating contaminants that may cause cosmetic effects (such as skin or tooth discoloration) or aesthetic effects (such as taste, odor or color) in drinking water. EPA recommends secondary standards for public water systems but does not require systems to comply. However, states may choose to adopt and enforce these standards.

Common Waterborne Diseases

Disease or Organism	Potential Sources and Description
Cholera	A major public health problem in many underdeveloped countries. Caused by the Vibrio cholera bacteria. Normal water disinfection will kill this organism.
Polio	Virus transmitted through sewage. Normal water disinfection will kill this organism.
Hepatitis A	Also known as "infectious hepatitis."
Entamoeba histolytica	An amoebae parasite transmitted when drinking water is contaminated with sewage. Normal water disinfection will kill this organism.
Norwalk virus	Associated with contamination of water wells after flooding. Any time flooding occurs, wells should be disinfected with chlorine and tested for the presence of coliform bacteria.
Shigella	Often called "traveler's diarrhea." Common in underdeveloped countries without modern sewage and water treatment facilities. Normal water disinfection will kill this organism.
Helicobacter pylori	Recently recognized as a cause of stomach ulcers. Investigators are now finding this organism in ground water supplies. Your ulcer may be caused by H. pylori instead of that high-stress job.
Escherichia coli O157:H7 (Toxigenic E. coli)	This organism produces a powerful toxin that can cause severe injury to the kidneys. Normally associated with undercooked hamburger meat, E. coli O157 has recently been linked to several major water-borne disease outbreaks. Normal water disinfection will kill this organism.
Giardiasis and Cryptosporidiosis	Also known as "hikers diarrhea." Caused by parasites in feces from wild animals (beavers, raccoons, bears, deer, other) From drinking water from a stream without disinfection. Assume all water in a stream is contaminated no matter how clear it may appear. This organism cannot be killed using normal methods of disinfection.

wells tested for coliform bacteria on an annual basis and after any construction or repair work or flooding.

Figure 5-9 A few of the waterborne diseases transmitted through contaminated drinking water. Rural homeowners need maximum separation between their on-site sewage disposal system and water well.

Testing the Waters

Now that you know more about water quality, you are probably asking, "Do I need to have my water tested for all of this?" It is both impractical and too costly for a homeowner to test for all possible contaminants listed in Figure 5-7. Having a private laboratory test for these contaminants could cost as much as $1,500.

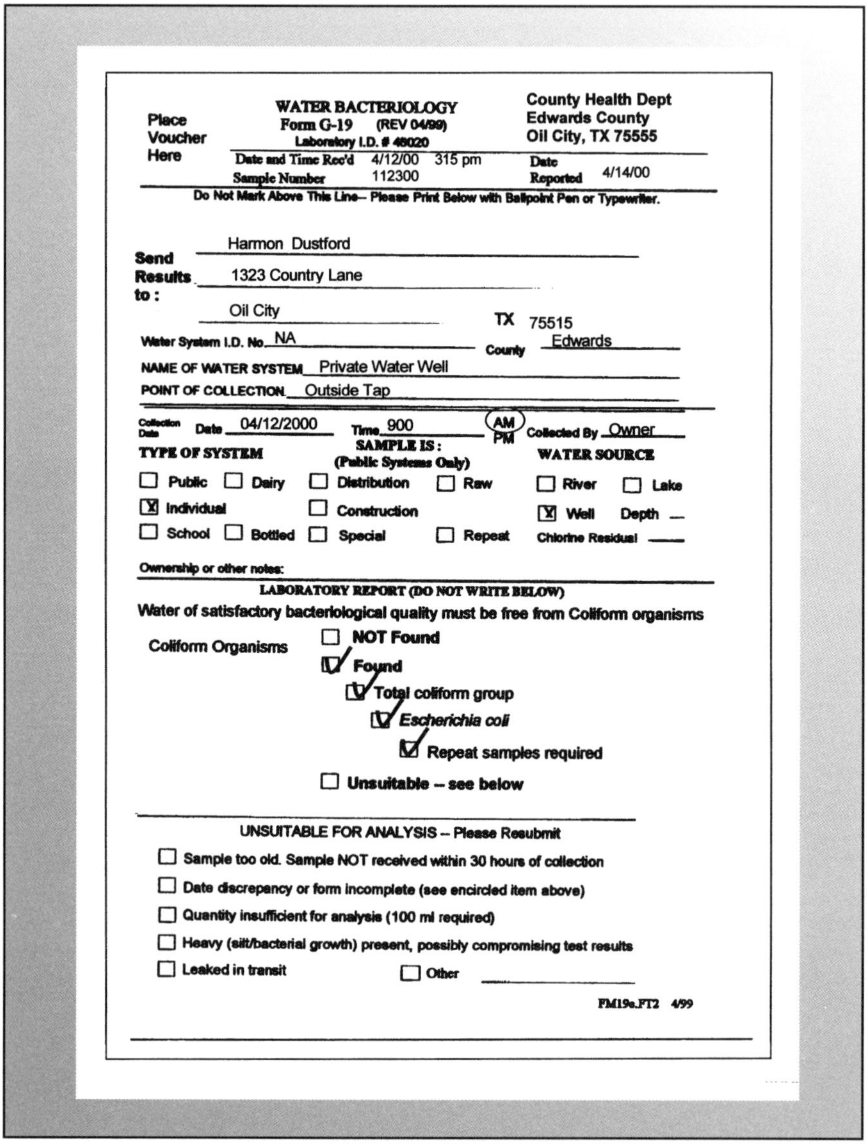

Place Voucher Here

WATER BACTERIOLOGY
Form G-19 (REV 04/99)
Laboratory I.D. # 46020

County Health Dept
Edwards County
Oil City, TX 75555

Date and Time Rec'd 4/12/00 315 pm
Sample Number 112300
Date Reported 4/14/00

Do Not Mark Above This Line– Please Print Below with Ballpoint Pen or Typewriter.

Send Results to: Harmon Dustford
1323 Country Lane
Oil City TX 75515

Water System I.D. No. NA County Edwards

NAME OF WATER SYSTEM Private Water Well

POINT OF COLLECTION Outside Tap

Collection Date Date 04/12/2000 Time 900 AM PM Collected By Owner

TYPE OF SYSTEM
☐ Public ☐ Dairy
☒ Individual
☐ School ☐ Bottled

SAMPLE IS: (Public Systems Only)
☐ Distribution ☐ Raw
☐ Construction
☐ Special ☐ Repeat

WATER SOURCE
☐ River ☐ Lake
☒ Well Depth —
Chlorine Residual —

Ownership or other notes:

LABORATORY REPORT (DO NOT WRITE BELOW)

Water of satisfactory bacteriological quality must be free from Coliform organisms

Coliform Organisms
☐ NOT Found
☑ Found
☑ Total coliform group
☑ *Escherichia coli*
☑ Repeat samples required
☐ Unsuitable -- see below

UNSUITABLE FOR ANALYSIS -- Please Resubmit

☐ Sample too old. Sample NOT received within 30 hours of collection
☐ Date discrepancy or form incomplete (see encircled item above)
☐ Quantity insufficient for analysis (100 ml required)
☐ Heavy (silt/bacterial growth) present, possibly compromising test results
☐ Leaked in transit ☐ Other

FM19a.FT2 4/99

Figure 5-10 A homeowner collected this water sample from a private well. Laboratory findings are positive for coliform bacteria and indicate possible contamination from an animal or human waste source. The owner should disinfect the well and ask for assistance in collecting repeat samples. If laboratory results continue to be positive, the owner should plan to install a chemical or UV disinfection system. Based on the results of this lab report, most public health professionals would likely recommend that water from this well be boiled prior to drinking, until the contamination problem is solved.

Some lenders may require that certain water quality tests be performed prior to approving a loan. As a minimum, the rural homeowner should have the following water quality testing performed on a new well: pH, hardness, TDS, chloride, nitrate and coliform bacteria. If you purchase an existing home with older plumbing, you should also check for lead. Figure 5-12 on page 98 provides recommendations for additional testing that may be indicated based on observations and problems experienced.

Disinfection of Domestic Water Wells

If the laboratory reports a water sample as being UNSATISFACTORY, due to the presence of coliform bacteria, you will need to disinfect your water system and collect additional samples. Prior to disinfecting and taking additional samples complete the following system checks:

✓ Check all pipes near the well and pump to make sure they are tight and in good repair.
✓ Check pump and well seals—replace or repair if found to be damaged.
✓ Check distances from possible sources of pollution, such as septic tanks, run off from animal pens or farm fields.
✓ Check filters, faucets and aerators – remove, clean and disinfect.
✓ Complete all repairs prior to the disinfection procedure.

The exact steps recommended for disinfection may vary among agencies. Several county health departments recommend the following procedure. This method can be used for shock disinfection using a liquid household bleach containing 5.25% chlorine. Do not use bleach with a "fresh scent," lemon fragrance or other cleaners added.

Steps in the Disinfection Procedure:

Caution: Avoid direct skin contact with bleach solutions. If it accidentally gets on your skin, flush immediately with clean water. Never mix chlorine bleach with other cleaners; it may produce a toxic gas. Follow directions on the product label.

(1) Mix 2 quarts bleach in 10 gallons of water; pour into well.
(2) Connect a garden hose to a nearby faucet and wash down the inside of the well.
(3) Open each faucet and let the water run until a strong chlorine odor is detected, then turn it off and go to the next one. Don't forget outdoor faucets and hydrants. Drain the water heater and let it refill with chlorinated water. If a strong odor is not detected at all outlets, add more chlorine to the well, (if you have an impaired sense of smell, use chlorine test strips sold with swimming pool supplies to detect chlorine at each outlet.)
(4) Flush the toilets.
(5) Mix an additional 2 quarts bleach in 10 gallons of water. Pour it into the well without pumping.
(6) Allow chlorinated water to stand in the well and pipes for at least 8 hours (preferably 12 to 24 hours).
(7) Run water from outdoor faucets to waste (away from desirable vegetation) until the chlorine odor is slight or not detected at each faucet. Then run indoor faucets until there is no chlorine odor. Minimize the amount of chlorinated water flowing into a septic tank.

During the disinfection process, water from the system is not suitable for consumption or extended contact by people or animals. Plan to perform the disinfection process when faucets and toilets will not be in use for at least 8 hours, preferably 12 to 24 hours.

If additional bacterial testing indicates persistent contamination, request assistance from a sanitarian at your local county health department.

Figure 5-11

Community water supply systems are required to provide "consumer confidence reports" (CCR) to consumers, with information about water quality. Ask for a copy of the CCR if your rural site will be provided water from a community system. An example of a CCR describing results of water sampling and testing is shown in Figure 5-13 on page 99.

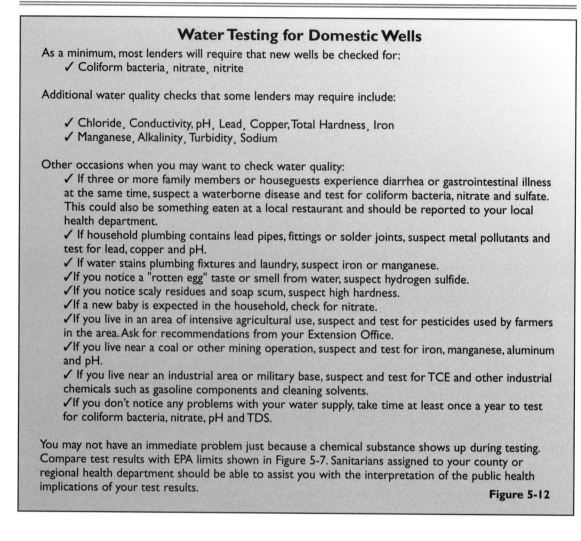

Water Testing for Domestic Wells

As a minimum, most lenders will require that new wells be checked for:
  ✓ Coliform bacteria, nitrate, nitrite

Additional water quality checks that some lenders may require include:

  ✓ Chloride, Conductivity, pH, Lead, Copper, Total Hardness, Iron
  ✓ Manganese, Alkalinity, Turbidity, Sodium

Other occasions when you may want to check water quality:
  ✓ If three or more family members or houseguests experience diarrhea or gastrointestinal illness at the same time, suspect a waterborne disease and test for coliform bacteria, nitrate and sulfate. This could also be something eaten at a local restaurant and should be reported to your local health department.
  ✓ If household plumbing contains lead pipes, fittings or solder joints, suspect metal pollutants and test for lead, copper and pH.
  ✓ If water stains plumbing fixtures and laundry, suspect iron or manganese.
  ✓ If you notice a "rotten egg" taste or smell from water, suspect hydrogen sulfide.
  ✓ If you notice scaly residues and soap scum, suspect high hardness.
  ✓ If a new baby is expected in the household, check for nitrate.
  ✓ If you live in an area of intensive agricultural use, suspect and test for pesticides used by farmers in the area. Ask for recommendations from your Extension Office.
  ✓ If you live near a coal or other mining operation, suspect and test for iron, manganese, aluminum and pH.
  ✓ If you live near an industrial area or military base, suspect and test for TCE and other industrial chemicals such as gasoline components and cleaning solvents.
  ✓ If you don't notice any problems with your water supply, take time at least once a year to test for coliform bacteria, nitrate, pH and TDS.

You may not have an immediate problem just because a chemical substance shows up during testing. Compare test results with EPA limits shown in Figure 5-7. Sanitarians assigned to your county or regional health department should be able to assist you with the interpretation of the public health implications of your test results.

Figure 5-12

It is highly recommended that you take time to visit your local health department or county extension office to ask about groundwater quality in the area. One of the most important questions to ask is "What is the name of the aquifer that will be my source of water?" Ask about known groundwater contamination problems due to past industrial activities, abandoned landfill waste disposal sites and nearby military installations. If you know the name of the aquifer, you may be able to obtain information related to both quality and quantity.

The United States Geologic Service (USGS) is another excellent source of information on what can be expected in terms of groundwater quality and quantity. Many states also have professional geologists working in state agencies responsible for conducting groundwater studies. The USGS has published detailed reports describing major aquifers in the U.S. See Figure 5-14 on page 100 for examples of aquifer descriptions obtained from the USGS and state geologic agencies.

Keep in mind that most problems related to poor quality water can be improved with home treatment units. Even seawater can be treated for drinking, if you can afford the cost to install and operate the system. Information on planning for home water treatment systems is provided later in this chapter.

SANTA MONICA WATER DIVISION
SUMMARY OF WATER QUALITY RESULTS FOR 1998

Parameter	MCLG/ (PHG)	Federal MCL	State MCL	LOCAL WELL WATER (a) Arcadia Plant Maximum	Range	IMPORTED SURFACE WATER Weymouth Plant Maximum	Range	IMPORTED SURFACE WATER Jensen Plant Maximum	Range	Dates Sampled if other than 1998
Secondary Drinking Water Standards - Aesthetic Standards										
Chemical Parameters										
Chloride (ppm)	NS	250	x500	95	74 - 95	86	62 - 86	53	44 - 53	
Color (units)	NS	15	15	<5	<5	3	1 - 3	2	1 - 2	
Iron (ppb)	NS	300	300	10	10	ND	ND	ND	ND	
Manganese (ppb)	NS	50	50	3	3	ND	ND	ND	ND	
Odor-Threshold (units)	NS	3	3	2	ND - 2	(b)	(b)	(b)	(b)	
pH (units)	NS	6.5-8.5	NS	8.6	8.1 - 8.6	8.1	8.0 - 8.1	8.3	8.2 - 8.3	
Specific Conductance (µmho/cm)	NS	NS	x1600	1338	782-1338	995	715 - 995	564	493 - 564	
Sulfate (ppm)	NS	250	x500	239	140 - 239	250	153 - 250	101	71 - 101	
Total Dissolved Solids (ppm)	NS	500	x1000	843	493 - 843	622	429 - 622	333	284 - 333	
Methyl tert-Butyl Ether (MTBE) (ppb)	NS	NS	5	ND	ND	ND	ND	ND	ND	
Additional Parameters										
Alkalinity (ppm)	NS	NS	NS	304	153 - 304	124	101 - 124	106	86 - 106	
Calcium (ppm)	NS	NS	NS	47	11 - 47	75	51 - 75	42	31 - 42	
Hardness (as CaCO3) (ppm)	NS	NS	NS	274	84 - 274	301	206 - 301	175	133 - 175	
Heterotropic Plate Count (cfu/ml)	NS	NS	NS	12	<1 -12	130	<1 - 130	2	<1 - 2	
Magnesium (ppm)	NS	NS	NS	30	19 - 30	28	19 - 28	17	14 - 17	
Perchlorate (ppb)	NS	NS	NS	ND	ND	6	ND -6	ND	ND	1997
Potassium (ppm)	NS	NS	NS	10.0	10.0	4.6	3.5 - 4.6	3.0	2.7 - 3.0	
Silica (ppm)	NS	NS	NS	21	21	N/A	N/A	N/A	N/A	
Sodium (ppm)	NS	NS	NS	222	172 - 222	93	64 - 93	48	44 - 48	
Total Chlorine Residual (ppm)	NS	NS	NS	1.3	0.4 - 1.3	N/A	N/A	N/A	N/A	

Key To Abbreviations

Secondary Drinking Water Standard = An MCL that applies to any contaminant in drinking water that adversely affects the taste, odor, or appearance of the water.

MCLG = Maximum Contaminant Level Goal, or the level of a contaminant in drinking water below which there is no known or expected risk to health. MCLGs are set by the U.S. Environmental Protection Agency.

PHG = Public Health Goal or the level of a contaminant in drinking water below which there is no known or expected risk to health. PHGs are set by the California Environmental Protection Agency

MCL = Maximum Contaminant Level, or the highest level of a contaminant that is allowed in drinking water. MCLs are set as close to the PHGs and MCLGs as is economically or technologically feasible.

N/A = Not Applicable
NS = No Standard
ND = Monitored for but Not Detected

ppb= parts per billion, or micrograms per liter (µg/l)
ppm= parts per million, or milligrams per liter (mg/l)
µmho/cm = micromhos per centimeter
cfu/ml = colony-forming units per milliliter
< = less than
x = upper limit - recommended level is lower

(a) = For 1998, the Arcadia well water treatment plant treated a blend of 65% well water and 35% imported surface water.
(b) = MWD has developed a flavor-profile analysis method that can more accurately identify odor occurences.

For additional water quality questions, contact Robert Harvey Superintendent of Water Production and Treatment at (310) 826-6712

Example of CCR   **Figure 5-13**

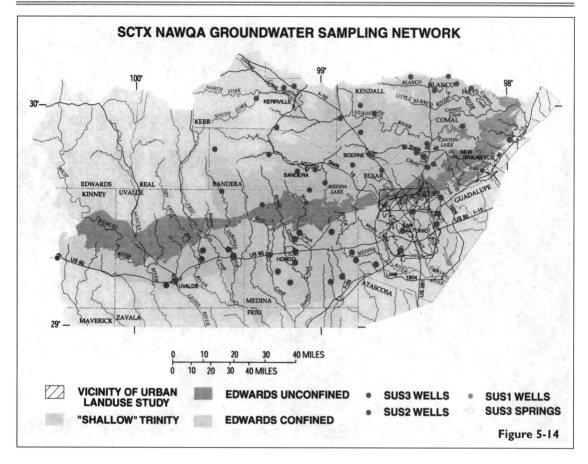

SCTX NAWQA GROUNDWATER SAMPLING NETWORK

Figure 5-14

After selecting a rural building site which offers the best potential for a safe and plentiful water supply, the next step is to start planning for the construction of an on-site water well.

Guidelines for Water Well Construction

If your rural building site will not be provided water from a community system, you will need to plan on drilling a well or constructing another type of on-site water system. The vast majority of rural homeowners have a well drilled on their property. Very few elect to filter and treat surface water from a nearby spring, stream or lake.

Recommendations for constructing a well on your site can be obtained from local health departments or county agricultural extension offices. In most states, the Department of Health or another agency regulates the water well industry with specific standards and requirements for installing a well. State regulations will likely cover all phases of water well construction to assure a safe and sanitary

The days of hand dug wells and the "community" tin drinking cup are long gone, but homeowners still face the same problems in finding a suitable groundwater supply in rural areas.

water supply. Obtain a copy of your state regulations as early in the process as possible.

Site Considerations

The first, and perhaps the most important, question to ask is, "Is this building site large enough to provide minimum separation distances between my well and sewage disposal systems (your own and neighbors)?" Most regulations specify a minimum separation distance between a water well and on-site sewage disposal systems. Typically the separation distance specified ranges from 75 to 150 feet. Keep in mind these are minimum distances to protect your family's health. As a rule of thumb, the greater the separation between your well and nearby sewage disposal systems, the better.

It may be difficult if not impossible to meet required separation distances on smaller lots. Regulations in some areas specify minimum lot size when private water wells are to be used. Building sites less than one acre in size may be a problem. Even larger-sized sites can be a problem when neighbors have already installed their well and sewage disposal system.

If the minimum separation distance cannot be met on a site that you have already purchased, it may be possible to obtain a waiver from the health authority. Some regulatory agencies will grant a waiver of the required separation distance if extra protection is provided for the well. There is no guarantee that a waiver will be granted.

Don't take the word of a real estate agent or salesperson that lot size is no problem. Your best course of action is to ask for a map of the subdivision, from the developer, showing your lot and adjacent lots. This map should be drawn to scale. Next, locate any existing wells and sewage disposal systems on surrounding properties as shown in Figure 5-15.

Existing sewage disposal systems or animal feed lots, on adjoining lots, may influence where you can locate your own well and sewage disposal system. In severe cases, you may find that you need to purchase two sites to provide the minimum separation distances required. The future value and sale of your home may be jeopardized when separation distances are neglected. If your site is large enough to provide the required separation distances, your next challenge will be to find water.

Without any knowledge about the hydrologic cycle you might be tempted to rely on the services of "water witches" that claim to have a special gift or power for finding groundwater. The USGS and the National Water Well Association have both published articles against water witching. Controlled field tests have shown that water witches do no better in locating water than random guessing.

Beware of drilling contractors who use the services of a water witch to locate potential drilling sites. This may be an indication that the contractor has little or no knowledge about local groundwater

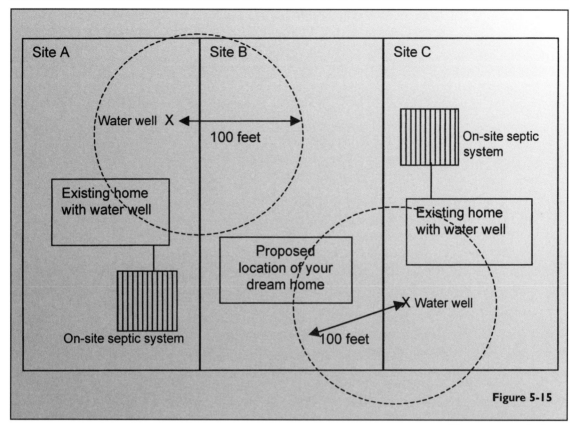

Site A

Site B

Site C

Water well X

100 feet

On-site septic
system

Existing home
with water well

Proposed
location of your
dream home

Existing home
with water well

On-site septic system

X Water well

100 feet

Figure 5-15

*Homeowners on site A
and site C have already
installed on-site sewage
treatment systems and
water wells. This will sev-
erly limit available options
for perspective owners of
site B. It may not be possible to install either system
on this site. Before buying
site B a site evaluation
should be performed by a
qualified professional.*

aquifers and how the hydrologic cycle works.

As discussed earlier in the "Hydrologic Cycle" portion of Chapter 5, groundwater occurrence is no mystery. In theory, groundwater can be found anywhere below the water table; but finding groundwater that is suitable in both quality and quantity can be a challenge. Meeting this challenge doesn't take the supernatural powers of a water witch; it simply takes a little homework.

Find out as much as possible about groundwater aquifers in the area in which you plan to build. It is possible in some states to obtain information on both the water quality and quantity to be expected at different sites. Ask about the density of wells in the area you plan to build as well as the ability of local aquifers to keep up with pumping demands. This information should be available from your local health department or county extension service.

During recent droughts, some aquifers in highly developed rural areas

103

have been literally "sucked dry." As long as the amount of water being pumped from an aquifer is recharged with rainwater percolating through soil and upper geological formations, homeowners will have a virtual "endless" supply. If the annual rate of pumping exceeds the annual rate of recharge, the water table will drop and the aquifer will begin to decline.

In rural areas undergoing rapid development, groundwater aquifers have been over pumped. This has resulted in water tables dropping and some wells being unable to meet peak pumping demands. In some cases, over pumping has resulted in water quality problems.

Along the coast, when fresh-water aquifers are over pumped, seawater can intrude and alter water quality. In the vicinity of Point Mugu, California, wells as far as 15 miles inland have experienced drastic increases in chloride levels as a result of over pumping. In east central Texas, over pumping some aquifers has allowed saline waters to lower water quality.

Aquifer authorities have been established in many areas to regulate the amount of groundwater being pumped from an aquifer. Such authorities may issue well permits and even assess fees for the amount of groundwater pumped.

The Role of the Driller

After you have done your homework and selected the building site with the best potential for providing your family with a suitable groundwater supply, your driller will do the rest. Selecting an experienced well driller and pump installation contractor is critical. If a license or certification is required in your state, make sure your contractor has all the necessary credentials. Drillers with membership in state and local well drillers associations are a plus. The contract with your driller should include specifications for every aspect of well construction and completion. Get every detail from casing and grouting to electrical connections fully specified in writing.

Your contract should also specify that well construction meets all state and county regulations in force at the time of construction. Some drillers will even include allowances for "dry" holes. If local aquifers are known for poor water quality or being able to only provide limited quantities of water, include contingencies for water treatment and water storage.

Well construction is normally accomplished in several phases consisting of drilling, testing and completion or development. Methods of well digging range from simple digging to the use of sophisticated high-tech drilling rigs.

Common methods of well digging in use today include: boring, driving, jetting, cable tool, hydraulic rotary drilling, reverse circulation drilling, air rotary drilling and down-hole hammer. Each method has certain advantages and disadvantages in different types of geologic formations. Commercial drillers are often equipped with at least two types of rigs and will use the one best suited for your conditions.

After several potential drill locations have been identified as meeting minimum separation distances, your driller will use his experience and knowledge of the local conditions to site the well. On smaller-sized lots located in developments where other homeowners have already installed on-site sewage disposal systems, the number of potential drill locations on your site may be limited.

Your driller should select a location situated on higher ground so that the well head is protected from flooding and surface drainage. Depending on site factors such as housing density, topography, topographic gradient and underground hydrogeological conditions, your drilling contractor may recommend a greater separation distance than the minimum requirement.

The Drilling Process
The rural homeowner doesn't need to have a detailed knowledge of the drilling process. However, it will be helpful to know what to expect when the drill rig arrives at your site.

As the drill bit cuts into soil, stones and rocks below the ground surface and drill cuttings will need to be removed. Pressurized air is used for removing cuttings in air rotary rigs. Most air rotary rigs are equipped to use water when sand and gravel are encountered.

Hydraulic rotary rigs use an additive mixed with water to form a drilling "mud." The mud is circulated in the drill hole to remove cuttings and also to help lubricate and cool the drill bit. As different types of soil and rock formations are encountered, the driller may change the mud formulation.

When drilling mud is to be used, check contract specifications to ensure that only drilling fluid additives approved by a recognized testing organization, such as the National Sanitation Foundation (NSF) are used. The NSF is a national testing and certification organization that has established standards for materials and chemicals used in potable water systems. The NSF also has established standards for water pipe and home water treatment devices.

Specifications should call for water piping and other components of the water system to meet NSF (National Sanitation Foundation) or similar testing and certification standards. This will help to ensure that components do not leach lead and other toxic chemicals into your water supply.

Contract specifications should also call for the use of fresh nonpolluted water in preparing the drill mud. Some state regulations may call for chlorine to be added to drilling fluids. Using non-approved drilling fluid additives or contaminated water to prepare the drilling fluid can result in contaminating your groundwater.

Recent incidents include a contractor who was using drilling mud not approved for potable water systems. Use of the non-approved drilling mud resulted in contaminating a school well with lead at levels considered a health hazard. Another contractor for a major water utility attempted to "recycle" drilling mud previously used in an oil well project. After the project was completed, it was found that the "recycled" drilling mud created severe taste and odor problems in the water supply. The utility lost use of the well for nearly a year and had to spend thousands of dollars in clean-up costs and legal fees.

During the drilling process, the contractor should obtain and record information on the depth, thickness, type of material and potential water yield of each formation encountered. Many state well drilling regulations require that this information be recorded on a well log. After the well has been completed, a copy of the well log may need to be submitted to a state or local regulatory agency. But the homeowner should also maintain their own permanent copy of the well log for future reference.

Once the desired aquifer and depth have been reached, your driller will conduct preliminary pump testing. If preliminary pump testing indicates that the well will be low yielding (less than 2 to 5 gpm), your driller may recommend trying another test hole. Individuals having a large building site of several acres and a large budget may decide to have another test hole drilled.

Those with a limited budget and small-sized building site should ask about the addition of a storage tank system. If you have already obtained information on local aquifers, you will know what to expect in terms of potential yield. If other wells in the area are also low producing, don't expect a gusher. In areas known to have low-producing aquifers, it may be better to have a storage tank installed instead of having another test hole drilled. The recommendations of an experienced driller can be valuable in making your decision.

Developing the Well

If preliminary testing indicates adequate yield, the driller will begin to "develop" the well. This phase of the process involves removing all the fine materials left over by drilling, installing a casing, grouting to seal the casing, installing a slab or pitless adapter, installing a sanitary well seal and taking any other measures to protect groundwater from surface contamination.

The casing can be a major cost factor and, in some cases, may account for 20 to 50 percent of the total well cost. The length, size, thickness and material (steel or plastic) of the casing is often specified in state and local regulations. A few well regulations call for the casing to be continuous from the ground level to the bottom of the well. Some regulations may only require that only upper portions of the well be cased. States without well drilling regulations leave the depth of the casing up to the driller and homeowner.

The well casing serves two purposes. At the top of the well, the casing helps to stop surface contamination from entering the well. Further down in the well, the casing keeps the well from caving in. The diameter of the casing is related to the type of well and type of pump. Shallow wells with a jet pump may be cased in smaller two-inch diameter casing. Deeper wells with deep-well jet pumps typically use a four-inch diameter casing. For submersible pumps, a casing diameter of four or six inches may be used. Some large community wells have casings over 30 inches in diameter.

To save a few dollars your driller may recommend using a casing left over from another project or installing used pipe as casing. A few unfortunate homeowners have had their groundwater supply contaminated from installing so-called bargain casing previously used for piping toxic chemicals.

All well casing should be of new material or in like-new condition. Casing should be long enough to protect your water supply from lower-quality water above the aquifer you are using. All joints in the casing should be watertight. Joints in steel casing should be welded or installed as screwed coupled joints. If state and local regulations fail to provide detailed standards for installing the well casing, you may want to consider having the driller adhere to specifications prescribed in the EPA's "Manual of Water Well Construction Practices."

After the casing has been set in the drilled hole, an open or "annular" space will exist between the casing and the sides of the hole. This annular space is filled with a nonshrinking cement grout to a depth sufficient to seal off any flow of surface water. State and local water well regulations will specify the depth to install grouting. As a minimum, grouting should extend at least ten feet below the surface.

When a well passes through an aquifer or water-bearing zone with poor quality water, grouting should be extended far enough to seal off any potential of contamination. In some cases grouting may need to extend beyond 50 feet. Trying to save a few dollars to minimize casing and grouting that will protect your groundwater may be regretted later on.

If the water-producing aquifer is composed of sand, gravel or other type of "unconsolidated" material, the driller may install one or more screens along the lower portion of the casing. The screen serves to protect the pump from sand and other fine material while allowing water to pass into the casing for pumping. In "consolidated" aquifers made up of rock, the screen may consist of slots in the casing. In some bedrock aquifers, a casing and screen may not be needed.

In some instances, the use of acids or other chemicals may be necessary for final well development to dissolve or loosen dense rock formations. If acids or other chemicals are used, the well water should be pumped until all traces of the chemical are dissipated. Potable water should be used if mixing of chemicals is necessary.

To increase potential water yields, your driller may recommend "rock fracturing." This practice may be able to increase yield, but may not be allowed in some states due to the potential for creating avenues for surface waters to enter and contaminate the aquifer. If rock fracturing is recommended, be sure to check local regulations.

Installing the Pump and Plumbing Components
After casing, grouting and screening installations have been complet-

ed, it will be time to install the pump system and plumbing components. Some drilling contractors will subcontract this portion of well construction to a licensed plumber. The use of a licensed plumber may be required in some jurisdictions.

Options for pump selection will depend on the depth of your well and the total distance and height water will need to be pumped. For very shallow wells less than 25 feet deep, a shallow-well jet pump with a single water line may work. A deep-well jet pump for depths down to 120 feet requires that two lines be installed. Jet pumps are located above ground and can be easily worked on if repair work is needed.

For deeper wells, a submersible pump can be used. Submersible pumps are harder to set and replace. Submersible pumps also require at least a four-inch casing. A major advantage of submersible pumps is that the right size unit can deliver water from virtually any depth. A 1/3 horsepower (HP) pump is capable of delivering 12 gallons per minute (gmp) from a depth of 100 feet. The same 1/3 HP pump would only be able to deliver 2 gmp from a depth of 200 feet. It would take a 3 HP unit to deliver 12 gpm from a depth of 400 feet.

In sizing your pump, the installer will also consider the "head loss" created by above-ground plumbing components. Different sizes of water pipe, connectors and the distance to the storage tank will influence pump size. It may be better to spend a few dollars more on a higher-rated pump than installing a smaller-sized unit that will only just meet your needs.

The majority of state regulations require that the well casing extend at least 12 inches above the ground surface. In North Dakota, the casing is required to extend at least two feet above the highest known flood elevation.

At the top of the casing, a cap and sanitary well seal will be installed. The sanitary well seal provides tight fitting openings for piping and electrical wiring. The seal consists of a rubber gasket that expands and completely seals off any open space. This prevents small animals and insects from falling into the well. County health department personnel have reported finding small animals ranging from dead rodents to baby skunks inside wells when the well seal was not installed.

A concrete slab should be poured around the casing, extending at least two feet in each direction. The slab will help to stabilize the casing and provide additional protection from surface runoff. A well house may be added for additional protection, but is not required in most circumstances.

After the driller has completed your on-site water well, request copies of the well log, yield testing and any chemical and bacterial analysis reports. Visit your local health department if you have any questions about these reports.

Several states allow the installation of a pitless adapter to support the pump and allow water pipes to be installed below the frost line (see Figure 5-16 on page 112). If a pitless adapter is used for a deep well, ensure that it meets all the specifications for the total weight of the pipe and pump it will support.

North Carolina and a few other states do not approve pitless adapters under any circumstances. Even though the pitless adapter may be allowed by state code some local jurisdictions may not approve its use. Be sure to check with local enforcement agencies.

Some homeowners will elect to simply have the pressure tank and pump controls installed outside without the expense of constructing a well house.

Testing for Yield

Bail testing or air lifting water for a minimum of one hour will normally be used in preliminary well testing to determine potential yield. In testing a well by means of a simple bail or air lift test, the amount of water taken out in a given time will be approximated following construction of the well.

Final pump testing will consist of pumping at a fixed rate for a number of specified hours. In a constant rate test the well discharge should remain constant for the duration of the test. The discharge rate after two hours of pumping is recorded as the yield.

Some states may require the driller to perform a well recovery test in addition to a constant rate test. Prior to starting the test, the water level in the well is measured and recorded on the drill log. Pumping is stopped abruptly throughout the test period with water level measured and recorded each time. Keep in mind that pump test results can vary considerably from season to season.

This homeowner had the wellhead and pump controls located in a well house to protect components from the environment and vandalism.

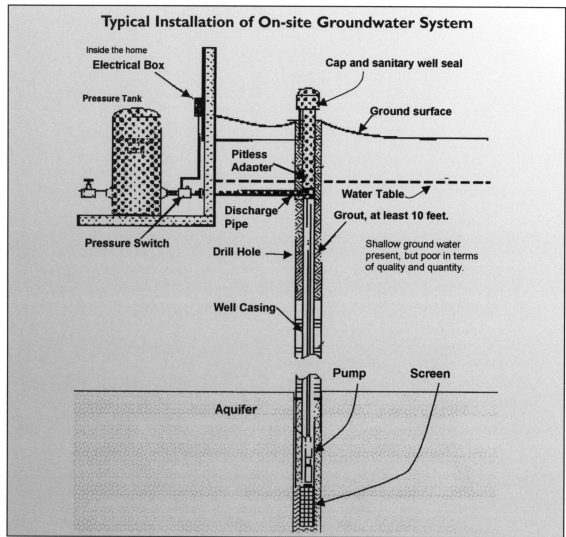

Typical Installation of On-site Groundwater System

Inside the home
Electrical Box

Pressure Tank

Cap and sanitary well seal

Ground surface

Pitless Adapter

Water Table

Discharge Pipe

Grout, at least 10 feet.

Pressure Switch

Drill Hole

Shallow ground water present, but poor in terms of quality and quantity.

Well Casing

Pump   **Screen**

Aquifer

Figure 5-16 Water well installations will vary. Some homeowners may elect to have a well house built over the well. In some cases the pressure tank may be installed outside or in a well house. When an aquifer is unable to produce more than five gallons per minute, a water storage tank may be needed.

Even though other wells in the same aquifer produce as much as 20 gpm, the well on your site may produce far less. It is possible for one neighbor to have an abundance of water, without the need for a large above-ground storage tank, while the next site must install a 1,000-gallon storage tank to meet peak demands.

The type of storage tank needed for your system depends on the constant rate at which your well can be pumped. For a low-yield well, producing less than 5 gpm, a large storage tank with an additional pump system may be indicated. The larger tank (up to 1,000 gallons) and extra pump will mean additional cost, but will help to ensure that your family has sufficient water to meet peak demands.

For wells able to provide a constant yield of more than 5 to 8 gpm, a smaller (less than 100 gallon) precharged or pressurized storage tank will be able to meet your needs. Precharged water storage tanks have a rubber bladder inside the tank case to maintain a constant pressure inside water pipes. When a water faucet is turned on, the pressure exerted by the bladder pushes water inside the tank through water pipes to the opened faucet. When the water level inside the storage tank reaches a certain level, an electrical relay automatically turns the well pump on to refill the tank and meet the peak demand. Some taste and odor from the rubber bladder may be noticed when water is first used. The use of Food and Drug Administration (FDA) approved materials in manufacturing the bladder will greatly reduce or eliminate taste and odor problems.

A pressurized storage tank without a precharged bladder also may be used. Air pressure on the tank will need to be maintained with an air compressor. Both types of storage tanks have their advantages and disadvantages. Your driller or licensed plumber will recommend the best option for your situation. In both types of storage tanks, a pressure relief valve is critical. Without a pressure relief valve, the storage tank can explode causing injury or serious property damage.

In time, bladders, electrical switches, relays and mechanical components will need to be repaired or replaced. Ask your plumber and driller about equipment manuals and maintenance schedules.

You may find your new well's ability to produce a given amount of water is significantly reduced after other wells are drilled on other sites. In rural areas undergoing rapid development, water levels have drastically dropped from over pumping during drought conditions. Wells located in or near aquifer recharge zones are likely to experience drastic changes in water levels depending on the amount of recent rainfall.

Water Analysis
Collecting water samples for biological (coliform bacteria) testing and chemical analysis will be one of the last procedures performed in completing your well. Samples may be collected from the discharge during test pumping or after the pump has been permanently installed. Typical costs for coliform bacteria testing will range from $15 to $30. The cost of chemical analysis will vary depending on the number of items tested. For aquifers without any known or expected industrial contamination problems, the cost for chemical analysis may range from $50 to $100.

Before a sample is taken for bacteriological analysis, the well must be disinfected to kill any biological organisms that may have been introduced during drilling. Pouring a chlorine solution of 50 to 100 ppm down the casing is the most common way to disinfect new wells.

Even though the driller will be responsible for initial disinfection, the homeowner should be familiar with the procedure for future reference. See Figure 5-11 on page 97 for information on mixing chlorine solutions for well disinfection.

Before collecting the sample for analysis, the chlorine solution must first be allowed to have sufficient contact time (preferably overnight) and then removed from the well by pumping. The chlorine residual should then be reduced to less than 2 ppm before the analysis sample is taken.

It is advisable to request a representative from the local public health department to collect the sample for bacteriological analysis. In situations where this is not possible, sample bottles and advice on sampling techniques may be provided. The health department staff may also be able to help interpret laboratory findings and advise on additional testing. Also review the information on biological concerns in the "Primer on Water Quality" in this chapter. If the biological analysis is negative, make plans for annual bacteriological sampling.

As already mentioned in the "Primer of Water Quality," while countless chemical compounds exist, less than 100 are a concern for community and public water supplies. For the private homeowner it isn't necessary to test groundwater for all chemical compounds regulated by the EPA. This would be very costly (about $1,500) and is not actually needed. As a minimum, initial chemical testing on your new well should include: pH, hardness, TDS, chloride and nitrate. Depending on the area in which you build, additional analysis may be advisable. If past industrial operations or abandoned landfills are known to be in the vicinity, testing for TCE should be considered. Ask the professional staff with your local health department or USGS regional office for advice about other chemical testing that they might recommend based on their knowledge of local aquifers.

Water Treatment Systems

Results of initial chemical testing may indicate the need for additional and follow-up testing. Test results will also help you decide if a home water treatment unit should be installed to improve water quality. Even before your well is completed you are likely to receive letters and phone calls from local water treatment firms warning you about the "impurities" in your water supply. Some may even offer free water testing or announce that you have won a free system. These types of offers are normally made to set an appointment with a salesperson. An untrained technician may do the free water testing, and that free treatment system is likely to require very expensive supplies and replacement filters and other parts every month.

During the 1980s there was a lot of consumer fraud in the home water treatment and conditioning industry. Homeowners were being promised that a particular treatment device would solve all their problems and make their water pure. The Federal Trade Commission (FTC) finally published consumer alerts and warnings about fraudulent and deceptive sales practices being used in the industry.

Today, the majority of firms in the home water conditioning industry act in a professional and responsible manner. Industry trade groups such as the Water Quality Association have promoted professionalism and encouraged the certification of technicians. Prior to having a salesperson "consult" with you about water quality, ask about membership in state and national professional associations and if technicians are certified and have passed written examinations. A professional water treatment consultant with trained and experienced technicians can be a big help in reducing water quality problems.

National Sanitation Foundation
In addition to industry professional groups, the National Sanitation Foundation (NSF), an independent laboratory, is now testing and certifying home water treatment devices and claims made by the manufacturers. For water treatment devices to be certified, the manufacturer must demonstrate that the unit meets test standards established by professional and public health NSF advisory committees.

NSF certification is strictly on a volunteer basis. Some manufacturers elect not to submit their products to the rigors of the NSF evaluation process. After a manufacturer has demonstrated that a device has been manufactured with approved components and the unit has passed specified testing, the product can bear the NSF Mark of Certification. The NSF Mark of Certification cannot be displayed on the product until the device has been tested and approved. The NSF Mark also indicates that claims made in product sales literature are not fraudulent.

The NSF has currently adopted several standards for different types of home water treatment devices and systems. The NSF has also developed a standard for "lead free" water faucets and other plumbing fixtures. The first question to ask the salesperson is, "Does this water treatment device bear the NSF Mark of Certification?"

The NSF International also maintains an Internet Web page at http://www.nsf.org where current information on certified products can be obtained.

Types of Systems

If you have a specific problem such as taste, odor, color, specific chemical substance or are concerned about water hardness, a home treatment system may help. Before a salesperson calls it is advisable to become familiar with the different types of treatment devices and systems. Most importantly, know what these different treatment devices can and cannot do. When a water consultant promises that a device can solve your problem, get it in writing and read the fine print. The device may work as promised but can only treat several gallons of water before needing to be replaced.

Home water treatment devices range from simple physical filters to reduce particles and ion exchange water softeners, to sophisticated membrane filters designed to remove chemicals and even harmful microorganisms. Some treatment devices using chlorine or ultraviolet (UV) light are designed to disinfect drinking water by destroying disease-causing microorganisms. Each device has certain advantages and disadvantages. No single device should be expected to solve all water quality problems.

Home treatment devices can be classified as being **"point of entry" (POE)** or **"point of use" (POU)**. POE devices treat all water entering the home, including water used for laundry, bathing, lawn watering, cooking and drinking. POU devices are installed at the point water is used, such as a pour-through filter on a pitcher, a faucet mounted or counter-top unit at the kitchen sink or an under-the-sink plumbed-in unit.

Water softeners designed to reduce hardness have been widely used in U.S. as POE units for many years. The majority of softening devices use an exchange resin, regenerated with sodium chloride (salt) or potassium chloride, to reduce the hardness caused by calcium and magnesium in the water. As calcium and magnesium are replaced with sodium or potassium, hardness is reduced to nearly zero. Softeners may, in some cases, be able to reduce small amounts of iron and manganese.

Hardness is a relative term. Some homeowners may wish to install a softener if water hardness exceeds 100 mg/l (5.9 grains per gallon). Other homeowners are happy without a softer with water hardness over 250 mg/l (14.7 grains per gallon). There are advantages and disadvantages of home softening units of which you should be aware.

As water hardness increases, the ability of soap to produce suds decreases. Cleaning tasks may become more difficult. Clothes washed in hard water may look dingy and begin to feel harsh and scratchy over time. Hard water also contributes to stains and spots on glasses and the build up of deposits inside hot water heaters and water pipes.

If a member of the family is on a sodium-restricted diet, ask your physician about the use of softeners using sodium as an exchange medium. Disposal of brine solutions produced when the softener is recharged may damage certain types of on-site sewage disposal systems. Some experts advise against using softened water for watering houseplants, lawns and gardens due to the sodium content. Softened water is not recommended for appliances such as steam irons or evaporative coolers.

With water hardness at nearly zero, some individuals may complain that shampoo is difficult to remove from the hair during a shower. You may find that your family is using more water just to remove extra soapsuds. Some individuals may not like the "slick" feel of very soft water as they drink.

Water treatment salespersons will be able to demonstrate how a water softener will literally pay for itself through savings in the cost of soap and cleaning supplies plus the reduced maintenance cost on appliances. Before making a final decision on a softening unit, visit a friend or neighbor with a similar unit. If possible, try the shower and a cup of coffee or tea made with softened water to be sure you like it.

Homeowners with on-site sewage disposal systems should also consult with their local health department prior to installation. Homeowners who want to reduce water hardness, but also want to avoid the disadvantages of a softening unit may want to consider a filter device capable of removing calcium and magnesium.

Physical filters have been used for some time to remove larger particles such as grit, sediment, dirt and rust that may impart a cloudy appearance to water. These filters are typically made of fabric, fiber or other screening material with small openings or pores. Particulate filters retain relatively large particles in the size range within the fiber material. These filters will not remove smaller disease-causing organisms or chemical substances.

The NSF International classifies particulate filters based on their ability to remove certain sizes of particulate matter measured in microns. A Class I filter can remove 85% of the particles present in the size range of 0.5 to less than 1 micron in size, while a Class VI filter can only remove 85% of the particles present larger than 50 microns. If small clay particles are the cause of your cloudy water, a Class VI filter device will not solve the problem. Filter classes designated by NSF International are shown in Figure 5-17.

Newer types of **membrane filter devices**, made from ceramic, celluloid films and membrane materials can remove extremely small particles down to less than 0.0001 microns in size. With ultra-small pore sizes, these filters have the ability to retain particles on the surface of the membrane. Depending on the size of surface pores, membrane filters can remove extremely small particles including disease-causing organisms and even certain chemical substances.

Membrane filter devices can be classified as microfilters, ultrafilters, nanofilters or reverse osmosis (RO), depending on pore size. Membrane filters with a pore size ranging from 0.03 microns to 1 micron are referred to as microfilters and have the capability of removing extremely small particles of sand, silt and clay. These devices typically require an operating pressure of 15 to 60 pounds per square inch (psi). The small pore size enables **microfilters** to remove larger disease-causing microorganisms such as *Cryptosporidium* (the bug that made Milwaukee sick) and *Giardia lamblia* (the bug causing "Hikers Diarrhea") and bacteria; however, viruses are not removed. Microfilters are also able to remove certain inorganic chemical substances such as TCE.

Figure 5-17 These types of filters are designed to remove only physical contaminants. A Class I filter would be able to remove small parasites such as Cryptosporidium, but would not be able to remove chemicals or reduce hardness. When making a decision on the purchase of water treatment devices ask about NSF certification.

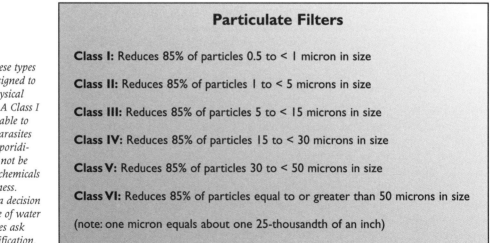

Particulate Filters

Class I: Reduces 85% of particles 0.5 to < 1 micron in size

Class II: Reduces 85% of particles 1 to < 5 microns in size

Class III: Reduces 85% of particles 5 to < 15 microns in size

Class IV: Reduces 85% of particles 15 to < 30 microns in size

Class V: Reduces 85% of particles 30 to < 50 microns in size

Class VI: Reduces 85% of particles equal to or greater than 50 microns in size

(note: one micron equals about one 25-thousandth of an inch)

Ultrafilters have even smaller pore size, ranging from 0.001 micron to 0.01 micron. This enables these devices to also remove larger viruses and chemical substances such as TCE and lead. Ultrafilters will normally require an operating pressure of 30 to 100 psi.

The pore size of **nanofilters** ranges from 0.001 micron to 0.0001 micron. These devices have all the capabilities of other membrane filters plus being able to remove most viruses with the smaller pore size. Nanofilters may require an operating pressure up to 300 psi.

Reverse osmosis (RO) devices are probably the best known of the membrane filter systems. As rural and city water worries increase, more and more of these units are being installed under kitchen sinks as POU devices. Larger RO units can be installed as POE devices to treat all water entering the home. Commercial-sized RO units, able to treat more than a million gallons a day, are used to treat seawater in many parts of the world.

While RO units have a wide range of capabilities, they have several disadvantages. A new homeowner may assume that a 25 gallon per day (gpd) RO unit can produce 25 gallons at any time and under any conditions. This is not the case because water temperature and water pressure affect RO performance.

RO filter capacity is rated by the NSF International as the amount of water treated in gallons per day (gpd), at a standard water temperature of 77° F. This means that a 25 gpd unit would be able to treat only about one gallon of water an hour (25 gpd/24 hrs. = 1.04 gal. per hour) at 77° F. This makes it necessary to include a storage tank in the design of the system. An RO unit rated at 25 gpd can fill a two-gallon storage tank in about two hours at a water temperature of 77° F. At a water temperature of 50°F it would take more than three hours to fill the same two-gallon storage tank.

Water pressure is another factor in RO filter performance. If an RO unit is designed to be operated at a water pressure of 60 psi and your water pressure is 40 psi, it could take up to seven hours to fill a two-gallon storage tank.

In the RO process, as water is applied to the membrane surface, only 25% to 50% may pass through the small membrane pores. Up to 75% of the water may be wasted as reject water. This means that for one gallon of RO treated water, up to three gallons goes down the drain. For a 25 gpd RO unit, as much as 75 gpd may go to your on-site sewage disposal system. If you plan to have an RO unit installed, the amount of reject water should be included in the design of your on-site sewage disposal system.

Most home units are designed as small POU **countertop or under-the-sink units**, capable of only treating enough water to use for drinking and cooking. Remember that some 25-gallon-a-day units may only be able to treat one to two gallons of water an hour.

All **membrane filters** are subject to decay and failure and must be replaced periodically. The best advice is to follow the manufacturer's recommendations about proper maintenance and use.

Carbon filter POU devices are typically designed as counter-top units and can help to improve smell, taste and appearance of drinking water. Activated carbon can reduce chlorine and certain organic chemicals. However, these units cannot remove most inorganic chemicals like salts or metals. Specially treated activated carbon units may be able to reduce lead. Look for the NSF International certification to support any claims made.

Carbon units eventually become saturated with the chemical substances being removed. Bacteria and other microorganisms can also collect and multiply on activated carbon filters when regular maintenance is neglected. Changing the filter cartridge according to the manufacturer's instructions will normally eliminate problems with bacterial growth. Some carbon filter units contain silver or another disinfectant and may be able to reduce certain nonharmful bacteria. The EPA must register these units as being bacteriostatic. Bacteriostatic carbon filters should not be used to disinfect water suspected of harboring disease-causing microorganisms.

Distillation units have been used for many years to "purify" water. These systems heat water to the boiling point, and then collect water vapor as it condenses. This process leaves many of contaminants behind, particularly the metals. Distillation removes most dissolved solids, such as salts, metals, minerals and particles, and reduces hardness. However, all chemical pollutants may not be removed by distillation. Other disadvantages of distillation units include high-energy requirements for boiling the water and maintenance to remove scale build-up when the source water is hard.

In rural areas undergoing rapid development, groundwater contamination from on-site sewage disposal systems is becoming a problem. In many areas it is now necessary to install a disinfection unit to destroy disease-causing organisms that may be present. If test results from your well continue to indicate the presence of coliform bacteria, a disinfection unit will be necessary to protect your family's health.

Chlorine feed units, similar to those used for small swimming pools can be used. The homeowner must maintain these units and ensure they are continually supplied with chlorine. The major disadvantage of chlorine is that normal application methods will not destroy the "Bug That Made Milwaukee Sick,"–*Cryptosporidum* (*Crypto* for short). This small protozoan, responsible for an estimated 400,000 cases of illness in Milwaukee, forms a protective spore and cannot be destroyed with normal levels of chlorine (1-5 ppm).

Ultraviolet treatment units use UV light to disinfect water. Like other water treatment units, UV disinfection units must be properly maintained by the homeowner. In hard water, dissolved and suspended solids may build up on the UV lamps, reducing the amount of ultraviolet light. To ensure proper disinfection, UV units must be cleaned periodically. Some states approve UV units for home use. However, the NSF International standard number 55, Ultraviolet Microbiological Water Treatment Systems, recommends their use to control only nonharmful types of bacteria.

When test results continue to show the presence of coliform bacteria, consult with local public health officials about recommendations for disinfection. A combination of chlorination or UV combined with membrane filtration or distillation may be recommended.

After you have determined which type of system is best to meet your needs, ask about cancellation and refund policies, maintenance requirements, warranties and the certification and training of installation technicians. Most importantly, ask if the unit bears the NSF International Mark of Certification. Be sure you receive the owner's manual or manufacturer's recommendations for care and maintenance. For complex systems it may be best to include a service and maintenance agreement as part of the contract.

When to Call a Professional

The majority of water quality problems will not likely be solved with a single treatment device. For difficult and complex situations you may want to hire the services of a professional water consultant. This will normally be a licensed engineer with experience in solving water quality problems. Larger water treatment firms may have professional consultants on their staff and offer consulting services at an hourly rate. It may be better to pay up to $100 an hour for an independent professional consultant than to rely on "free" consulting services from a firm selling a specific water treatment device.

When it comes to a water supply for your new rural home, do not take anything for granted. Even if your site will be provided water from a community system ask questions before you make your final decision. Using information in Chapter 5 will assist you in asking these important questions. Chapter 6 will assist you in asking the right questions about sewage disposal for your home in the country.

Your source of drinking water will either be from a community central system or from an on-site well located on your property.

If water is to be supplied from a community system, ask if homeowners will be responsible for future operation and maintenance costs. Ask for copies of the consumer confidence report (CCR). If a CCR is not available ask the state environmental agency if the system complies with drinking water regulations. You may want to request copies of past regulatory inspection reports.

ON-SITE SEWAGE DISPOSAL FOR RURAL SITES

Large municipal, sewage treatment facilities provide a vital service for homeowners in the city. Rural homeowners are likely to be responsible for the care and maintenance of their own on-site sewage treatment.

When it comes to selecting a building site in the country the last thing that most people think about is sewage disposal. For the city dweller, this vital necessity is out of sight and out of mind. By paying a monthly disposal fee, the homeowner gives little thought to proper treatment, how much water goes down the drain or operation and maintenance problems. All of this is left to city utility crews.

Because sewage contains human waste, a number of human diseases can be transmitted when food, drinking water or hands become contaminated. Diseases such as typhoid, cholera, *cryptosporidium* and hepatitis, to name a few, can be transmitted when disposal of sewage is neglected. Sewage treatment systems must be designed to collect, treat and dispose of household waste to remove contaminants and eliminate direct contact with food, drinking water and humans.

The History of Sewage Disposal

Historically, man has sought to find better and easier methods to take care of this vital necessity. A number of terms and phrases have been used to describe the methods and facilities used for taking care of mankind's vital necessities. Our early ancestors had their "chamberpot," "thunderpot" or "thundermug." In more recent times, terms such as "outhouse," "privy," "cesspool," "septic tank," "washroom," "bathroom," "restroom" and "toilet" have been used. Today we even use terms such as "waste engineering" or "waste management."

Early Methods

The mythical King Minos of Crete is credited with having the world's first flushing water closet more than 2,500 years ago. The Romans had a highly developed water management system and an underground sewage drain system, part of which is still in use today.

The American Way

As American cities developed and as more settlers moved West, the outdoor privy (outhouse) became a common feature in every backyard. The design and construction of privies ranged from a simple shack with a hole in the ground to elaborate structures with vented vaults to allow noxious sewer gases to escape into the atmosphere. When the amount of collected human waste began to overflow, another privy was constructed in the backyard.

Indoor Plumbing Comes of Age

In the mid-1800s, the "germ theory of disease" led to improvements in water systems and piping to bring drinking water indoors. Thomas Crapper, owner of a successful plumbing business in England during the late 1800s to 1907, is often credited with inventing the flush toilet. While Crapper did hold a number of plumbing patents for water closets, he was not the first to design this necessity of the modern age.

Bringing the outhouse in house did have its advantages, but also had its problems. One obstacle that had to be overcome with the advent of indoor plumbing was getting rid of "sewer gases" produced inside the sewage collection system. Initially indoor plumbing systems, designed by trial and error, allowed these foul smelling gases to enter the home. The development of sanitary plumbing designs to vent sewer gases into the atmosphere soon overcame this obstacle.

Early Problems of Disposal

With ever increasing amounts of wastewater being produced in American cities, proper disposal became a problem. City building lots were too small and did not have adequate space for on-site disposal of

The outdoor privy (outhouse) was once a common sight in rural America. Today, the privy has been replaced with a variety of on-site sewage treatment system designs for use by rural homeowners.

household sewage. Larger cities began to construct underground collection systems to remove and transport household sewage to a remote location outside the city for disposal in a nearby stream or river. In some cases, the point of disposal was upstream from the city's drinking water supply inlet line.

The city of Chicago is often credited with constructing the first major sewage project in the U.S. in 1885. Ironically, the city was also the site of a major disease outbreak caused by indoor plumbing problems.

By the 1920s, plumbing health codes for the licensing and examination of plumbers were being proposed in major American cities. Unfortunately, a few individuals were still designing and installing indoor plumbing systems by trial and error. In 1933, a major outbreak of amoebic dysentery occurred in Chicago during the World's Fair.

The outbreak, with more than 90 deaths, was traced to two hotels with flawed plumbing designs that had water lines directly connected to sewer drain lines.

As a result of the 1933 Chicago outbreak, stricter plumbing codes and inspection techniques were instituted in the U.S. Today, builders must schedule city plumbing inspections during different phases of construction when building inside the city limits. In rural areas, similar plumbing inspections may not be required.

The introduction of indoor plumbing to rural America led to a gradual decline in the use of the outdoor privy. Increased amounts of wastewater now had to be disposed of on-site. This was often accomplished by the use of a "cesspool" which was merely a large covered hole where sewage was allowed to collect with excess liquid leaching into the surrounding soil, rocks and groundwater.

In some instances excess liquid waste from the cesspool was allowed to drain across the land or flow into nearby streams without further treatment. When the cesspool became filled with solid material another one was dug nearby. Cesspools were often constructed too close to water wells and were frequently linked to illness outbreaks.

In rural areas, plumbing system inspections may not be required.

Early on-site sewage disposal systems often failed, resulting in pools of sewage in the back-yard.

The First On-Site System

In 1881, Louis Mouras of France was given a patent for an improved method of on-site sewage disposal consisting of a buried tank with underground drain lines, known as the septic tank. At the end of WWII, as a new rural migration was taking place, the installation of septic tank disposal systems dramatically increased in the U.S.

On-site sewage disposal became vital for developing new housing areas beyond the limits of municipal collection systems. By 1950, the septic tank was a common backyard feature in rural America. Today more than 25% of the U.S. population relies on some type of on-site sewage disposal system.

The Introduction of Regulations

Initially, on-site sewage disposal systems consisted of small 500-gallon septic tanks with poorly designed underground drain lines. In some cases, 50-gallon drums were used as septic tanks with liquid waste allowed to drain to a nearby stream or roadside ditch. These open-pipe systems were a particular problem in recreational areas where poorly treated sewage was allowed to drain into lakes and streams.

Reports of public health hazards resulting from undersized and poorly designed on-site sewage disposal systems for entire housing developments became headline news. Until the 1970s the majority of states did not have strict rules and regulations covering the design and installation of septic tanks and other on-site sewage disposal systems. Each state tended to develop its own design criteria for on-site sewage disposal systems in an attempt to resolve local public health problems.

While the EPA has established strict regulatory requirements when it comes to constructing and operating municipal sewage treatment works, there are no similar federal regulations for on-site sewage disposal systems. Instead, each state must still develop its own rules and regulations for the construction and operation of these systems.

Today, rules and regulations for the construction of on-site sewage disposal systems vary considerably from state to state and even vary from county to county within the same state. This hodgepodge of regulations can be confusing for homeowners as well as builders.

In some regulatory jurisdictions, it may be possible to install an on-site sewage disposal system on a building site as small as one acre, while across the state or county line a two-acre minimum lot size will be required. Surface irrigation may be approved in one county but not approved for use in an adjacent county. To make regulatory matters more confusing, rules and regulations for constructing on-site sewage treatment systems are continually being changed.

Rules and regulations for the installation of on-site sewage disposal systems vary from state to state. Rules may also vary in the same state. What may be allowed in one county may be prohibited just across the county line.

A low-pressure dosing disposal system was the right solution for this site with shallow soils and fragmented rock. Following treatment in an ATU, the low-pressure dosing system allows effluent to be distributed in the upper soil for evaporation and uptake by grass and other plants.

It is advisable to visit the regulatory agency responsible for approving the installation of on-site sewage disposal systems in your area to obtain a copy of current rules and regulations. Keep in mind that no matter what may be allowed in the next county, local rules will apply to your site and will determine your options for the installation of an on-site system.

Types of Sewage Disposal Systems

In most states, on-site sewage disposal systems are generally described as being "conventional" (standard)" or "non-conventional" (alternative). Conventional systems consist of the typical septic tank with gravity flow to subsurface drain lines for final disposal. Non-conventional systems can range from aerated treatment units (ATU) to recirculating biological filters with elaborate pumps and electrical controls. Final disposal of treated waste in non-conventional systems may involve additional components requiring more attention and maintenance (see Appendix Two). Conventional septic tank systems are suitable for building sites with deep well-drained soils and gentle slopes. Installing a conventional system on a site with shallow soil, high groundwater or having fractured rocks near the surface may result in public health and environmental problems.

This is a dual chamber ATU. Homeowners decided to reuse treated wastewater by installing a surface irrigation system. The reuse irrigation system will be an advantage during drought conditions.

Differences in the Two Types

For the homeowner the biggest difference is the cost to install and maintain. Conventional septic tank systems cost less to install and are easier to maintain than non-conventional systems. The typical cost for the installation of a conventional septic tank with subsurface drain lines for a family of four may range from $4,000 to $8,000 depending on site conditions. The cost to install non-conventional systems may be as high as $10,000 to $20,000 and higher. Non-conventional on-site systems will also require more homeowner operation and maintenance. Some jurisdictions may require homeowners to have written maintenance contracts with commercial firms on ATUs and other types of non-conventional systems.

Science of Sewage

Septic tanks and other on-site sewage disposal systems are more than just concrete boxes and some drain line buried in the backyard. These systems must be designed based on basic principles of engineering and microbiology to provide primary and secondary treatment of household waste. The following "Science of Sewage Primer" will provide the new homeowner with a better understanding of these principles.

The Composition of Waste

Household sewage is composed of liquid waste (from bathing and showering, dishwashing, food preparation and human liquid waste) and solid waste (from paper, kitchen food waste, laundry waste and human solid waste). It may be surprising, but after biological treatment by bacteria and other microorganisms (microbes), only 0.01% solids remain with 99.99% water left for disposal. For a treatment system to properly function, the right conditions must be provided for microbes to work.

Relative Strength of Sewage (BOD)

The relative strength of sewage is expressed in terms of biochemical oxygen demand (BOD). Typical household sewage has a BOD ranging from 200 ppm to 250 ppm. Some industrial waste may have a BOD of over 1,000 ppm.

BOD is a measure of how much oxygen will be needed by microbes to break down or treat the waste without creating a nuisance or polluting the environment. When sewage having a high BOD is allowed to enter a stream or lake, microbes feeding on the waste will begin to consume available dissolved oxygen (DO). Fish and other aquatic organisms will start to die when the DO level begins to fall below 4 ppm. As DO is depleted, portions of the stream will become "septic zones" with foul odors and may experience massive fish kills.

Today, the EPA requires municipal, publicly owned treatment works (POTW) to reduce BOD prior to discharge to surface waters. The BOD of wastewater discharged from a POTW may be as low as 3 to 5 ppm. In some cases this will be lower than the natural BOD in the receiving stream.

The BOD of wastewater from a conventional septic tank may range from 120 to 240 ppm. As long as this waste can be disposed of underground, fish kills and other environmental problems will be avoided. Where clay soils and other site conditions prohibit the installation of a conventional septic tank, a non-conventional on-site system may be an option. When designed and operated properly, non-conventional on-site systems can reduce BOD levels to as low as 5 to 20 ppm.

The Problem of Nitrogen

Nitrogen is a major chemical concern when it comes to sewage treatment. Nitrogen in groundwater may cause "blue-baby syndrome" (methemoglobinemia) in infants. As a nutrient and fertilizer, nitrogen can lead to excessive growths of algae in surface streams and lakes. Crystal clear lakes and streams have literally turned green overnight

Nutrient pollution from on-site sewage treatment systems around the shores of this popular lake has promoted the rapid growth of algae. What was once crystal clear water is now murky green. Improved system designs and strict on-site regulations will help to improve water quality.

from algae feeding on nitrogen rich wastewater. Lakeside homes with poorly designed on-site sewage disposal systems can turn pristine lakes and streams into virtual septic tanks.

Algae blooms and other water quality problems in Chesapeake Bay have been linked to failing on-site sewage disposal systems. Older conventional septic tank systems along several shoreline communities have been described as "nutrient time bombs." It has been estimated that these systems contribute more than 12 million pounds of nitrogen a year to the Bay.

In the septic tank, microbes convert nitrogen that is present in human waste to ammonia-nitrogen. As wastewater enters the subsurface drain lines and percolates down through the soil, other types of microbes begin to convert ammonia to nitrates. Nitrates are able to move quickly through the soil into groundwater supplies. Shallow aquifers near the surface are a special problem for nitrate pollution.

Groundwater aquifers have been subject to nitrate pollution from high-density housing developments with on-site septic tank systems. Fertilizers used by farmers to increase crop production and nitrogen rich runoff from farm animal waste have also contaminated groundwater supplies. In some rural areas groundwater aquifers can no longer be used for public water supplies due to nitrate contamination.

The sample on the left is from a conventional septic tank and has a total suspended solids (TSS) concentration of about 95 to 155 ppm. The sample on the right was collected from a non-conventional on-site system using sand filtration and has a lower TSS concentration.

Studies have shown that wastewater from a conventional septic tank system has a typical nitrogen level of about 45 ppm. This can be a problem for building sites with high groundwater or fractured rock near the surface. This level of nitrogen can also be a problem for building sites in coastal areas or sites adjacent to lakes and streams. These building sites may require the installation of non-conventional on-site systems such as a recirculating sand filter, which is capable of reducing nitrogen.

Total Suspended Solids (TSS)

Total suspended solids (TSS) are another concern in treating wastewater. TSS are the very small particles that remain suspended in wastewater after treatment. Prior to treatment the TSS level in household sewage may be as high as 200 to 290 ppm. Reducing TSS will also reduce problems associated with dissolved toxic metals such as lead, copper and mercury that may be adsorbed and carried by suspended solids.

For on-site sewage disposal systems the major problem posed by TSS is the physical clogging of soil pores in underground disposal drains. When pumps and other devices must be installed, high TSS levels may lead to early failure and maintenance problems. The TSS level in

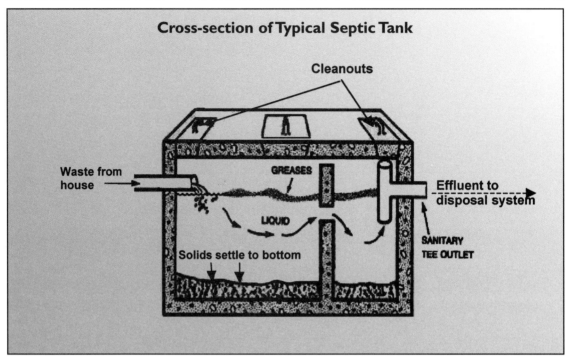

Cross-section of Typical Septic Tank

Cleanouts

Waste from house

GREASES

LIQUID

Solids settle to bottom

Effluent to disposal system

SANITARY TEE OUTLET

Septic tanks are more than just concrete boxes. They must be designed to allow waste to settle and biological microbes to begin the treatment process.

wastewater from the typical septic tank can be as high as 95 to 155 ppm. Installation of effluent filters can further reduce TSS, prolonging the life of disposal drain lines.

Proper Design

No matter what the size, a sewage treatment system must be designed to reduce BOD, nitrogen, TSS and other pollutants to levels that will not create public health problems and environment nuisances. Large municipal POTWs treating several million gallons of waste per day as well as small on-site sewage disposal systems are designed to provide primary and secondary treatment. In environmentally sensitive areas, additional tertiary or advanced treatment may be required.

During primary treatment in a septic tank, heavier solids are allowed to settle to the bottom of the tank. Grease and smaller light particles float to the top forming a scum. By use of a baffle system or T-fitting, liquid waste with reduced TSS is allowed to drain from the tank for final disposal.

As household sewage is collected in the septic tank, sufficient retention time must be provided to allow heavier solids to settle to the bottom (normally 48 to 60 hours). For a family of four, generating 400 gallons per day (gpd) of wastewater, a 1,000-gallon septic tank will provide a retention time of about 60 hours. For a family of six, generating 600 gallons gpd of wastewater, a 1,500-gallon tank would be needed to provide a 60-hour retention time.

As soon as solids begin to settle to the bottom of the septic tank, microbes begin to feed on waste. When it comes to oxygen, microbes may be classified as being anaerobic (not requiring oxygen) or aerobic (requiring oxygen). Some are able to survive with or without oxygen and are classified as facultative microbes.

Methane and Other Gases

When sewage enters the septic tank, the demand for oxygen by aerobic and facultative microbes is so great that available oxygen is quickly depleted. Conditions inside the tank soon become "septic" with an easily recognizable and familiar rotten egg odor (hence, the name septic tank). Without the presence of oxygen, anaerobic microorganisms begin to flourish producing more water and "sewer" gases as they feed on waste. Not only do these sewer gases have a very distinct and noxious odor, but they also contain methane and hydrogen sulfide gas.

Methane is flammable and will burn when concentrated. In some countries methane produced in septic tanks has been used as a fuel for cooking and heating. Hydrogen sulfide gas is toxic and can be deadly at low levels.

Sewer gases produced by anaerobic microbes inside the septic tank must be vented to the atmosphere through vents in the household plumbing system located on the roof. If the vents for the household plumbing system are lower than the pitch of the roof, sewer gases may not be sufficiently vented. If you detect the unpleasant odor of sewer gas in your backyard, the most likely cause is the design of the household plumbing vents on the roof. Under no circumstance should a homeowner attempt to self-inspect the inside of a septic tank due to the hazards of the hydrogen sulfide gas.

Secondary Treatment

Wastewater leaving the conventional septic tank undergoes limited secondary treatment by microbes as water percolates through the soil. If the septic tank is to be located uphill from the building foundation, a sewage-pumping unit with electrical controls will need to be installed. Some non-conventional on-site systems require the installation of elaborate pumping and aeration units with sophisticated electrical controls.

Plumbing system vents on the roof allow hydrogen sulfide and other sewer gases to escape to the atmosphere. Your septic tank system is designed to produce hydrogen sulfide and other types of sewer gas. If you smell sewer-like odors, roof vents may need to be extended above the pitch of the roof.

Regulations for Disposal Systems

State rules and regulations for both conventional and non-conventional on-site disposal systems are based on the basic principles of engineering and microbiology discussed in the "Science of Sewage Primer." For conventional systems the size of the septic tank is based on the time required for solids to settle. The size of the underground disposal system is based on soil conditions and amount of water used. The same principles are applied in the design of non-conventional on-site systems where additional secondary or advanced treatment may be required to further reduce BOD, nitrates and TSS.

For building sites having deep, well-drained soils, the installation of a conventional septic tank to provide primary treatment followed by limited secondary treatment in subsurface drain lines may be suitable. Additional secondary and advance treatment by non-conventional systems may be needed for sites having high groundwater, shallow soils, clay soils or other environmental challenges.

A typical conventional on-site system is compared to a non-conventional system in Figure 6-1 on page 138. Descriptions of other conventional and non-conventional on-site systems are provided in Appendix Two. Advantages and disadvantages of each system are discussed. The type of system that will best fit your needs is based on a number of factors.

Deciding on the Right System

The first step in making a decision on which type of on-site system is best for your situation is to have a "qualified professional" conduct a site evaluation. Individuals who are qualified to perform site evaluations vary from state to state and within local jurisdictions. In some cases only licensed engineers or registered professional sanitarians (individuals trained and experienced in public health) may be allowed to perform site evaluations and system design. Some states may also allow soil scientists, geologists, septic tank installers and other professionals to conduct site evaluations.

Some licensed engineers currently charge over $1,000 for performing a site evaluation and designing an on-site system. Other qualified individuals may quote a fee as little as $200. Most prospective homeowners tend to shop around to find the individual with the lowest fee; however, this may not be your best strategy for problem sites. Keep in mind that the fee charged for a site evaluation reflects the amount of time expended on the site evaluation and the skills required for design. You may wind up with a design that is quick and easy for the site evaluator but a system that's more costly to install and maintain.

Some homeowners will leave finding a site evaluation to their builder and not even talk with the site evaluator. Whatever method you use in obtaining a site evaluation and system design, keep in mind that it is best to have this done as early as possible in your homebuilding project. Once the site evaluation is completed it will be possible to select the best option from Appendix Two. Even if your builder has arranged for the site evaluation, take the time to meet and discuss your options with the professional designing the system.

Conducting a Site Evaluation

You may want to take 30 to 60 minutes to conduct your own site evaluation. The checklist shown in Appendix One can be used to determine if a conventional septic tank with underground absorption is indicated versus one of the more complex non-conventional systems described in Appendix Two. While you won't be able to use your site evaluation to obtain a permit, you will better know what level of professional services you need for site evaluation and system design. Building sites with limited space, steep slopes, clay or shallow

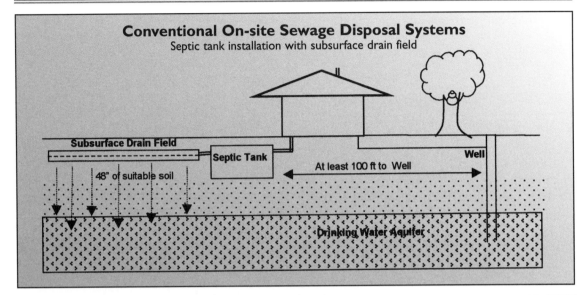

Conventional On-site Sewage Disposal Systems
Septic tank installation with subsurface drain field

Subsurface Drain Field

Septic Tank

48" of suitable soil

At least 100 ft to Well

Well

Drinking Water Aquifer

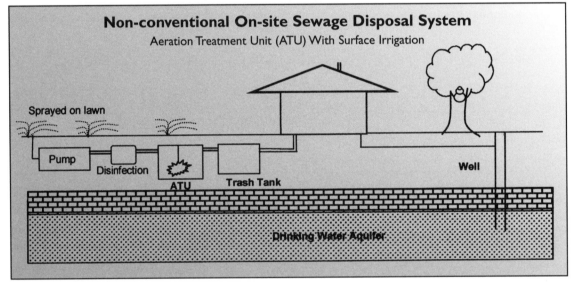

Non-conventional On-site Sewage Disposal System
Aeration Treatment Unit (ATU) With Surface Irrigation

Sprayed on lawn

Pump

Disinfection

ATU

Trash Tank

Well

Drinking Water Aquifer

Figure 6-1 A conventional system may be installed when soil conditions and other site factors allow.

If soil and site conditions warrant, a non-conventional system may need to be installed.

soils or other environmental challenges will be more likely to require the services of a site evaluator with experience and technical skills.

If your site has a number of environmental challenges where a non-conventional system is indicated, it may be better to pay a few dollars more for a site evaluator with the experience and the advanced design skills needed. Whatever the case may be, you will still need to have a qualified professional perform a site evaluation and develop a system design.

Building sites with steep slopes, rock formations or other environmental challenges will require a site evaluator with extensive experience and technical skills.

During the professional site evaluation, factors such as soil texture and structure; topography and slopes; location of floodplains; depth to groundwater; and location of water wells will be assessed. In addition, the evaluator will obtain information related to lot size, easements and setbacks, and estimates of family water use for the final design.

Soil conditions determine the method and amount of area required for disposing of liquid waste from the treatment unit. Sandy and loam type soils will require a smaller-sized soil absorption area than soils with large amounts of clay. For example, a family of four using 400 gallons of water per day would need about 160 feet of absorption lines in sandy soil but may need more than 350 feet in other type soils. The difference in cost could be as high as $1,000 - $1,500.

The Perc Test

The soil percolation test or "perc" test is a method that has been used in many states to estimate of the amount of wastewater that soils can absorb in a given time. Several test holes are dug in the area of the proposed disposal system, filled with water and allowed to soak. After soaking for a specified time (normally overnight), additional water is added to the test hole and the time required for a one-inch drop is then recorded.

The amount of time test holes are allowed to soak, weather conditions and other factors can influence perc test results. A few unscrupulous site evaluators have been known to skip the soaking (dry hole test) and instead rely on their "technical expertise" to estimate the perc results.

USDA Soil Texture Analysis

The majority of state regulatory authorities now require the use of USDA soil analysis techniques to evaluate soil conditions. In some states, the regulatory authority may require both a perc test and a USDA soil texture analysis as part of the site evaluation.

Soils can vary a great deal on the same building site. Changes in surface color are one indication of changes in soil. Soils can also drastically change with depth. A site evaluation is the only way to determine if soils are suitable for conventional on-site sewage treatment systems.

A number of states require site evaluators to attend formal training and pass a field examination. Using USDA techniques, the site evaluator will assess soil permeability, soil texture and soil structure at a depth specified by the regulatory authority (normally 48 to 60 inches). With the aid of a soil auger, the evaluator will bore two to four holes to the required depth. At specified intervals, soil texture, structure, color and other information will be recorded to produce a soil profile. If solid or fractured rock or groundwater is encountered, a conventional subsurface disposal system will not be suitable.

Sandy soils will allow water to move rapidly to lower depths. If the movement is too rapid, bacteria in the soil will not have time to

Proper evaluation of soil and site conditions takes a lot of time, hard labor and professional experience.

reduce pollutants before reaching groundwater. Water movement through clay soils will be slow. Soils with a clay content greater than 40 to 50 percent will not be suitable for a conventional subsurface absorption system.

The USDA has identified eleven classes of soil texture (see soil textural chart Figure 6-2 on next page). The site evaluator using a variety of field techniques will determine the class of soil found at various depths. Soils classified as sand, loamy sand, sandy loam, silt loam, loam, sandy clay loam, silty clay loam, clay loam, or sandy clay soils will be suitable for the installation of a conventional subsurface disposal system if shallow groundwater or fractured rocks are not encountered. Silty clay or clay are not suitable for conventional subsurface disposal systems.

Soil Structure

Soil structure (see Figure 6-3 on next page) will also be determined during the site evaluation. Structure that is massive or platy may impede the flow of water through soil and will make the site unsuitable for a conventional system. Structure that is columnar, blocky or granular will not interfere with water movement.

141

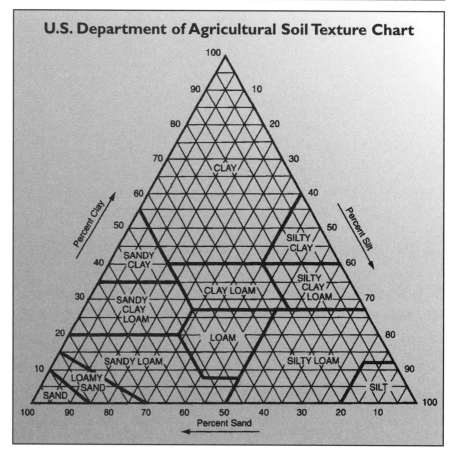

U.S. Department of Agricultural Soil Texture Chart

Figure 6-2 In some states, soil texture analysis has replaced the standard percolation test. The site evaluator will collect soil samples to determine texture and other soil characteristics. As the percent of clay increases more area will be required for the disposal of septic tank effluent. Soils classified as clay or silty clay will not be suitable for conventional septic tank systems using subsurface drain lines. Most site evaluators will determine soil texture based on a field dexterity "feel" test. Some evaluators may elect to use a more sophisticated laboratory hydrometer procedure.

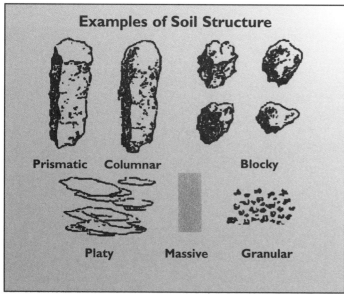

Examples of Soil Structure

Prismatic   Columnar   Blocky

Platy   Massive   Granular

Figure 6-3 Movement of water and air through the soil depends on soil structure. Granular, blocky, columnar and prismatic types of soil structure allow water and air to move freely. Platy and massive soil types of structure hinder the free flow of water and air through soil. These types of structure are not suitable for some types of on-site treatment systems.

Soils subject to groundwater saturation during part of the year may develop color patterns with streaks of orange and brown on a bluish or gray background. This type of color pattern, known as mottling, may indicate a condition

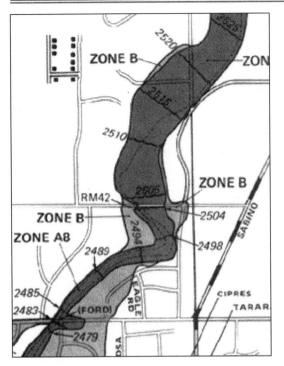

Example of a floodplain map showing areas prone to flooding. Assistance in interpreting maps can be obtained from your County Floodplain Administrator.

known as a gley soil. Gley soil is generally unsuitable for conventional disposal systems because of seasonal high groundwater.

Flood Plains or Floodways

Using maps prepared by the Federal Emergency Management Agency (FEMA), the site evaluator will determine if the site is located in a 100-year flood plain. Some jurisdictions may not allow any on-site system to be installed within a 100-year flood plain. Other jurisdictions may require special engineering designs for installing an on-site system within a 100-year flood plain or floodway.

Other Locational Factors

The presence of flat or low lying areas where rainwater can collect will also be identified. The location of property lines, easements and setbacks for the site will also be identified. A blueline survey map may need to be submitted to the approval authority.

Existing and planned water wells on your site must be identified. Existing water wells on adjacent properties also need to be located. On a small-sized lot (less than an acre) you may find that a neighbor's existing well on an adjacent site restricts locations where you can install your disposal system. In severe cases, water wells on adjacent properties may even prohibit the installation of a disposal system on your site. The site evaluator should use a tape measure or other device to determine all distances not shown on a survey map.

Topography

Topography (lay of the land) is evaluated to identify depressions, slope, relief and features such as roads, creeks, rivers or lakes. Slope is the rate of rise or fall of the ground surface from the horizontal and is expressed in terms of degrees or percent. Depressions and nearly flat sites with slopes of less than 2% may be subject to standing water after rain. Sites with a slope of 2% to 6% are ideal for surface drainage. When slopes exceed 6% a contour design may need to be used for disposal trenches. Slopes in excess of 30% may not be suitable for conventional subsurface disposal systems. Sites with rolling hills and steep slopes will require the use of pumps to move wastewater uphill.

Building sites with excessive slopes may require the installation of an additional tank and pump unit to move waste water uphill.

Information obtained during the site evaluation will be used to determine available options for the final design of your on-site sewage system. In most jurisdictions the site evaluator will also provide the design and layout for your on-site system.

Discussing the Site Evaluation

No matter whom you select to perform the site evaluation arrange to meet and discuss all your options before making a final decision on the type of system to be designed and installed. The majority of homeowners simply leave this decision to the site evaluator, builder or installer. The site evaluator may make this decision based on which system requires less time to design. Installers will tend to recommend an on-site system based on their capability to install the system. A few may recommend systems giving them the higher profit margin. In ideal circumstances, the final decision will be based on a conference between the homeowner, site evaluator, installer and builder prior to starting any construction work on the new home.

When a non-conventional on-site system must be installed use Appendix Two to discuss the advantages and disadvantages of all your options. If a non-conventional on-site system is indicated, ask if any changes could be made that would allow the installation of a conventional septic tank system. In some cases repositioning the planned location of your foundation a few feet or relocating the site for a planned well may make it easier and less expensive to install a disposal system. This can also mean the difference in having to install a system with pumps or other components that will require more maintenance for the homeowner.

Installation of this on-site system is nearly completed. The yellow flags outline the treatment system. The light-colored sand indicates the location of the effluent disposal system. Homeowners need to keep information and maps on the location of all underground components. Driveways, lawn irrigation systems and patios should not be installed over any part of the system.

During the conference to discuss the design of your on-site system ask how water use was estimated for your family. Estimating the amount of water a family will use is more of an art than an exact science. If reducing the amount of water for disposal will allow you to install a conventional septic tank system, ask about the possibility of using a "grey water" disposal system, for laundry and other liquid waste.

Figure 5-5 on page 81 provides water usage estimates for a number of different activities. The estimates in Figure 5-5 are based on long-term studies and reflect averages. The age of family members, frequent weekend visits from friends and relatives, Saturday washdays and other factors will influence the actual amount of water used by your family. Site evaluators will use similar tables to estimate the amount of water your family will use.

If you think your family may use more water that the average family, talk it over with the person designing the system. Attempting to "low ball" water use estimates may result in problems later. The majority of septic tank failures can be traced to underestimating the amount of water a family will use.

Maintenance

Once an on-site sewage disposal is installed the homeowner will be responsible for routine operation and maintenance. Conventional septic tank systems will need to have accumulated solids pumped every three to four years. Non-conventional systems with pumps and other components will need more frequent maintenance. Many regu-

Non-conventional on-site sewage treatment systems, such as aerobic treatment units (ATU) may require extensive electrical controls and other components. Some states now require that homeowners with these systems have a contract with a qualified maintenance firm.

Publications for the Care and Maintenance of On-site Sewage Systems
Available From the National Small Flows Clearinghouse

The following brochures can be downloaded from the NSFC Web site at http://www.estd.wvu.edu/nsfc/NSFC_homepage.html:
- So...now you own a septic tank.
- The care and feeding of your septic system.
- Groundwater protection and your septic system.

These products can be obtained by writing to the NSFC, West Virginia University, P.O. Box 6064, Morgantown, WV, 26506:
- Your Septic System: A Reference Guide for Homeowners, free.
- Homeowner's Septic Tank Information Package, $2.15.
- Homeowner's Septic Tank System Guide & Record Keeping Folder, $0.50.
- Introduction to Water Quality Standards, free.
- Xeriscape Landscaping: Using Resources Efficiently, free.
- Your Septic System: A Guide for Homeowners, Video. $10.00
- The Care and Feeding of Your Septic Tank, Video. $10.00

Figure 6-4 Funded by the EPA, the National Small Flows Clearinghouse (NSFC) provides information about low-cost waste-water treatment for small communities generating one million gallons or less of waste-water. The NSFC also provides private home-owners with publications, training videos and other educational material on the care and maintenance of on-site sewage systems.

latory agencies are now requiring homeowners to have maintenance contracts for non-conventional on-site systems such ATUs.

Neglecting maintenance can lead to early failure and costly repair bills. Recent surveys have shown that many rural homeowners do not know or understand maintenance requirements for the type of on-site system they own. Many of the homeowners surveyed didn't even know where their system was located.

Sources for More Information
A number of excellent homeowner training materials and maintenance guides for on-site sewage disposal systems are available from the EPA-sponsored National Small Flows Clearinghouse in West Virginia. Educational materials available from the Clearinghouse are described in Figure 6-4. A summary of recommended homeowner practices for the "care and feeding" of on-site sewage disposal systems is provided in Figure 6-5 on page 148.

The Dwindling Availability of Suitable Site Conditions
As the demand for rural building sites continues to increase it may not be easy to find site conditions allowing the installation of a conventional septic tank system. More regulatory jurisdictions can be

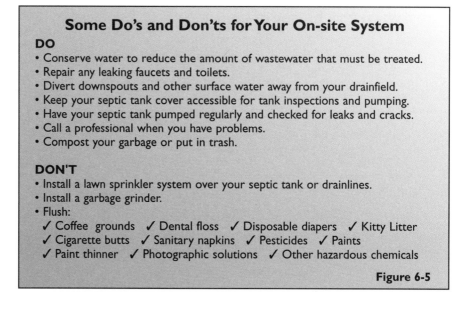

Some Do's and Don'ts for Your On-site System

DO
- Conserve water to reduce the amount of wastewater that must be treated.
- Repair any leaking faucets and toilets.
- Divert downspouts and other surface water away from your drainfield.
- Keep your septic tank cover accessible for tank inspections and pumping.
- Have your septic tank pumped regularly and checked for leaks and cracks.
- Call a professional when you have problems.
- Compost your garbage or put in trash.

DON'T
- Install a lawn sprinkler system over your septic tank or drainlines.
- Install a garbage grinder.
- Flush:
  ✓ Coffee grounds ✓ Dental floss ✓ Disposable diapers ✓ Kitty Litter
  ✓ Cigarette butts ✓ Sanitary napkins ✓ Pesticides ✓ Paints
  ✓ Paint thinner ✓ Photographic solutions ✓ Other hazardous chemicals

Figure 6-5

expected to become stricter when it comes to inspecting and approving the installation of non-conventional system designs.

For non-conventional systems such as ATUs with sophisticated mechanical and electrical units, routine operation and maintenance can be expected to become more costly. Rural homeowners responsible for these systems may someday be required to obtain training and certification in their proper operation to ensure that sensitive groundwater supplies are not contaminated.

A Final Word of Advice

Congratulations on deciding to build in the country. Hopefully, the information presented in *Building Your Country* Home will help you in this journey. Keep in mind that no building site will be "perfect" when it comes to all the environmental concerns discussed in this book. It is only when potential problems are neglected in planning that they later become headaches.

Don't be reluctant to ask questions. When it comes to making decisions about potential building sites and building in rural areas there are no dumb questions. Take the time to visit with nearby neighbors to ask about their experiences with water and on-site sewage disposal. Visit with local regulatory officials and ask about any known problems in the area that you are planning to build. Figure 6-6 on page 150 provides a summary of people and places you may want to visit and key questions to ask as you plan to build in the country.

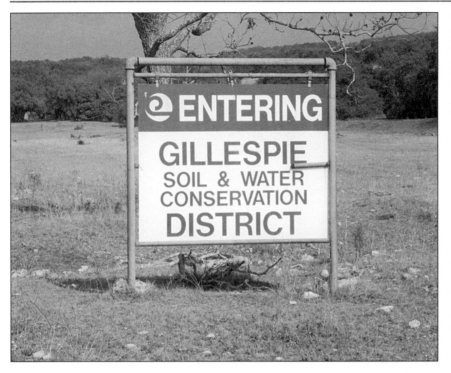

Take time to visit with the professional staff at local and county agencies. Most will have information and free publications that may help you prepare for life in the country.

Developers of this rural development elected to provide homeowners with a centralized sewage treatment lagoon system. Careful operation and maintenance has made the treatment lagoon a valuable community asset.

Figure 6-6
Local Offices to Visit for Assistance

(1) County or State Health Department: Sanitarians and other environmental specialists can assist in answering public health questions related to water quality and local environmental health issues. Some county health departments may also be the regulatory authority responsible for inspecting and approving on-site sewage disposal systems. Most local health departments will be able to perform bacteriological testing of drinking water, free of charge or for a minimal fee.

(2) Regional or State Department of Environmental Quality (DEQ) Office: Provides similar services as local health departments. Instead of focusing on public health issues, the DEQ emphasizes environmental protection.

(3) County Floodplain Administrator: Normally assigned to a county or local planning department to provide information to homeowners on the location of flood-prone areas and the National Flood Insurance Program (NFIP).

(4) State University Cooperative Extension Service: Extension agents will be available to answer questions on a variety of agricultural, natural resource and environmental subjects. The County Extension Service office should have publications and information on a variety of agricultural subjects as well as on groundwater and waste disposal for rural homeowners.

(5) Natural Resources Conservation Service (NRCS): First established in 1933, as the Soil Erosion Service, the NRCS works with rural residents on a wide range of environmental issues. While, their primary mission is still focused on the farm community the NRCS staff at state and county field offices can provide information on local soils and help interpret the results of soil profile analysis.

(6) U.S. Geological Survey: State and regional offices may have detailed technical reports on the quality and quantity of local groundwater aquifers.

(7) U.S. Fish and Wildlife Service: The staff at Regional and State USFWS field offices will be able to provide information related to endangered wildlife species that might be encountered on proposed building sites. In some areas, rural homebuilding has been halted due to the presence of threatened or endangered sub-terrarium cave crickets and wild rice.

One final word of advice, keep in mind the first word and last word when it comes to water–**conservation**. No matter if you have your own well or are supplied by a community water system, water conservation needs to be a way of life for the rural homeowner. Using water like you had an endless supply not only depletes limited groundwater sources, but may also overload your on-site sewage disposal system. Water conservation is a small price to pay to escape that city haze and those bright city lights.

Your new address in the country will be worth all the hard work and effort as you get used to life beyond the bright city lights.

COUNTRY HOMES YOU CAN BUILD

Design by
© Home Planners

Width: 84'-6"
Depth: 64'-0"

QUOTE ONE®
Cost to build? See page 184
to order complete cost estimate
to build this house in your area!

Design HPT09001
Square Footage: 2,090

L D

◆ This classic farmhouse enjoys a wraparound porch that's perfect for enjoyment of the outdoors. To the rear of the plan, a sun terrace with a spa opens from the owners suite and the morning room. A grand great room offers a sloped ceiling and a corner fireplace with a raised hearth. A low wall and graceful archways set off by decorative columns define the formal dining room. The tiled kitchen has a centered island counter with a snack bar and adjoins a laundry area. Two family bedrooms reside to the side of the plan, and each enjoys private access to the covered porch. A secluded owners suite nestles in its own wing and features a sitting area with access to the rear terrace and spa.

To Order Blueprints see pages 182-191

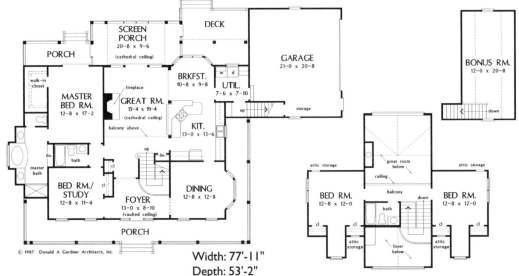

Width: 77'-11"
Depth: 53'-2"

Design HPT09002

First Floor: 1,743 square feet
Second Floor: 555 square feet
Total: 2,298 square feet
Bonus Space: 350 square feet

Design by
Donald A. Gardner
Architects, Inc.

◆ A lovely arch-top window and a wraparound porch set off this country exterior. Inside, formal rooms open off the foyer, which leads to a spacious great room. This living area provides a fireplace and access to a screened porch with a cathedral ceiling. Bay windows allow natural light into the breakfast area and formal dining room. The owners suite features a spacious bath and access to a private area of the rear porch. Two second-floor bedrooms share a bath and a balcony hall that offers an overlook to the great room.

To Order Blueprints see pages 182-191

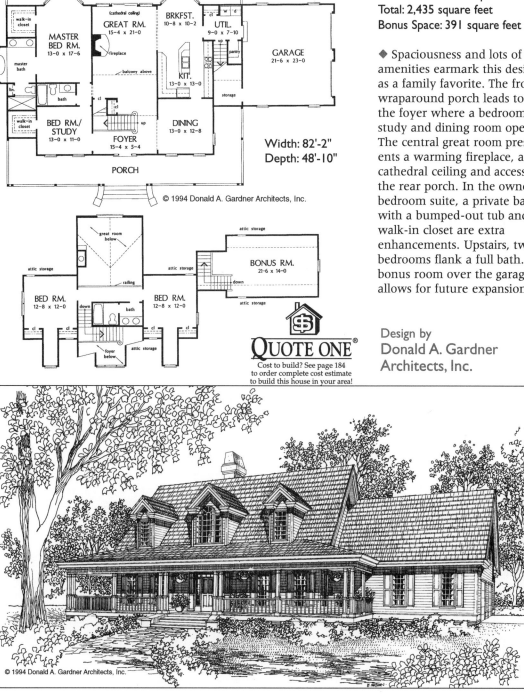

skylights

(cathedral ceiling)

walk-in closet

MASTER BED RM.
13-0 x 17-6

master bath

lin.

bath

walk-in closet

GREAT RM.
15-4 x 21-0

fireplace

balcony above

BRKFST.
10-8 x 10-2

UTIL.
9-0 x 7-10

w d

a

pantry

up

KIT.
13-0 x 13-0

storage

GARAGE
21-6 x 23-0

cl

cl

up

BED RM./ STUDY
13-0 x 11-0

FOYER
15-4 x 5-4

DINING
13-0 x 12-8

PORCH

© 1994 Donald A. Gardner Architects, Inc.

great room below

attic storage

attic storage

attic storage

attic storage

BONUS RM.
21-6 x 14-0

down

railing

BED RM.
12-8 x 12-0

down

bath

BED RM.
12-8 x 12-0

cl

cl

cl

cl

attic storage

foyer below

attic storage

QUOTE ONE®

Cost to build? See page 184
to order complete cost estimate
to build this house in your area!

Design HPT09003

First Floor: 1,841 square feet
Second Floor: 594 square feet
Total: 2,435 square feet
Bonus Space: 391 square feet

◆ Spaciousness and lots of
amenities earmark this design
as a family favorite. The front
wraparound porch leads to
the foyer where a bedroom or
study and dining room open.
The central great room pres-
ents a warming fireplace, a
cathedral ceiling and access to
the rear porch. In the owners
bedroom suite, a private bath
with a bumped-out tub and a
walk-in closet are extra
enhancements. Upstairs, two
bedrooms flank a full bath. A
bonus room over the garage
allows for future expansion.

Design by
Donald A. Gardner
Architects, Inc.

Width: 82'-2"
Depth: 48'-10"

© 1994 Donald A. Gardner Architects, Inc.

© 1993 Donald A. Gardner Architects, Inc.

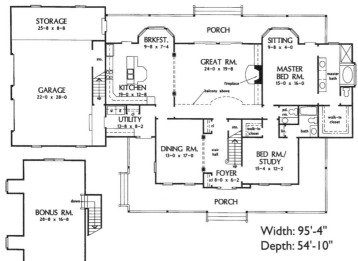

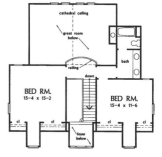

Design HPT09004
First Floor: 2,316 square feet
Second Floor: 721 square feet
Total: 3,037 square feet
Bonus Space: 545 square feet

Width: 95'-4"
Depth: 54'-10"

Design by
Donald A. Gardner
Architects, Inc.

Cost to build? See page 184
to order complete cost estimate
to build this house in your area!

◆ This gracious farmhouse with its wraparound porch offers a touch of symmetry in a well-defined, open plan. The entrance foyer has a Palladian clerestory window that gives an abundance of natural light to the interior. The vaulted great room furthers this feeling of airiness, along with two sets of sliding glass doors leading to the porch out back. The country kitchen, with an island countertop, the bayed breakfast nook and the dining room all enjoy nine-foot ceilings. Upstairs, each family bedroom has two closets. For privacy, the owners suite occupies the right side of the first floor. With a sitting room and all the amenities of a spa-style bath, this room won't fail to please.

To Order Blueprints see pages 182-191

©1993 Donald A. Gardner Architects, Inc.

S. NATHAN

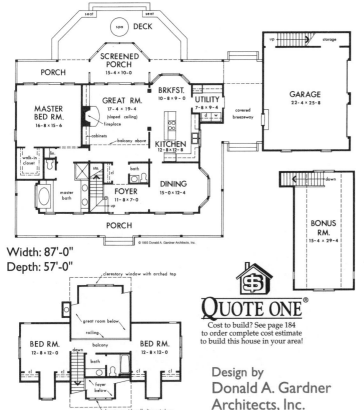

Width: 87'-0"
Depth: 57'-0"

Design HPT09005

First Floor: 1,618 square feet
Second Floor: 570 square feet
Total: 2,188 square feet
Bonus Space: 495 square feet

◆ A wraparound covered porch, open deck with a spa and seating, arched windows and dormers enhance the already impressive character of this three-bedroom farmhouse. The entrance foyer and great room have Palladian window clerestories to allow natural light to enter. The spacious two-story great room boasts a fireplace. The kitchen, with a cooking island, is conveniently located between a dining room and a breakfast room with an open view of the great room. A generous owners bedroom has plenty of closet space as well as an expansive owners bath. Bonus room over the garage allows for room to grow.

QUOTE ONE®

Cost to build? See page 184 to order complete cost estimate to build this house in your area!

Design by
Donald A. Gardner
Architects, Inc.

157

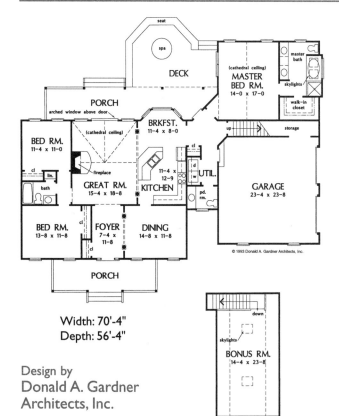

Width: 70'-4"
Depth: 56'-4"

Design by
**Donald A. Gardner
Architects, Inc.**

BONUS RM.
14-4 x 23-8

Design HPT09006
Square Footage: 1,864
Bonus Space: 438 square feet

◆ Quaint and cozy on the outside with porches front and back, this three-bedroom country home surprises with an open floor plan featuring a large great room with a cathedral ceiling. Nine-foot ceilings add volume throughout the home. A central kitchen with an angled counter opens to the breakfast and great rooms for easy entertaining. The privately located owners bedroom has a cathedral ceiling and adjacent access to the deck. Operable skylights over the tub accent the luxurious owners bath. Two secondary bedrooms share a full hall bath. A bonus room makes expanding easy.

Cost to build? See page 184
to order complete cost estimate
to build this house in your area!

To Order Blueprints see pages 182-191

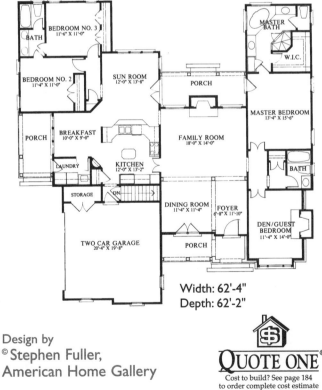

Width: 62'-4"
Depth: 62'-2"

Design by
© Stephen Fuller,
American Home Gallery

QUOTE ONE®
Cost to build? See page 184
to order complete cost estimate
to build this house in your area!

Design HPT09007
Square Footage: 2,170

◆ This classic cottage features a stone and wooden exterior with an arch-detailed porch and a box-bay window. From the foyer, double doors open to the den with built-in bookcases and a fireplace. A full bath is situated next to the den, allowing for an optional guest room. The family room is centrally located, just beyond the foyer. The owners bedroom opens to the rear porch. The owners bath, with a large walk-in closet, double vanities, a corner tub and separate shower completes this relaxing retreat. Left of the family room awaits a sun room with access to the covered porch. A breakfast area complements the attractive and efficiently designed kitchen. Two secondary bedrooms with large closets share a full bath featuring double vanities. This home is designed with a basement foundation.

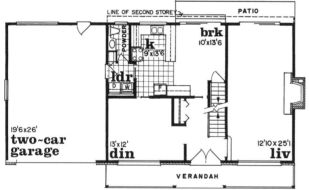

LINE OF SECOND STOREY   PATIO

brk
10'x13'6

k
9'x13'6

POWDER

ldr
D | W

F

two-car garage
19'6x26'

din
13'x12'

liv
12'10 x 25'1

VERANDAH

Design HPT09008

First Floor: 1,026 square feet
Second Floor: 994 square feet
Total: 2,020 square feet
Bonus Space: 377 square feet

Width: 58'-0"
Depth: 32'-0"

◆ This inviting country home is enhanced by a full-width covered front porch, a fieldstone exterior and a trio of dormers on the second floor. Double doors open to a foyer flanked by a living room and a dining room. The living room extends the full depth of the house and has a fireplace and sliding glass doors to the rear patio. A U-shaped kitchen adjoins a breakfast room with sliding glass doors to the patio. A laundry and a half-bath connect the home to a two-car garage. Second-floor space includes two family bedrooms with a shared bath and an owners suite that features a full bath and walk-in closet. A large bonus room adds 377 square feet of living space on the second floor.

bonus room
18'x19'7

br 2
13'x11'8

BATH

W.I. CLOSET

ENS.

br3
13'x10'4

GALLERY

mbr
12'10 x14' & 16'

Design by
©Select Home Designs

To Order Blueprints see pages 182-191

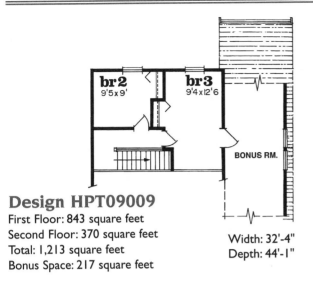

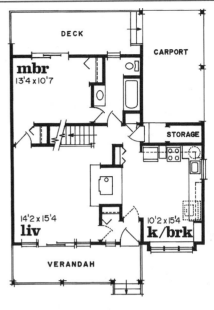

Design HPT09009

First Floor: 843 square feet

Second Floor: 370 square feet

Total: 1,213 square feet

Bonus Space: 217 square feet

Width: 32'-4"
Depth: 44'-1"

◆ This country-style vacation home is economical to build and offers additional space for future development. A bonus room may be used as an extra bedroom, play room or media center. The front veranda opens to a living room with wood stove and vaulted ceiling. The kitchen and breakfast room are nearby; the kitchen has an L-shaped work counter. The owners bedroom is on the first floor for privacy and has its own deck, accessed through sliding glass doors, and a private bath. Note the storage room just beyond the carport. Family bedrooms and the bonus room occupy the second floor.

Design by
© Select Home Designs

QUOTE ONE®

Cost to build? See page 184
to order complete cost estimate
to build this house in your area!

Design by
© Home Planners

HPT09029

First Floor: 1,592 square feet
Second Floor: 1,054 square feet
Total: 2,646 square feet

◆ This Colonial home has all the exteri-
or charm of its Early American ancestors. To
the immediate left of the entry is a living room
with a music alcove and a fireplace. To the right is
the formal dining room. In its own wing, a few steps
down from the living room is a cheery sun room. The
country kitchen, with an island range, built-in china
cabinets and a fireplace, offers plenty of space for informal eating. Upstairs, two family bedrooms share a full
bath, while the owners suite pampers with a whirlpool
tub, twin vanities and plenty of closet space.

Width: 64'-0"
Depth: 48'-8"

QUOTE ONE®

Cost to build? See page 184
to order complete cost estimate
to build this house in your area!

To Order Blueprints see pages 182-191

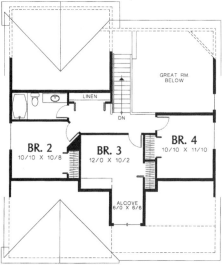

GREAT RM. BELOW

LINEN

DN

BR. 2
10/10 X 10/8

BR. 3
12/0 X 10/2

BR. 4
10/10 X 11/10

ALCOVE
6/0 X 6/6

VAULTED MASTER
11/8 X 15/0

UP

GREAT RM.
15/8 X 16/8

DINING
11/0 X 10/0 +/-

GARAGE
19/0 X 21/6

DISPLAY

PREF PAN

13/0 X 9/6

RANGE

Width: 40'-0"
Depth: 47'-0"

Design HPT09010

First Floor: 1,198 square feet
Second Floor: 673 square feet
Total: 1,871 square feet

Design by
© Alan Mascord Design
Associates, Inc.

◆ This petite bungalow would be perfect for either empty-nesters or those just starting out. The charm of the exterior is echoed inside, where a comfortable floor plan is very accommodating with its layout. A G-shaped kitchen has no cross-room traffic and serves the dining room with a pass-through. The spacious great room features a corner fireplace and sliding glass doors to the rear yard. The vaulted owners bedroom, on the first floor, offers a walk-in closet and private bath. Upstair, three secondary bedrooms are available—one with an alcove—and share a full hall bath and a large linen closet.

Design HPT09011

Square Footage: 1,389

L

◆ A double dose of charm, this special farm-house plan offers two elevations in its blueprint package. Though rooflines and porch options are different, the floor plan is the same. A formal living room has a warming fireplace and a delightful bay window. The U-shaped kitchen shares a snack bar with the bayed family room. Note the sliding glass doors to the rear yard here. Sleeping quarters include two family bed-rooms served by a full bath and a lovely owners suite with its own private bath.

Design by
© Home Planners

Width: 44'-8"
Depth: 54'-6"

Alternate Elevation

To Order Blueprints see pages 182-191

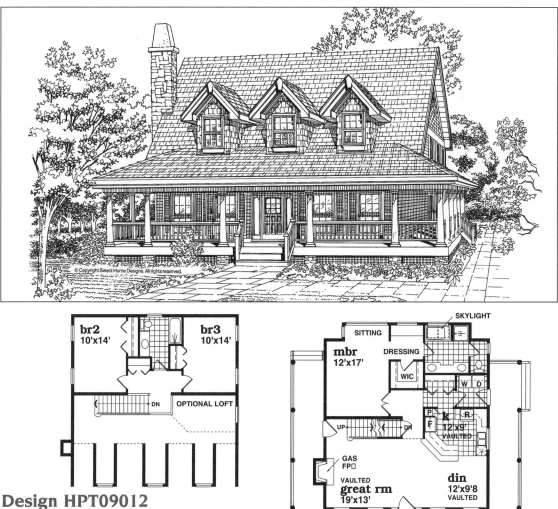

br2 10'x14'
br3 10'x14'

DN

OPTIONAL LOFT

SKYLIGHT

SITTING

mbr 12'x17'

DRESSING

WIC

W D

UP

DN

k 12'x9' VAULTED

P F R

GAS FP

VAULTED
great rm 19'x13'

din 12'x9'8 VAULTED

COVERED VERANDAH

Design HPT09012

First Floor: 1,099 square feet
Second Floor: 535 square feet
Total: 1,634 square feet

Width: 44'-8"
Depth: 41'-4"

◆ This design offers several different options to make the floor plan exactly as you like it. The exterior is graced by a wrapping veranda, round columns and a trio of dormers. Inside, the open plan includes a vaulted great room with fireplace, a vaulted dining room, a vaulted kitchen and three bedrooms. The kitchen provides a pass-through to the dining room and large pantry. The owners bedroom—found on the first floor for privacy—contains a walk-in closet with dressing room, sitting area and full skylit bath. Family bedrooms reside on the second floor. If you choose, you can reconfigure the owners bath to allow for a half bath in the laundry.

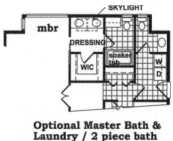

SKYLIGHT

mbr

DRESSING

WIC

soaker tub

W D

**Optional Master Bath &
Laundry / 2 piece bath**

Design by
© **Select Home Designs**

Design by
©R.L. Pfotenhauer

Design HPT09013
Square Footage: 1,550

Width: 62'-9"
Depth: 36'-1"

◆ If you like the rustic appeal of ranch-style homes, you'll love this version. Both horizontal and vertical siding appear on the exterior and are complemented by a columned covered porch and a delightful cupola as accent. The entry opens to a huge open living/dining room combination. A fireplace in the living area is flanked by windows and doors to one of two rear decks. A vaulted ceiling runs the width of this area. The kitchen also accesses the deck and features counter space galore. Look for a private deck behind the owners suite. A vaulted ceiling graces the owners bedroom. Two family bedrooms have good closet space and share a full bath at the opposite end of the hall.

To Order Blueprints see pages 182-191

Design HPT09014
Square Footage: 1,830

L **D**

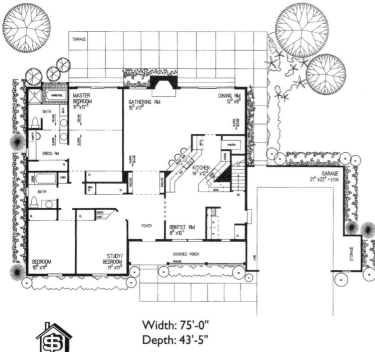

TERRACE

MASTER BEDROOM 11'×17'⁸

GATHERING RM 15'×17'

DINING RM 12'×9'⁸

WHIRLPOOL

BATH

DRESS RM

PANTRY

KITCHEN 14'×12'⁰

GARAGE 21'×22'⁴ + STOR

BATH

LINEN

BOOKS CART

FOYER

BRKFST RM 8'⁸×10'⁴

DESK

STORAGE

BEDROOM 10'⁶×11'⁸

STUDY/ BEDROOM 11'×11'⁸

COVERED PORCH
RAILING

CAR

Width: 75'-0"
Depth: 43'-5"

QUOTE ONE®

Cost to build? See page 184
to order complete cost estimate
to build this house in your area!

Design by
© Home Planners

◆ This charming one-story traditional home greets visitors with a covered porch. A uniquely shaped galley-style kitchen shares a snack bar with the spacious gathering room where a fireplace is the focal point. The dining room provides sliding glass doors to the rear terrace as does the owners suite. This bedroom area also includes a luxury bath with a whirlpool tub and separate dressing room. Two additional bedrooms, one that could double as a study, are located at the front of the home. The two-car garage features a large storage area and can be reached through the service entrance or from the rear terrace.

167

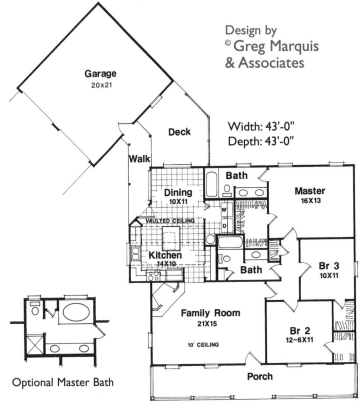

Design by
© Greg Marquis
& Associates

Width: 43'-0"
Depth: 43'-0"

Optional Master Bath

Design HPT09015
Square Footage: 1,475

◆ This home-sweet-home features a welcoming front porch across it's entire length. Once you enter, you'll be greeted by ten-foot ceilings and a cozily angled fireplace in the large family room. The vaulted eat-in kitchen with its popular L-shape and work island includes an ample pantry and a laundry room. But there's more to this easy-to-build house. Note the large owners bedroom with a walk-in closet. Each of the other two bedrooms also have walk-in closets. Out back, a covered walk runs next to the deck and connects the angled two-car garage with the living space in a most charming way.

To Order Blueprints see pages 182-191

Design by
© Greg Marquis
& Associates

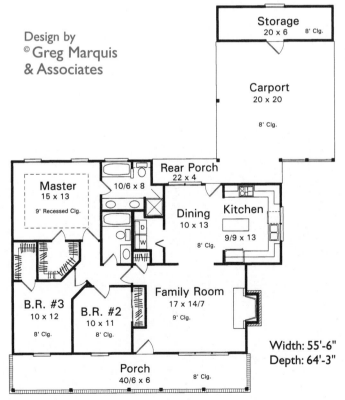

Storage
20 x 6   8' Clg.

Carport
20 x 20

8' Clg.

Rear Porch
22 x 4

Master
15 x 13

9' Recessed Clg.

10/6 x 8

Dining
10 x 13

8' Clg.

Kitchen

9/9 x 13

D
W

Family Room
17 x 14/7

9' Clg.

B.R. #3
10 x 12

8' Clg.

B.R. #2
10 x 11

8' Clg.

Porch
40/6 x 6   8' Clg.

Width: 55'-6"
Depth: 64'-3"

Design HPT09016
Square Footage: 1,333

◆ This country cottage is sure to please with its many amenities! Included in the long list are a fireplace in the family room, a work island in the U-shaped kitchen and a convenient—yet hidden—laundry room. Two family bedrooms—one with walk-in closet—share a full bath while the owners suite offers a private bath, with a spa tub and double sinks, and a large walk-in closet. The rear porch connects to a carport, where there is a large storage space.

Design HPT09017
Square Footage: 2,090

◆ This traditional home features board and batten and cedar shingles in an attractively proportioned exterior. Finishing touches include a covered entrance and porch with column detailing and an arched transom, flower boxes and shuttered windows. The foyer opens to both the dining room and the great room beyond with French doors opening to the porch. To the right of the foyer is the combination bedroom/study. A short hallway leads to a full bath and a secondary bedroom with ample closet space. The spacious owners bedroom enjoys walk-in closets on both sides of the entrance to the owners bath. This home is designed with a basement foundation.

Design by
© Stephen Fuller, American Home Gallery

Width: 61'-0"
Depth: 70'-6"

Quote One®
Cost to build? See page 184
to order complete cost estimate
to build this house in your area!

170

To Order Blueprints see pages 182-191

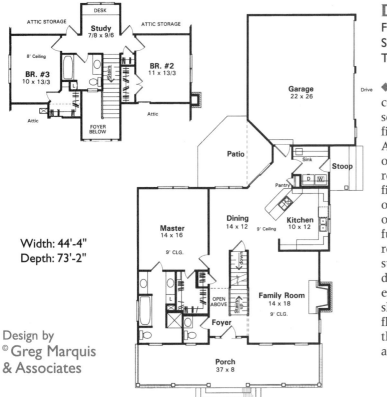

Width: 44'-4"
Depth: 73'-2"

Design by
© Greg Marquis
& Associates

Design HPT09018
First Floor: 1,271 square feet
Second Floor: 537 square feet
Total: 1,808 square feet

◆ The foyer of this traditional country design is open to the second-floor dormer above to fill the house with natural light. A powder room sits to the left of the foyer and the family room with high ceilings and a fireplace is to the right. The open dining room and kitchen offer an angled cooking area, full pantry and access to the rear patio. The owners bedroom suite features a walk-in closet, double vanities and a linen closet in the bath. Two bedrooms share a hall bath on the second floor, plus a built-in desk under the windows in the study area at the top of the stairs.

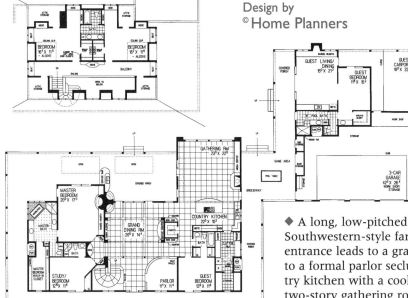

Design by
© Home Planners

QUOTE ONE®

Cost to build? See page 184
to order complete cost estimate
to build this house in your area!

Width: 154'-0"
Depth: 94'-8"

Design HPT09019

First Floor: 3,166 square feet
Second Floor: 950 square feet
Total: 4,116 square feet
Guest House: 680 square feet

L

◆ A long, low-pitched roof distinguishes this Southwestern-style farmhouse design. The tiled entrance leads to a grand dining room and opens to a formal parlor secluded by half-walls. A country kitchen with a cooktop island overlooks the two-story gathering room with its full wall of glass, fireplace and built-in media shelves. The owners suite satisfies the most discerning tastes with a raised hearth, an adjacent study or exercise room, access to the wraparound porch, and a bath with corner whirlpool tub. Rooms upstairs can serve as secondary bedrooms for family members, or can be converted to home office space or used as guest bedrooms.

To Order Blueprints see pages 182-191

Design HPT09020

First Floor: 1,700 square feet
Second Floor: 1,585 square feet
Total: 3,285 square feet
Bonus Space: 176 square feet

Design by
© Stephen Fuller, American
Home Gallery

QUOTE ONE®
Cost to build? See page 184
to order complete cost estimate
to build this house in your area!

Width: 60'-0"
Depth: 47'-6"

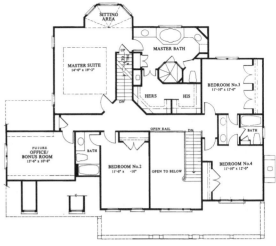

◆ The covered front stoop of this two-story traditionally styled home gives way to the foyer and formal areas inside. A cozy living room with a fireplace sits on the right and an elongated dining room is on the left. For fine family living, a great room and a kitchen with breakfast area account for the rear of the first-floor plan. A guest room with a nearby full bath finishes off the accommodations. Upstairs, four bedrooms include an owners suite fit for a king. A bonus room rests near Bedroom 3. This home is designed with a basement foundation.

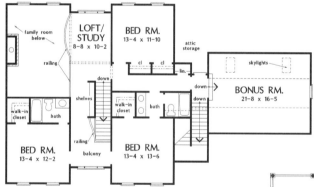

Design HPT09021

First Floor: 2,086 square feet
Second Floor: 1,077 square feet
Total: 3,163 square feet
Bonus Space: 403 square feet

Design by
Donald A. Gardner
Architects, Inc.

◆ This beautiful farmhouse, adds just the right amount of country style. The owners suite is quietly tucked away downstairs. The family cook will love the spacious U-shaped kitchen and adjoining bayed breakfast nook. A bonus room is easily accessible from the back stairs or from the second floor, where three large bedrooms share two full baths. Storage space abounds with walk-ins, half-shelves and linen closets. A curved balcony borders a versatile loft/study, which overlooks the stunning two-story family room.

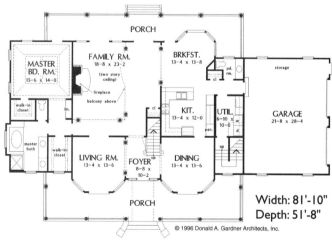

Width: 81'-10"
Depth: 51'-8"

© 1996 Donald A. Gardner Architects, Inc.

To Order Blueprints see pages 182-191

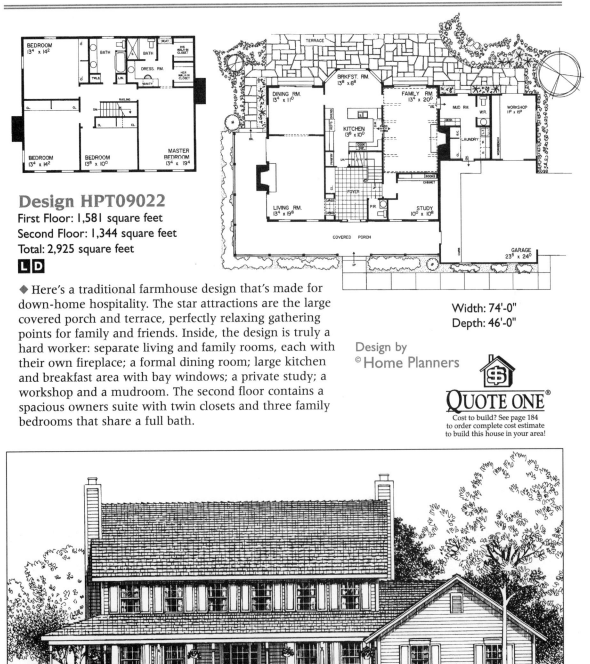

Design HPT09022

First Floor: 1,581 square feet
Second Floor: 1,344 square feet
Total: 2,925 square feet

L D

◆ Here's a traditional farmhouse design that's made for down-home hospitality. The star attractions are the large covered porch and terrace, perfectly relaxing gathering points for family and friends. Inside, the design is truly a hard worker: separate living and family rooms, each with their own fireplace; a formal dining room; large kitchen and breakfast area with bay windows; a private study; a workshop and a mudroom. The second floor contains a spacious owners suite with twin closets and three family bedrooms that share a full bath.

Width: 74'-0"
Depth: 46'-0"

Design by
© Home Planners

QUOTE ONE®
Cost to build? See page 184
to order complete cost estimate
to build this house in your area!

Design HPT09023

First Floor: 586 square feet
Second Floor: 486 square feet
Total: 1,072 square feet

◆ This quaint, country-style cottage would make a fine vacation retreat. Balusters and columns deck out the wraparound porch, while the glass-paneled entry offers an elegant welcome. With a cozy fireplace and plenty of views in the great room, the interior is warmed by more than just heat—it enjoys a charming sense of the outdoors. A well-organized kitchen has its own door to the wraparound porch, as well as a dining nook which also leads outdoors. Each of two bedrooms on the second floor contains a private bath.

Design by
© Home Planners

QUOTE ONE®
Cost to build? See page 184
to order complete cost estimate
to build this house in your area!

Width: 40'-0"
Depth: 40'-0"

To Order Blueprints see pages 182-191

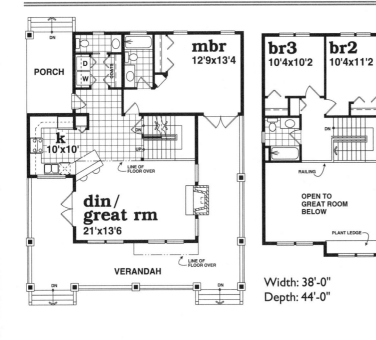

PORCH

mbr
12'9x13'4

k
10'x10'

LINE OF
FLOOR OVER

UP

DN

din/
great rm
21'x13'6

LINE OF
FLOOR OVER

VERANDAH

DN   DN

br3
10'4x10'2

br2
10'4x11'2

DN

RAILING

OPEN TO
GREAT ROOM
BELOW

PLANT LEDGE

Width: 38'-0"
Depth: 44'-0"

Design HPT09024

First Floor: 995 square feet
Second Floor: 484 square feet
Total: 1,479 square feet

◆ What an appealing plan! The great room/dining room combination is reached through double doors off the veranda and features a fireplace towering two stories to the lofty ceiling. A U-shaped kitchen has an angled snack counter that serves this area and loads of space for a breakfast table—or use the handy side porch for alfresco dining. To the rear is the owners bedroom with a full bath and double doors to the veranda. An additional half-bath sits just beyond the laundry room. Two family bedrooms and a full bath occupy the second floor.

QUOTE ONE®

Cost to build? See page 184
to order complete cost estimate
to build this house in your area!

Design by
©Select Home Designs

Design HPT09025

First Floor: 1,223 square feet
Second Floor: 1,163 square feet
Total: 2,386 square feet
Bonus Space: 204 square feet

Design by
©Frank Betz Associates, Inc.

Width: 50'-0"
Depth: 46'-0"

◆ Classic capstones and arched windows complement rectangular shutters and pillars on this traditional facade. The family room offsets a formal dining room and shares a see-through fireplace with the keeping room. The gourmet kitchen boasts a food preparation island. Upstairs, a sensational owners suite with a tray ceiling and a vaulted bath with a plant shelf, whirlpool spa and walk-in closet, opens from a gallery hall with a balcony overlook. Bonus space offers the possibility of an adjoining sitting room. Three additional bedrooms share a full bath. Please specify basement or crawlspace foundation when ordering.

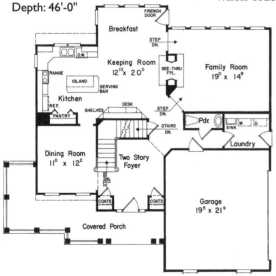

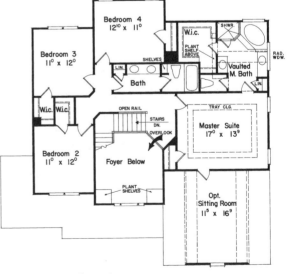

To Order Blueprints see pages 182-191

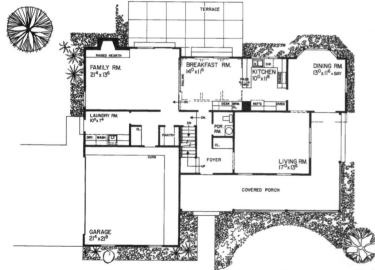

Width: 59'-6"
Depth: 46'-0"

Design HPT09026

First Floor: 1,366 square feet
Second Floor: 969 square feet
Total: 2,335 square feet

L D

Design by
© Home Planners

QUOTE ONE®
Cost to build? See page 184
to order complete cost estimate
to build this house in your area!

◆ Here's a great farmhouse adaptation. The quiet corner living room opens to the sizable dining room. This room will enjoy plenty of natural light from the delightful bay window overlooking the rear yard and is conveniently located near the efficient U-shaped kitchen. The kitchen features many built-ins and a pass-through to the beam-ceilinged nook. Sliding glass doors to the terrace are found in both the family room and nook. Four bedrooms and two baths reside on the second floor. The owners bedroom offers a dressing room and double vanity.

Design HPT09027

First Floor: 3,560 square feet
Second Floor: 1,783 square feet
Total: 5,343 square feet

◆ Multi-pane windows complement the porte cochere and
dress up the natural stone
facade on this French country
estate. A two-story foyer leads
to a central grand room with
French doors to the terrace. A
formal dining room to the front
offers a fireplace. To the left, a
cozy study with a second fireplace features built-in cabinetry
and is close to a convenient
powder room. The sleeping
quarters offer luxurious
amenities. The owners bath
includes a whirlpool tub in
a bumped-out bay, twin
lavatories and two walk-in closets. Upstairs, three suites, each
with a walk-in closet and one
with its own bath, share a balcony hall that leads to a home
theater. A guest apartment over
the garage will house visiting or
live-in relatives, or may be used
as a maid's quarters.

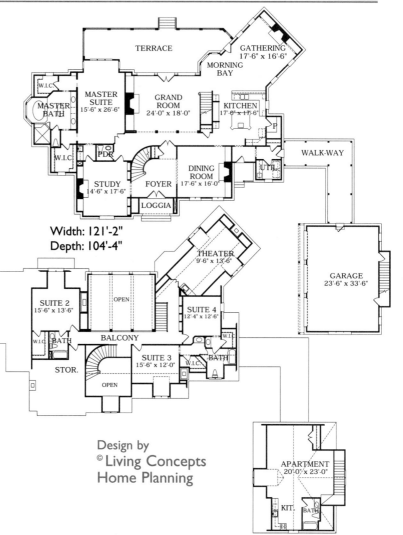

Width: 121'-2"
Depth: 104'-4"

Design by
© Living Concepts
Home Planning

To Order Blueprints see pages 182-191

Design HPT09028

First Floor: 3,387 square feet
Second Floor: 1,799 square feet
Total: 5,186 square feet
Bonus Space: 379 square feet

Width: 110'-10"
Depth: 84'-6"

GATHERING ROOM 17'-0" x 17'-0"
BKFST. 12'-6" x 9'-0"
TERRACE
BAR
W.I.C.
KITCHEN 21'-0" x 15'-6"
MASTER SUITE 15'-0" x 20'-6"
SCREENED PORCH
GRAND ROOM 24'-6" x 17'-0"
MASTER BATH
W.I.C.
2-CAR GARAGE 21'-0" x 22'-6"
PDR.
LAUN.
DINING ROOM 15'-0" x 16'-6"
FOYER
STUDY 16'-6" x 16'-6"
PDR.
W.I.C.
1-CAR GARAGE 11'-8" x 21'-0"
STOR.
PORTICO

SUITE 3 18'-8" x 16'-6"
OPEN TO BELOW
SUITE 4 15'-0" x 16'-0"
W.I.C.
W.I.C.
BATH
BATH
BALCONY
W.I.C.
BONUS ROOM 21'-0" x 17'-4"
BATH
W.I.C.
SUITE 2 14'-8" x 12'-8"
OPEN TO BELOW
SUITE 5 14'-8" x 11'-8"
BAR

◆ A stone-accented entrance welcomes you to this impressive French country estate. A sunken grand room combines with a bay-windowed dining room to create the formal living area. A multi-level terrace links formal and informal areas and the owners suite. A screened porch off the gathering room has a pass-through window from the kitchen. The owners wing includes a study with a fireplace as well as a bayed sitting area and an amenity-laden bath. Two of the four bedrooms have private baths, while the others have separate dressing and vanity areas within a shared bath. A bonus recreation room with a corner bar completes the plan.

Design by
© Living Concepts
Home Planning

181

WHEN YOU'RE READY TO ORDER...

LET US SHOW YOU OUR HOME BLUEPRINT PACKAGE.

Building a home? Planning a home? Our Blueprint Package has nearly everything you need to get the job done right, whether you're working on your own or with help from an architect, designer, builder or subcontractors. Each Blueprint Package is the result of many hours of work by licensed architects or professional designers.

QUALITY

Hundreds of hours of painstaking effort have gone into the development of your blueprint set. Each home has been quality-checked by professionals to insure accuracy and buildability.

VALUE

Because we sell in volume, you can buy professional quality blueprints at a fraction of their development cost. With our plans, your dream home design costs only a few hundred dollars, not the thousands of dollars that architects charge.

SERVICE

Once you've chosen your favorite home plan, you'll receive fast, efficient service whether you choose to mail or fax your order to us or call us toll free at 1-800-521-6797. For customer service, call toll free 1-888-690-1116.

SATISFACTION

Over 50 years of service to satisfied home plan buyers provide us unparalleled experience and knowledge in producing quality blueprints.

ORDER TOLL FREE 1-800-521-6797

After you've looked over our Blueprint Package and Important Extras on the following pages, simply mail the order form on page 191 or call toll free on our Blueprint Hotline: 1-800-521-6797. We're ready and eager to serve you. For customer service, call toll free 1-888-690-1116.

Each set of blueprints is an interrelated collection of detail sheets which includes components such as floor plans, interior and exterior elevations, dimensions, cross-sections, diagrams and notations. These sheets show exactly how your house is to be built.

AMONG THE SHEETS INCLUDED MAY BE:

FRONTAL SHEET

This artist's sketch of the exterior of the house gives you an idea of how the house will look when built and landscaped. Large floor plans show all levels of the house and provide an overview of your new home's livability, as well as a handy reference for deciding on furniture placement.

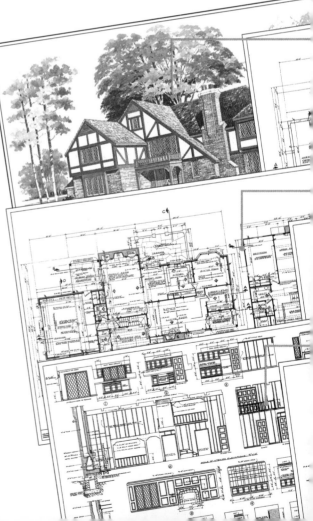

FOUNDATION PLANS

This sheet shows the foundation layout including support walls, excavated and unexcavated areas, if any, and foundation notes. If slab construction rather than basement, the plan shows footings and details for a monolithic slab. This page, or another in the set, may include a sample plot plan for locating your house on a building site.

DETAILED FLOOR PLANS

These plans show the layout of each floor of the house. Rooms and interior spaces are carefully dimensioned and keys are given for cross-section details provided later in the plans. The positions of electrical outlets and switches are shown.

HOUSE CROSS-SECTIONS

Large-scale views show sections or cut-aways of the foundation, interior walls, exterior walls, floors, stairways and roof details. Additional cross-sections may show important changes in floor, ceiling or roof heights or the relationship of one level to another. Extremely valuable for construction, these sections show exactly how the various parts of the house fit together.

INTERIOR ELEVATIONS

Many of our drawings show the design and placement of kitchen and bathroom cabinets, laundry areas, fireplaces, bookcases and other built-ins. Little "extras," such as mantelpiece and wainscoting drawings, plus moulding sections, provide details that give your home that custom touch.

EXTERIOR ELEVATIONS

These drawings show the front, rear and sides of your house and give necessary notes on exterior materials and finishes. Particular attention is given to cornice detail, brick and stone accents or other finish items that make your home unique.

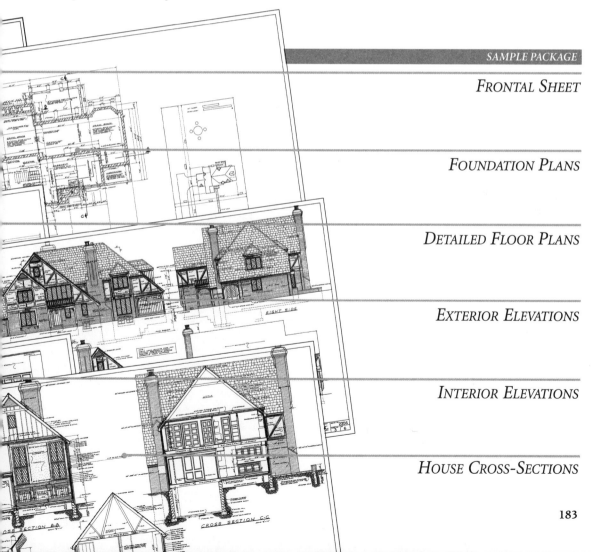

SAMPLE PACKAGE

FRONTAL SHEET

FOUNDATION PLANS

DETAILED FLOOR PLANS

EXTERIOR ELEVATIONS

INTERIOR ELEVATIONS

HOUSE CROSS-SECTIONS

183

INTRODUCING EIGHT IMPORTANT PLANNING AND CONSTRUCTION AIDS DEVELOPED BY OUR PROFESSIONALS TO HELP YOU SUCCEED IN YOUR HOME-BUILDING PROJECT

MATERIALS LIST

For many of the designs in our portfolio, we offer a customized materials take-off that is invaluable in planning and estimating the cost of your new home. This Materials List outlines the quantity, type and size of materials needed to build your house (with the exception of mechanical system items). Included are framing lumber, windows and doors, kitchen and bath cabinetry, rough and finish hardware, and much more. This handy list helps you or your builder cost out materials and serves as a reference sheet when you're compiling bids. A Materials List cannot be ordered before blueprints are ordered.

(Note: Because of the diversity of local building codes, our Materials List does not include mechanical materials.)

SPECIFICATION OUTLINE

This valuable 16-page document is critical to building your house correctly. Designed to be filled in by you or your builder, this book lists 166 stages or items crucial to the building process. It provides a comprehensive review of the construction process and helps in choosing materials. When combined with the blueprints, a signed contract, and a schedule, it becomes a legal document and record for the building of your home.

QUOTE ONE®

SUMMARY COST REPORT / MATERIALS COST REPORT

A new service for estimating the cost of building select designs, the Quote One® system is available in two separate stages: The Summary Cost Report and the Materials Cost Report.

The **Summary Cost Report** is the first stage in the package and shows the total cost per square foot for your chosen home in your zip-code area and then breaks that cost down into various categories showing the costs for building materials, labor and installation. The report includes three grades: Budget, Standard and Custom. These reports allow you to evaluate your building budget and compare the costs of building a variety of homes in your area.

Make even more informed decisions about your home-building project with the second phase of our package, our **Materials Cost Report.** This tool is invaluable in planning and estimating the cost of your new home. The material and installation (labor and equipment) cost is shown for each of over 1,000 line items provided in the Materials List (Standard grade), which is included when you purchase this estimating tool. It allows you to determine building costs for your specific zip-code area and for your chosen home design. Space is allowed for additional estimates from contractors and subcontractors, such as for mechanical materials, which are not included in our packages. This invaluable tool includes a Materials List. For most plans, a Materials Cost Report cannot be ordered before blueprints are ordered. Call for details. In addition, ask about our Home Planners Estimating Package. The Quote One® program is continually updated with new plans. If you are interested in a plan that is not indicated as Quote One®, please call and ask our sales reps. They will be happy to verify the status for you. To order these invaluable reports, use the order form on page 191 or call 1-800-521-6797.

If you want to know more about techniques—and deal more confidently with subcontractors—we offer these useful sheets. Each set is an excellent tool that will add to your understanding of these technical subjects. These helpful details provide general construction information and are not specific to any single plan.

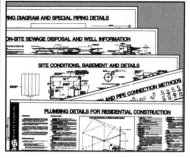

PLUMBING

The Blueprint Package includes locations for all the plumbing fixtures, including sinks, lavatories, tubs, showers, toilets, laundry trays and water heaters. However, if you want to know more about the complete plumbing system, these Plumbing Details will prove very useful. Prepared to meet requirements of the National Plumbing Code, these fact-filled sheets give general information on pipe schedules, fittings, sump-pump details, water-softener hookups, septic system details and much more. Sheets also include a glossary of terms.

ELECTRICAL

The locations for every electrical switch, plug and outlet are shown in your Blueprint Package. However, these Electrical Details go further to take the mystery out of household electrical systems. Prepared to meet requirements of the National Electrical Code, these comprehensive drawings come packed with helpful information, including wire sizing, switch-installation schematics, cable-routing details, appliance wattage, doorbell hookups, typical service panel circuitry and much more. A glossary of terms is also included.

PLAN-A-HOME® is an easy-to-use tool that helps you design a new home, arrange furniture in a new or existing home, or plan a remodeling project. Each package contains:

✓ **MORE THAN 700 REUSABLE PEEL-OFF PLANNING SYMBOLS** on a self-stick vinyl sheet, including walls, windows, doors, all types of furniture, kitchen components, bath fixtures and many more.

✓ **A REUSABLE, TRANSPARENT, ¼" SCALE PLANNING GRID** that matches the scale of actual working drawings (¼" equals one foot). This grid provides the basis for house layouts of up to 140'x92'.

✓ **TRACING PAPER** and a protective sheet for copying or transferring your completed plan.

✓ **A FELT-TIP PEN**, with water-soluble ink that wipes away quickly.

Plan-A-Home® lets you lay out areas as large as a 7,500 square foot, six-bedroom, seven-bath house.

CONSTRUCTION

The Blueprint Package contains everything an experienced builder needs to construct a particular house. However, it doesn't show all the ways that houses can be built, nor does it explain alternate construction methods. To help you understand how your house will be built—and offer additional techniques—this set of Construction Details depicts the materials and methods used to build foundations, fireplaces, walls, floors and roofs. Where appropriate, the drawings show acceptable alternatives.

MECHANICAL

These Mechanical Details contain fundamental principles and useful data that will help you make informed decisions and communicate with subcontractors about heating and cooling systems. Drawings contain instructions and samples that allow you to make simple load calculations, and preliminary sizing and costing analysis. Covered are today's most commonly used systems from heat pumps to solar fuel systems. The package is filled with illustrations and diagrams to help you visualize components and how they relate to one another.

To Order, Call Toll Free
1-800-521-6797

To add these important extras to your Blueprint Package, simply indicate your choices on the order form on page 191. Or call us toll free 1-800-521-6797 and we'll tell you more about these exciting products. For customer service, call toll free 1-888-690-1116.

THE DECK BLUEPRINT PACKAGE

Many of the homes in this book can be enhanced with a professionally designed Home Planners Deck Plan. Those home plans highlighted with a **D** have a matching Deck Plan, sold separately, which includes a Deck Plan Frontal Sheet, Deck Framing and Floor Plans, Deck Elevations and a Deck Materials List. A Standard Deck Details Package, also available, provides all the how-to information necessary for building *any* deck. Our Complete Deck Building Package contains one set of Custom Deck Plans of your choice, plus one set of Standard Deck Building Details, all for one low price. Our plans and details are carefully prepared in an easy-to-understand format that will guide you through every stage of your deck-building project. This page contains a sampling of six different Deck layouts (and a front-yard landscape) to match your favorite house. See page 188 for prices and ordering information.

EUROPEAN-FLAIR HOME
Landscape OLA088

WEEKEND-ENTERTAINER DECK
Deck ODA013

CENTER-VIEW DECK
Deck ODA015

KITCHEN-EXTENDER DECK
Deck ODA016

SPLIT-LEVEL ACTIVITY DECK
Deck ODA018

TRI-LEVEL DECK WITH GRILL
Deck ODA020

CONTEMPORARY LEISURE DECK
Deck ODA021

THE LANDSCAPE BLUEPRINT PACKAGE

For the homes marked with an **L** in this book, Home Planners has created a front-yard Landscape Plan that matches or is complementary in design to the house plan. These comprehensive blueprint packages include a Frontal Sheet, Plan View, Regionalized Plant & Materials List, a sheet on Planting and Maintaining Your Landscape, Zone Maps and Plant Size and Description Guide. These plans will help you achieve professional results, adding value and enjoyment to your property for years to come. Each set of blueprints is a full 18" x 24" in size with clear, complete instructions and easy-to-read type. Six of the forty front-yard Landscape Plans to match your favorite house are shown below.

Regional Order Map

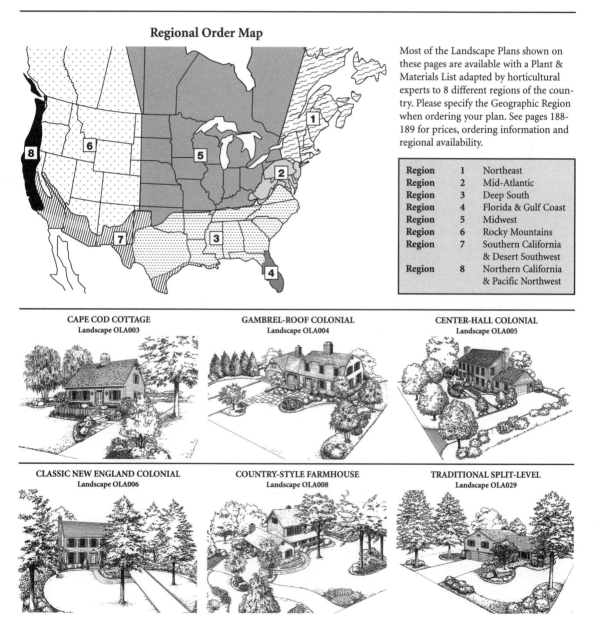

Most of the Landscape Plans shown on these pages are available with a Plant & Materials List adapted by horticultural experts to 8 different regions of the country. Please specify the Geographic Region when ordering your plan. See pages 188-189 for prices, ordering information and regional availability.

Region	1	Northeast
Region	2	Mid-Atlantic
Region	3	Deep South
Region	4	Florida & Gulf Coast
Region	5	Midwest
Region	6	Rocky Mountains
Region	7	Southern California & Desert Southwest
Region	8	Northern California & Pacific Northwest

CAPE COD COTTAGE
Landscape OLA003

GAMBREL-ROOF COLONIAL
Landscape OLA004

CENTER-HALL COLONIAL
Landscape OLA005

CLASSIC NEW ENGLAND COLONIAL
Landscape OLA006

COUNTRY-STYLE FARMHOUSE
Landscape OLA008

TRADITIONAL SPLIT-LEVEL
Landscape OLA029

HOUSE BLUEPRINT PRICE SCHEDULE

(Prices guaranteed through December 31, 2001)

TIERS	1-SET STUDY PACKAGE	4-SET BUILDING PACKAGE	8-SET BUILDING PACKAGE	1-SET REPRODUCIBLE	HOME CUSTOMIZER® PACKAGE
P1	$20	$50	$90	$140	N/A
P2	$40	$70	$110	$160	N/A
P3	$60	$90	$130	$180	N/A
P4	$80	$110	$150	$200	N/A
P5	$100	$130	$170	$230	N/A
P6	$120	$150	$190	$250	N/A
A1	$420	$460	$520	$625	$680
A2	$460	$500	$560	$685	$740
A3	$500	$540	$600	$745	$800
A4	$540	$580	$640	$805	$860
C1	$585	$625	$685	$870	$925
C2	$625	$665	$725	$930	$985
C3	$675	$715	$775	$980	$1035
C4	$725	$765	$825	$1030	$1085
L1	$785	$825	$885	$1090	$1145
L2	$835	$875	$935	$1140	$1195
L3	$935	$975	$1035	$1240	$1295
L4	$1035	$1075	$1135	$1340	$1395

OPTIONS FOR PLANS IN TIERS A1–L4

Additional Identical Blueprints in same order for "A1–L4" price plans..$50 per set

Reverse Blueprints (mirror image) with 4- or 8-set order
  for "A1–L4" price plans ....$50 fee per order

Specification Outlines ....$10 each

Materials Lists for "A1–C3" price plans ....$60 each

Materials Lists for "C4–L4" price plans ....$70 each

OPTIONS FOR PLANS IN TIERS P1–P6

Additional Identical Blueprints in same order for "P1–P6" price plans ....$10 per set

Reverse Blueprints (mirror image) for "P1–P6" price plans..$10 per set

1 Set of Deck Construction Details...$14.95 each

Deck Construction Package ....add $10 to Building Package price
  (includes 1 set of "P1–P6" price plans, plus
  1 set Standard Deck Construction Details)

1 Set of Gazebo Construction Details...$14.95 each

Gazebo Construction Package ....add $10 to Building Package price
  (includes 1 set of "P1–P6" price plans, plus
  1 set Standard Gazebo Construction Details)

IMPORTANT NOTES

The 1-set study package is marked "not for construction."
Prices for 4- or 8-set Building Packages honored only at time of original order. All Donald A. Gardner basement foundations will incur a $225 surcharge. Right-reading reverse blueprints, if available, will incur a $165 surcharge.

INDEX

To use the Index below, refer to the design number listed in numerical order (a helpful page reference is also given). Note the price index letter and refer to the House Blueprint Price Schedule above for the cost of one, four or eight sets of blueprints or the cost of a reproducible drawing. Additional prices are shown for identical and reverse blueprint sets, as well as a very useful Materials List for some of the plans. Also note in the Index below those plans that have matching or complementary Deck Plans or Landscape Plans. Refer to the schedules above for prices of these plans. All plans in this publication are customiz-

able. However, only Home Planners plans can be customized with the Home Planners Home Customizer® Package. These plans are indicated below with the letter "Y." See page 191 for more information. The letter "Y" also identifies plans that are part of our Quote One® estimating service and those that offer Materials Lists. See page 184 for more information.

To Order: Fill in and send the order form on page 191—or call toll free 1-800-521-6797 or 520-297-8200. FAX: 1-800-224-6699 or 520-544-3086

DESIGN	PRICE	PAGE	MATERIALS LIST	CUSTOMIZABLE®	QUOTE ONE®	DECK	DECK PRICE	LANDSCAPE	LANDSCAPE PRICE	REGIONS
HPT09001	C1	153	Y	Y	Y	ODA012	P3	OLA010	P3	1234568
HPT09002	A4	154	Y							
HPT09003	A4	155	Y		Y					
HPT09004	C3	156	Y		Y					
HPT09005	A4	157	Y		Y					
HPT09006	A3	158	Y		Y					
HPT09007	C2	159	Y		Y					
HPT09008	A4	160	Y							
HPT09009	A2	161	Y		Y					
HPT09010	A3	163								
HPT09011	A3	164	Y	Y				OLA001	P3	123568
HPT09012	A3	165	Y							
HPT09013	A3	166								
HPT09014	A4	167	Y	Y	Y	ODA013	P2	OLA001	P3	123568
HPT09015	A2	168	Y							
HPT09016	A2	169								
HPT09017	C2	170	Y		Y					
HPT09018	A3	171	Y							
HPT09019	L1	172	Y	Y	Y	OLA037	P4	OLA037	P4	347
HPT09020	C4	173	Y							
HPT09021	C3	174	Y							
HPT09022	C2	175	Y	Y	Y	ODA015	P2	OLA008	P4	1234568
HPT09023	A4	176	Y	Y	Y					
HPT09024	A2	177	Y		Y					
HPT09025	A4	178								
HPT09026	C1	179	Y	Y	Y	ODA001	P2	OLA008	P4	1234568
HPT09027	L1	180								
HPT09028	L3	181								
HPT09029	C3	162	Y	Y	Y					

BEFORE FILLING OUT THE COUPON AT RIGHT OR CALLING US ON OUR TOLL-FREE BLUEPRINT HOTLINE, YOU MAY WANT TO LEARN MORE ABOUT OUR SERVICES AND PRODUCTS. HERE'S SOME INFORMATION YOU WILL FIND HELPFUL.

OUR EXCHANGE POLICY

Since blueprints are printed in response to your order, we cannot honor requests for refunds. However, we will exchange your entire first order for an equal or greater number of blueprints within our plan collection within 90 days of the original order. The entire content of your original order must be returned to our offices before an exchange will be processed. If the returned blueprints look used, redlined or copied, we will not honor your exchange. Fees for exchanging your blueprints are as follows: 20% of the amount of the original order...*plus* the difference in cost if exchanging for a design in a higher price bracket or *less* the difference in cost if exchanging for a design in lower price bracket. (**Reproducible blueprints are not exchangeable.**) Please add $25 for postage and handling via Regular Service; $35 via Priority Service; $45 via Express Service. Shipping and handling charges are not refundable.

ABOUT REVERSE BLUEPRINTS

If you want to build in reverse of the plan as shown, we will include any number of reverse blueprints (mirror image) from a 4- or 8-set package for an additional fee of $50. Although lettering and dimensions will appear backward, reverses will be a useful aid if you decide to flop the plan.

REVISING, MODIFYING AND CUSTOMIZING PLANS

The wide variety of designs available in this publication allows you to select ideas and concepts for a home to fit your building site and match your family's needs, wants and budget. Like many homeowners who buy these plans, you and your builder, architect or engineer may want to make changes to them. Some changes may be made by your builder, but we recommend that most changes be made by a licensed architect or engineer. If you need to make alterations to a design that is customizable, you need only order our Home Customizer® Package to get you started. As set forth below, we cannot assume any responsibility for blueprints which have been changed, whether by you, your builder or by professionals selected by you or referred to you by us, because such individuals are outside our supervision and control.

ARCHITECTURAL AND ENGINEERING SEALS

Some cities and states are now requiring that a licensed architect or engineer review and "seal" a blueprint, or officially approve it, prior to construction due to concerns over energy costs, safety and other factors. Prior to application for a building permit or the start of actual construction, we strongly advise that you consult your local building official who can tell you if such a review is required.

ABOUT THE DESIGNS

The architects and designers whose work appears in this publication are among America's leading residential designers. Each plan was designed to meet the requirements of a nationally recognized model building code in effect at the time and place the plan was drawn. Because national building codes change from time to time, plans may not comply with any such code at the time they are sold to a customer. In addition, building officials may not accept these plans as final construction documents of record as the plans may need to be modified and additional drawings and details added to suit local conditions and requirements. We strongly advise that purchasers consult a licensed architect or engineer, and their local building official, before starting any construction related to these plans.

LOCAL BUILDING CODES AND ZONING REQUIREMENTS

At the time of creation, our plans are drawn to specifications published by the Building Officials and Code Administrators (BOCA) International, Inc.; the Southern Building Code Congress (SBCCI) International, Inc.; the International Conference of Building Officials (ICBO); or the Council of American Building Officials (CABO). Our plans are designed to meet or exceed national building standards. Because of the great differences in geography and climate throughout the

United States and Canada, each state, county and municipality has its own building codes, zone requirements, ordinances and building regulations. Your plan may need to be modified to comply with local requirements regarding snow loads, energy codes, soil and seismic conditions and a wide range of other matters. In addition, you may need to obtain permits or inspections from local governments before and in the course of construction. Prior to using blueprints ordered from us, we strongly advise that you consult a licensed architect or engineer—and speak with your local building official—before applying for any permit or beginning construction. We authorize the use of our blueprints on the express condition that you strictly comply with all local building codes, zoning requirements and other applicable laws, regulations, ordinances and requirements. **Notice: Plans for homes to be built in Nevada must be re-drawn by a Nevada-registered professional. Consult your building official for more information on this subject.**

FOUNDATION AND EXTERIOR WALL CHANGES

Depending on your specific climate or regional building practices, you may wish to change a full basement to a slab or crawlspace foundation. Most professional contractors and builders can easily adapt your plans to alternate foundation types. Likewise, most can easily change 2x4 wall construction to 2x6, or vice versa.

DISCLAIMER

We and the designers we work with have put substantial care and effort into the creation of our blueprints. However, because we cannot provide on-site consultation, supervision and control over actual construction, and because of the great variance in local building requirements, building practices and soil, seismic, weather and other conditions, WE CANNOT MAKE ANY WARRANTY, EXPRESS OR IMPLIED, WITH RESPECT TO THE CONTENT OR USE OF OUR BLUEPRINTS, INCLUDING BUT NOT LIMITED TO ANY WARRANTY OF MERCHANTABILITY OR OF FITNESS FOR A PARTICULAR PURPOSE.

TERMS AND CONDITIONS

These designs are protected under the terms of United States Copyright Law and may not be copied or reproduced in any way, by any means, unless you have purchased Sepias or Reproducibles which clearly indicate your right to copy or reproduce. We authorize the use of your chosen design as an aid in the construction of one single family home only. You may not use this design to build a second or multiple dwellings without purchasing another blueprint or blueprints or paying additional design fees.

HOW MANY BLUEPRINTS DO YOU NEED?

A single set of blueprints is sufficient to study a home in greater detail. However, if you are planning to obtain cost estimates from a contractor or subcontractors—or if you are planning to build immediately—you will need more sets. Because additional sets are cheaper when ordered in quantity with the original order, make sure you order enough blueprints to satisfy all requirements. The following checklist will help you determine how many you need:

____ Owner

____ Builder (generally requires at least three sets; one as a legal document, one to use during inspections, and at least one to give to subcontractors)

____ Local Building Department (often requires two sets)

____ Mortgage Lender (usually one set for a conventional loan; three sets for FHA or VA loans)

____ TOTAL NUMBER OF SETS

Have You Seen Our Newest Designs?

At least 50 of our latest creations are featured in each edition of our New Design Portfolio. You may have received a copy with your latest purchase by mail. If not, or if you purchased this book from a local retailer, just return the coupon below for your FREE copy. Make sure you consider the very latest of what Home Planners has to offer.

Yes! Please send my FREE copy of your latest New Design Portfolio.

Offer good to U.S. shipping address only.

Name _____

Address_____

City _____ State _____ Zip _

HOME PLANNERS, LLC
Wholly owned by Hanley-Wood, LLC
3275 WEST INA ROAD, SUITE 110
TUCSON, ARIZONA 85741

Order Form Key

HPT09

190

☎ TOLL FREE 1-800-521-6797

REGULAR OFFICE HOURS:

8:00 a.m.-12:00 a.m. EST, Monday-Friday, 10:00 a.m.-7:00 p.m. EST Sat & Sun.

If we receive your order by 3:00 p.m. EST, Monday-Friday, we'll process it and ship within **two business days**. When ordering by phone, please have your credit card ready. We'll also ask you for the Order Form Key Number at the bottom of the coupon.

By FAX: Copy the Order Form on the next page and send it on our FAX line:
1-800-224-6699 or 520-544-3086.

Canadian Customers — Order Toll Free 1-877-223-6389

For faster service, Canadian customers may now call in orders directly to our Canadian supplier of plans and charge the purchase to a credit card. Or, you may complete the order form at right, adding the current exchange rate to all prices and mail in Canadian funds to:

Home Planners Canada, c/o Select Home Designs
301-611 Alexander Street • Vancouver, BC, Canada • V6A 1E1

OR: Copy the Order Form and send it via our FAX line: 1-800-224-6699.

The Home Customizer®

"This house is perfect...if only the family room were two feet wider." Sound familiar? In response to the numerous requests for this type of modification, Home Planners has developed **The Home Customizer® Package**. This exclusive package offers our top-of-the-line materials to make it easy for anyone, anywhere to customize any Home Planners design to fit their needs. Check the index on page 189 for those plans which are customizable.

Some of the changes you can make to any of our plans include:

- exterior elevation changes
- kitchen and bath modifications
- roof, wall and foundation changes
- room additions and more!

The Home Customizer® Package includes everything you'll need to make the necessary changes to your favorite Home Planners design. The package includes:

- instruction book with examples
- architectural scale and clear work film
- erasable red marker and removable correction tape
- ¼"-scale furniture cutouts
- 1 set reproducible drawings
- 1 set study blueprints for communicating changes to your design professional
- a copyright release letter so you can make copies as you need them
- referral letter with the name, address and telephone number of the professional in your region who is trained in modifying Home Planners designs efficiently and inexpensively.

The Home Customizer® Package will not only save you 25% to 75% of the cost of drawing the plans from scratch with an architect or engineer, it will also give you the flexibility to have your changes and modifications made by our referral network or by the professional of your choice. Now it's even easier and more affordable to have the custom home you've always wanted.

ORDER TOLL FREE!
FOR INFORMATION ABOUT ANY OF OUR SERVICES OR TO ORDER CALL

1-800-521-6797 OR 520-297-8200
Browse our website:
www.homeplanners.com

BLUEPRINTS ARE NOT REFUNDABLE EXCHANGES ONLY

FOR CUSTOMER SERVICE,
CALL TOLL FREE **1-888-690-1116.**

HOME PLANNERS, LLC wholly owned by Hanley-Wood, LLC
3275 WEST INA ROAD, SUITE 110 • TUCSON, ARIZONA • 85741

THE BASIC BLUEPRINT PACKAGE
Rush me the following (please refer to the Plans Index and Price Schedule in this section):
___Set(s) of blueprints for plan number(s) _____. $_____
___Set(s) of reproducibles for plan number(s) _____. $_____
___Home Customizer® Package for plan(s)_____. $_____
___Additional identical blueprints (standard or reverse) in same order @ $50 per set. $_____
___Reverse blueprints @ $50 fee per order. Right-reading reverse @ $165 surcharge. $_____

IMPORTANT EXTRAS
Rush me the following:
___Materials List: $60 (Must be purchased with Blueprint set.) Add $10 for Schedule C4–L4 plans. $_____
___**Quote One®** Summary Cost Report @ $29.95 for one, $14.95 for each additional, for plans _____ $_____
    Building location: City_____ Zip Code _____
___**Quote One®** Materials Cost Report @ $120 Schedules P1–C3; $130 Schedules C4–L4, for plan _____ (Must be purchased with Blueprints set.) $_____
    Building location: City_____ Zip Code _____
___Specification Outlines @ $10 each. $_____
___Detail Sets @ $14.95 each; any two $22.95; any three $29.95; all four for $39.95 (save $19.85). $_____
    ❏ Plumbing ❏ Electrical ❏ Construction ❏ Mechanical
___Plan-A-Home® @ $29.95 each. $_____

DECK BLUEPRINTS
(Please refer to the Plans Index and Price Schedule in this section)
___Set(s) of Deck Plan _____. $_____
___Additional identical blueprints in same order @ $10 per set. $_____
___Reverse blueprints @ $10 per set. $_____
___Set of Standard Deck Details @ $14.95 per set. $_____
___Set of Complete Deck Construction Package (Best Buy!) Add $10 to Building Package
    Includes Custom Deck Plan _____ Plus Standard Deck Details

LANDSCAPE BLUEPRINTS
(Please refer to the Plans Index and Price Schedule in this section)
___Set(s) of Landscape Plan _____. $_____
___Additional identical blueprints in same order @ $10 per set. $_____
___Reverse blueprints @ $10 per set. $_____
Please indicate the appropriate region of the country for Plant & Material List.
(See map on page 187): Region _____

POSTAGE AND HANDLING	1–3 sets	4+ sets
Signature is required for all deliveries. **DELIVERY** No CODs (Requires street address—No P.O. Boxes)		
•Regular Service (Allow 7–10 business days delivery)	❏ $20.00	❏ $25.00
•Priority (Allow 4–5 business days delivery)	❏ $25.00	❏ $35.00
•Express (Allow 3 business days delivery)	❏ $35.00	❏ $45.00
OVERSEAS DELIVERY	fax, phone or mail for quote	

Note: All delivery times are from date Blueprint Package is shipped.

POSTAGE (From box above) $_____
SUBTOTAL $_____
SALES TAX (AZ & MI residents, please add appropriate state and local sales tax.) $_____
TOTAL (Subtotal and tax) $_____

YOUR ADDRESS (please print)

Name _____

Street _____

City _____ State _____ Zip_____

Daytime telephone number (_____) _____

FOR CREDIT CARD ORDERS ONLY

Credit card number _____ Exp. Date: (M/Y) _____

Check one ❏ Visa ❏ MasterCard ❏ Discover Card ❏ American Express

Signature _____

Please check appropriate box: ❏ Licensed Builder-Contractor ❏ Homeowner | HPT09 |

Checklist for Rural Building Sites

In selecting a site, make a list of key questions and details on which to check. Ask as many questions as possible about your water supply and sewage treatment. Also include those items most important to your lifestyle and family needs. For younger families, schools and youth recreational facilities may be high on the list. For others, commute time to work may be a major priority.

A "score card" is also provided to use in comparing environmental factors for different building sites. The checklist and score card are meant to be a general guide and are not designed to identify every single item that prospective homeowners should consider prior to making a final decision. If legal, medical, engineering or other expert assistance is required, the services of a competent professional should be sought.

Checklist for Rural Building Sites

Water Supply	✓ If water is to be provided from a public or community water system ask for a copy of the most recent consumer confidence report (CCR). When was the community water system last inspected? Are operators trained and certified? Will homeowners have to pay for the cost of complying with new water quality regulations? ✓ If your water supply will be on-site, make sure the site is large enough for the installation of both a well and an on-site sewage system. ✓ What permits will be needed for drilling? Who will obtain permits? ✓ How deep will you need to drill to find a suitable aquifer? What can you expect the "finished" well cost to be? ✓ Ask about the name of the aquifer that will supply your water. Ask if any USGS reports have been published on this aquifer. Are there any limits on pumping? ✓ Check with neighbors and local agencies about the quality and quantity of water in your local aquifer. ✓ Have recent droughts affected the area? ✓ Can you expect a pumping rate lower than 5 gpm? If so, plan for a storage tank. ✓ Will your builder require the plumber to follow the Uniform Plumbing Code or a similar plumbing code? (see Chapter 5 for additional questions to ask)
Sewage System	✓ If a community system is available, ask if homeowners will be responsible for future operation and maintenance. Ask if the community system has had any violations of environmental rules and regulations. ✓ Where is the community system located? If the community sewage system is close to your site, will you notice any odors? ✓ If you will need an on-site sewage disposal system, will soil and site conditions allow the installation of a conventional septic tank system? (see Site Evaluation Chart page 195) ✓ Will a permit be required to install a system? Who will apply for permit? ✓ What do local regulations allow for the installation of non-conventional on-site systems? Will you be able to reuse treated waste water for landscape irrigation? ✓ Will you need a maintenance contract for a non-conventional on-site system? (see Chapter 6 for additional questions to ask)
Services	✓ If natural gas is not available, will this home be all electric or use propane for cooking and heating? ✓ Will mail be delivered to the door, to a mailbox in the front yard or a community mailbox some distance from your house? ✓ How is trash disposal service provided? Is trash picked up once or twice a week? What is the cost of service? ✓ Is cable TV service available? Will the homeowner association allow the installation of a satellite TV dish? ✓ Is fire service available? What is the approximate response time? What is the annual cost for this service? ✓ How close is the nearest hospital and emergency treatment facility? (see Chapter 4 for additional questions to ask)

Checklist (continued)

Environmental Factors	✓ Did the developer have a Phase I Environmental Site Assessment conducted? If so, ask to review a copy of the Phase I Report. ✓ Are there any sources of noise (airports, highways railroads)? ✓ Is there any past history of industrial activity on this site or adjacent sites? ✓ Is there any past history of the site or adjacent sites being used as an industrial waste or municipal waste landfill? Are there any waste disposal landfills within one mile of the property? ✓ Do any pipelines cross the site or adjacent sites? If so, what types of chemical substances are transported? What's the company's safety record? ✓ Are any stained or discolored soils on the site that could indicate past chemical spills? ✓ Will the presence of endangered species have an impact on your building plans? ✓ Are there any parts of the property in the floodplain? ✓ Does the area have any history of flooding in the last 100 years? ✓ Is the area subject to flash flooding with low-water crossings? ✓ Will runoff from adjacent properties flood this site during heavy rains? ✓ Are there mature trees that you want to protect during construction? ✓ If site is located in a known radon area, have your builder use designs that allow radon to vent to the atmosphere.
Other Factors	✓ Are there any animal restrictions or pet control requirements? Some states have laws stating, "Dogs running livestock against the wish of the owner of the livestock may be killed at once..." ✓ Is site located in a known rabies or Lyme Disease area? ✓ Are there any easements, setbacks or rights-of-way that may impact use of property? ✓ Are roads to property subject to frequent flooding? Are roads closed during snow and inclement weather?

After construction is completed, check to make sure that you have:

✓ Detailed records and location for all components of the on-site sewage disposal system. This includes owner maintenance manuals that may come with pumps and other major items.

✓ Detailed records and location for all components of the water supply system. This includes owner maintenance manuals that may come with pumps and other major items.

Site Evaluation for On-site Sewage Disposal

This checklist can be used to make a preliminary evaluation of potential sites for the installation of an on-site sewage disposal system. Building sites with shallow groundwater, clay soil, excessive slopes or other limiting conditions will likely require the installation of a non-conventional on-site system. It may not be possible to install an on-site sewage disposal system on some sites. Before you purchase any site, make sure that an on-site system can be installed.

Check the size of building sites	
Determine the overall size of proposed building site. Include all easements, setbacks and rights-of-way that could limit your options for installing an on-site system.	If site is less than an acre and you need both on-site water and sewage disposal, recommend that a professional site evaluator confirm that systems can be installed meeting all distance requirements. Be sure to include wells and septic tanks on adjoining properties. A professional site evaluator will confirm.
Check for limiting conditions	
Step 1: Dig a hole with an auger or posthole digger to a depth of 48 inches to determine presence of groundwater or fractured rocks.	If you find moist, saturated soil or water, a non-conventional system is indicated. If fractured rock is encountered a non-conventional system is indicated. A professional site evaluator will confirm.
Step 2: Evaluate soil texture at 18-inch intervals. Take a small amount of soil in your hand and add a small amount of water to moisten until you can roll into a ball.	a) If soil texture feels gritty and falls apart without forming a ball, sandy soil is indicated. (b) If soil texture feels like modeling clay and forms a solid, plastic-like ball, clay soil is indicated. (c) If neither (a) or (b), loamy soil is indicated. If you find clay soils, a non-conventional system is indicated. A professional site evaluator will confirm.
Check for excessive slope	
Determine if site is on a hillside or appears to have a slope.	(a) If enough space is available for the system to be installed with gravity flow, distribution boxes or T-inverts will need to distribute effluent along contours. (b) If gravity flow cannot be used, an effluent pump system may be needed to lift effluent for disposal along side contours. A professional site evaluator will confirm.

In most states, a professional engineer, soil scientist or registered sanitarian will be required to conduct a site evaluation. Based on the results of this site evaluation, an on-site sewage disposal system similar to the examples described in Appendix Two will be designed.

Score Card for Evaluating Potential Sites

Rate each factor for the sites being considered:
3 points = fully meets my requirements
2 points = meets some of my requirements
1 points = will require additional work and money
0 points = does not meet my requirements

Site Factor	Sites Considered			Important notes to remember
	A (0-3 pts)	B (0-3 pts)	C (0-3 pts)	
Meets My Budget				
Location				
Water Supply				
Sewage Disposal				
Environmental Factors A-Z				
Services				
Schools				
Recreational Facilities				
Commute Time				
Other (add your own)				
Other (add your own)				
Other (add your own)				
Total points for site				

Description of On-site Sewage Disposal Systems

Rural building sites with soils suitable for the installation of conventional septic tank systems are becoming harder to find. Newer, non-conventional on-site sewage treatment designs are now being used in rural areas having rocky soils, shallow groundwater or other site limitations. The on-site systems described in Appendix Two are just a few of the examples of designs now being installed in many rural areas. These non-conventional systems tend to cost more to install and maintain, but help to prevent pollution of streams and groundwater.

Your local regulatory authority may not approve some of the examples shown in Appendix Two. The experience and training of local installers may also limit your options for on-site systems. Some installers may only be experienced in the installation of conventional septic tank systems with underground drain lines. Newer, non-conventional on-site systems may require installers to be factory trained and certified.

When it comes to on-site systems, you need to know your options and the advantages and disadvantages of each option. If a system will require a pump or other electrical components, you may need to severely limit water usage and avoid flushing during power outages or when repairs are needed. Before making a decision on the type of on-site sewage system to install, it is advisable to meet with your site evaluator, builder and system installer.

Conventional On-site Sewage Disposal Systems
Septic tank installation with subsurface drain field

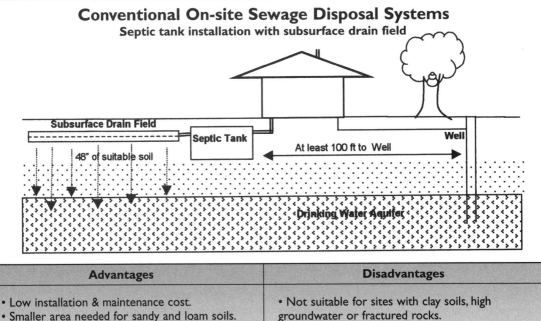

Advantages	Disadvantages
• Low installation & maintenance cost. • Smaller area needed for sandy and loam soils. • On sites with slope of less than 6% easy to install. • Your best choice when site conditions allow.	• Not suitable for sites with clay soils, high groundwater or fractured rocks. • Provides limited secondary treatment /effluent has high BOD (120-140 ppm), TSS (95-155 ppm) & nitrates (45 ppm).

Conventional septic tank with subsurface drain lines using drop boxes
(Allows installation on sites with 6-30% slope)

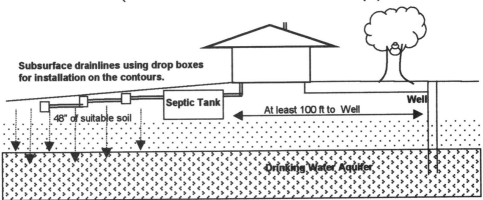

Advantages	Disadvantages
• Allows installation on slopes of 6-30%. May vary among approval authorities. • Low installation & maintenance cost.	• Not suitable for sites with clay soils, high groundwater or fractured rocks. • Provides limited secondary treatment /effluent has high BOD (120-140 ppm), TSS (95-155 ppm) & nitrates (45 ppm).

Septic tank using soil substitution

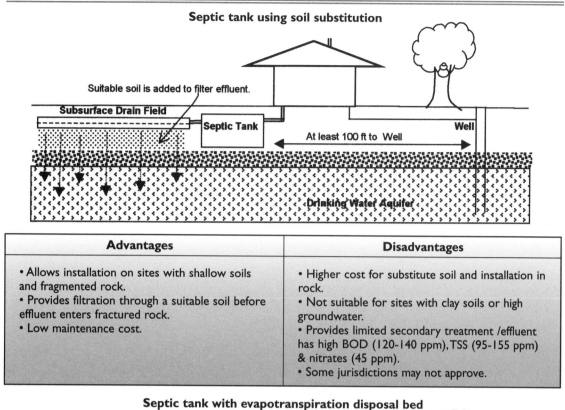

Advantages	Disadvantages
• Allows installation on sites with shallow soils and fragmented rock. • Provides filtration through a suitable soil before effluent enters fractured rock. • Low maintenance cost.	• Higher cost for substitute soil and installation in rock. • Not suitable for sites with clay soils or high groundwater. • Provides limited secondary treatment /effluent has high BOD (120-140 ppm), TSS (95-155 ppm) & nitrates (45 ppm). • Some jurisdictions may not approve.

Septic tank with evapotranspiration disposal bed

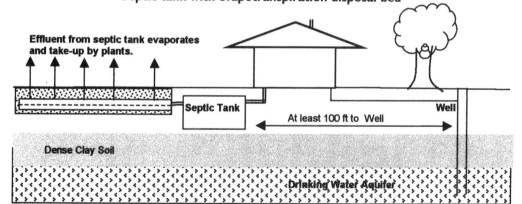

Advantages	Disadvantages
• Suitable for sites with clay soils. Can also be used on sites with fractured rock or shallow groundwater if a plastic liner is installed. • Works best in dry, low humidity areas.	• Large area needed for installation of evapo-tran-spiration bed. • Not suitable for areas with high annual rainfall. • Not suitable for installation on slopes. • Requires more design experience. • History of early failure. • Some jurisdictions may not approve.

Non-conventional On-site Sewage Disposal Systems

Septic tank with intermittent sand filter

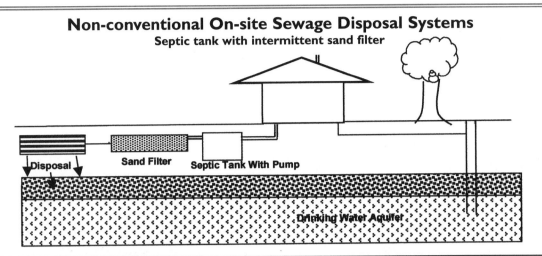

Advantages	Disadvantages
• Greater removal of BOD & TSS. • Some reduction in pathogenic bacteria. • May reduce size of area required for final disposal. • May be used on sites with fractured rock or shallow groundwater.	• Higher cost to install and maintain. • Normally requires pump system with electrical controls. • Some odors may be experienced • Some jurisdictions may not approve.

Septic tank with recirculating intermittent sand filter

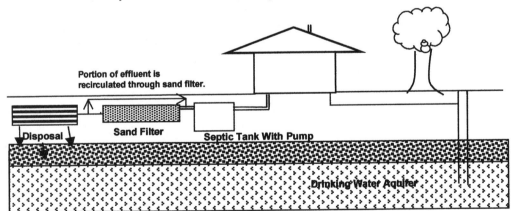

Advantages	Disadvantages
• Greater removal of BOD, TSS and nitrate. • Some reduction in pathogenic bacteria. • May reduce size of area required for final disposal. • May be used on sites with fractured rock or shallow groundwater.	• Higher cost to install and maintain. • Requires pump system with electrical controls. • Some odors may be experienced. • May require design by an engineer. • Some jurisdictions may not approve.

Septic tank with effluent disposal to mound system

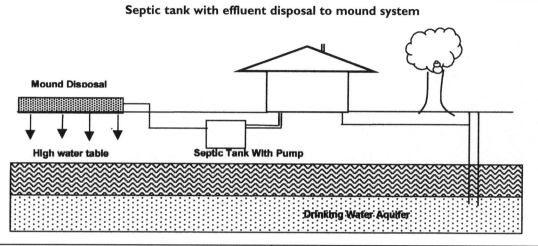

Advantages	Disadvantages
• Allows installation on sites with high ground water and other limitations.	• Higher cost to install and maintain. • Requires pump system with electrical controls. • Some jurisdictions may not approve.

Aerobic Treatment Unit (ATU)

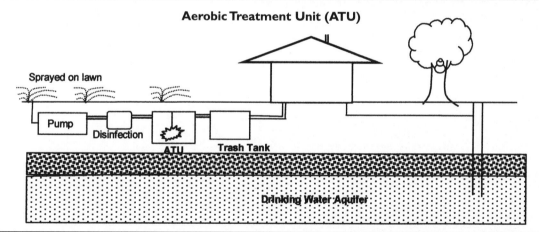

Advantages	Disadvantages
• Allows reuse of water for landscape irrigation. • Reduces BOD and TSS. • Where allowed final disposal can be by surface irrigation. • Easier to install in rock. Note: some ATU designs may not require a separate trash tank.	• Higher cost to purchase and maintain. • Some ATUs require small septic tank as a pretreatment to remove "trash." • Requires pump system with electrical controls. • Most jurisdictions require maintenance contract. • Requires disinfectant unit if final disposal is by surface irrigation. Without proper disinfection may be a potential health hazard. • Homeowner neglect can lead to serious problems.

Low-pressure dosing system

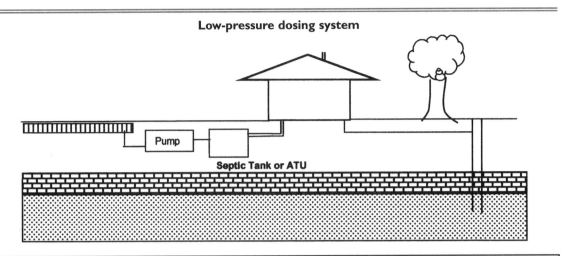

Advantages	Disadvantages
• Easier to install on sites with shallow soils. • No disinfectant unit is required. • May be used on sites with shallow ground-water or shallow soils.	• Larger area for disposal needed. • Higher cost to purchase and maintain. • Requires pump system with electrical controls. • Most jurisdictions require maintenance contract.

Septic tank with biofilter

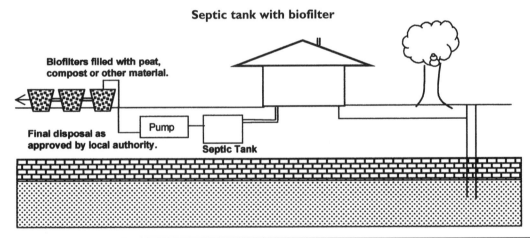

Advantages	Disadvantages
• Able to produce high quality effluent with BOD below 10 ppm, TSS 16, low nitrates. • May reduce amount of drain line needed. • Low operating cost to produce high quality effluent.	• Biofilter material (peat, compost) has a limited useful life and has to be replaced. • Still requires final disposal of effluent. • Some local authorities may not approve. Some may approve as an experimental system. • Local installers may not be experienced in construction and installation. • Cost is higher than conventional system.

Sample of State Regulations for On-site Sewage Disposal Systems

TITLE 252. DEPARTMENT OF ENVIRONMENTAL QUALITY
CHAPTER 641. INDIVIDUAL AND SMALL PUBLIC ON-SITE SEWAGE
DISPOSAL SYSTEMS

The sample state regulation is from the Oklahoma Department of Environmental Quality (DEQ). The Oklahoma DEQ has developed its on-site rules in a concise, ten-page document with several appendices. The DEQ rules are flexible, allowing site evaluators to use the standard soil percolation test or a soil profile description. Homeowners with large building sites are also provided options for surface irrigation or the installation of on-site lagoons.

Keep in mind that on-site sewage regulations may vary from state to state. Your state rules may be similar, but may not be the same. Your first step in planning your on-site sewage disposal system should be to obtain a copy of your local regulations.

Section
252:641-1-1.   Purpose, authority and applicability
252:641-1-2.   Definitions
252:641-1-3.   General requirements for on-site sewage
                disposal systems
252:641-1-4.   Operation, repairs and maintenance
252:641-1-5.   Enforcement

252:641-1-1.   Purpose, authority and applicability
(a) **Purpose.** This Chapter establishes procedures for the construction, installation and operation of individual and small public on-site sewage disposal systems. This Chapter also establishes procedures for persons seeking certification as installers of individual sewage disposal systems.
(b) **Authority.** 252:641 is authorized by 27A O.S.Supp. 1998, §§ 2-1-101, 2-6-402 and 403.
(c) **Applicability.** The rules in this Chapter apply to:
    (1) Any person who owns, constructs, installs or operates an on-site sewage disposal system; and
    (2) Any person who seeks certification from the DEQ to install individual sewage disposal systems.
(d) **Disclaimer.** The design standards contained in this Chapter are established as minimum criteria and do not guarantee an individual system's performance.
(e) **Appendices.**   All references to appendices are appendices to this Chapter.

252:641-1-2.   Definitions
    In addition to the definitions contained in the Environmental Quality Code (27A O.S.Supp. 1998, § 2-1-101 *et seq.*), the following words and terms, when used in this Chapter, shall have the following meaning, unless the context clearly indicates otherwise:
    "Absorption field" means an area which contains soils suitable for the installation of a subsurface absorption system.
    "Aerobic system" means a sewage disposal system which treats sewage in an aerobic treatment unit and then applies the treated sewage to the surface as described in 252:641-13.
    "Aerobic treatment" means the digestion of organic matter and settleable solids in an oxygenated environment to produce a clarified liquid.
    "Aerobic treatment unit" means a watertight covered receptacle designed to receive, store, and provide aerobic treatment to sewage prior to its disposal.
    "Alternative system" means an on-site sewage disposal system that does not meet the requirements of on-site sewage disposal systems described in this Chapter.
    "Certified installer" means a person in the business of installing or constructing individual sewage disposal systems who has been certified by the DEQ to inspect his/her installations.
    "DEQ" means the Department of Environmental Quality.

    "Distribution structure" means a watertight compartment, box, or solid piping which receives sewage and distributes it evenly.
    "French Drain (Curtain Drain)" means a subsurface installation of perforated pipe and filter material used to divert groundwater.
    "Individual sewage disposal system" means a sewage disposal system which serves one individual residence or duplex and is not available for use by the general public.
    "Installer" means a person who installs or who is in the business of contracting to install or furnishing labor to install on-site sewage disposal systems.
    "Lift station" means a short-term storage reservoir, containing an automatically controlled pump, that pumps sewage to a higher elevation for treatment or disposal.
    "Major earth fill area" means any area where soil has been added to change the elevation from the original ground level by more than one (1) foot.
    "On-site sewage disposal system" means an individual or small public sewage disposal system as defined in this Chapter.
    "Retention structure" is a structure that retains sewage until it reaches a depth of ten inches (10") and then allows it to flow to another trench.
    "Sewage" means wastewater that generally originates as human waste from certain activities including using toilet facilities, washing, bathing, preparing foods and washing laundry, excluding industrial wastewater.
    "Soil profile description" means the identification and characterization of soils at a specific site.

252:641-1-3.   General requirements for on-site sewage disposal systems
(a) **Disposal.** On-site sewage disposal systems shall only be used for disposal of sewage, as defined in 252:641-1-2. All sewage must be disposed of according to this Chapter.
(b) **Application.**   An applicant seeking a permit to construct, repair or modify an individual or small public on-site sewage disposal system shall submit a completed and signed DEQ Form 641-581 "Report for On-Site Sewage Disposal" to the local DEQ office for approval before construction. The detail needed varies with each system design; guidance will be provided by the local DEQ office.
(c) **Minimum lot size.** The applicant shall comply with the minimum lot size requirements as set forth in Appendix A. Plats recorded before January 1, 1974, are not subject to minimum lot size requirements but systems built in those platted areas must meet the construction requirements of this Chapter.
(d) **Estimation of sewage flow.**
    (1) Small public systems shall be designed using the information in Appendix F to estimate flow unless actual flow data or a more accurate estimation method is available.
    (2) Individual sewage disposal systems shall be

designed for a water usage of 6,000 gallons per month for a residence of two (2) bedrooms or less, and an additional two thousand (2,000) gallons per month for each additional bedroom.

(e) **Separation distances.** The applicant must comply with the required separation distances listed in the table in Appendix E.

(f) **Primary treatment.** All disposal systems in this Chapter must include a septic tank or an aerobic treatment unit as primary treatment.

(g) **Pipe specifications.** All pipe and chambers shall meet the minimum specifications listed in Appendix C.

(h) **Final inspection.** All on-site sewage disposal systems shall be inspected and approved by the DEQ or installed and certified by a certified installer. The installer shall not backfill subsurface systems or place any system into operation until the system has been approved by the DEQ or a certified installer.

(1) The installer shall be responsible for requesting that the DEQ do a final inspection or, if certified, shall conduct a self-inspection.

(2) The installer shall be responsible for payment of fees associated with inspection of the system.

252:641-1-4.   Operation, repairs and maintenance

(a) **Proper operation.** On-site sewage disposal systems shall be maintained and operated properly so that sewage or effluent from the system does not surface, pool, flow across the ground or
discharge to surface waters.

(b) **Failing systems.** The person owning or otherwise responsible for a system shall take prompt action to repair a failing system, prevent further violations and remediate the site.

(c) **Repairs and modifications.** Repairs, modifications or additions to existing on-site sewage disposal systems shall be inspected and approved by the DEQ or installed and certified by a certified installer.

252:641-1-5.   Enforcement

Violations of this chapter are subject to enforcement actions and penalties set forth in 27A O.S.Supp. 1998, §§ 2-3-502, 2-3-504 and 2-6-206.

SUBCHAPTER 3. PERCOLATION TESTS AND SOIL PROFILES

Section
252:641-3-1.   General provisions
252:641-3-2.   Percolation test method
252:641-3-3.   Linear feet requirements
252:641-3-4.   Soil profile descriptions

252:641-3-1.   General provisions.

(a) **General purpose.** A percolation test shall be used to identify an acceptable area for an absorption field. Percolation tests are not required for lagoons, aerobic systems or evapotranspiration/absorption (ET/A) systems. All percolation tests shall be performed in accordance with this Subchapter. For further explanation, see Appendix B.

(b) **Percolation tests.** Percolation tests must be performed by a Registered Professional Engineer, Registered Land Surveyor, Registered Professional Sanitarian or Registered Professional Environmental Specialist licensed to practice in Oklahoma.

(c) **Submission to the DEQ.** When a percolation test is required, the results shall be submitted to the local DEQ office on DEQ Form #641-581 or in a format approved by the DEQ prior to the construction of the on-site sewage disposal system.

(d) **Corroborative tests.** The DEQ may perform corroborative tests or require additional tests if there is reason to believe the original test results are inaccurate.

(e) **Excavations and major earth fill areas.** No percolation tests shall be performed in major earth fill areas. Once an acceptable absorption field has been identified, any subsequent modification to that area may require an additional percolation test.

252:641-3-2.   Percolation test method

(a) **Test hole requirements.** The following test hole requirements shall be met:

(1) **Number.** Three (3) acceptable test holes are required to define an absorption field area.

(2) **Size.** Test holes shall be dug or bored, four to twelve inches (4"-12") in diameter with vertical sides, to the same depth, within a range of eighteen to thirty inches (18"-30").

(3) **Placement.** Test holes shall be placed at the approximate corners of an isosceles triangle having two (2) sides fifty feet (50') long and one side seventy-five feet (75') long. The DEQ may approve alternative configurations.

(4) **Soil surfaces.** The bottoms and sides of the test holes shall be scratched with a sharp-pointed instrument to relieve any smeared soil surfaces. Loose material shall be removed from the hole.

(5) **Prohibitions.** Test holes dug through animal burrows, root channels or cracked soil due to dry weather conditions shall not be used.

(b) **Presoak period.** Each test hole shall be filled with water and refilled as necessary to maintain a water depth of at least twelve inches (12") in the holes for at least four (4) hours before testing.

(c) **Percolation test procedure.** At the completion of the presoak, the depth of the water shall be adjusted to approximately ten inches (10") above the bottom of the test holes. The water level shall be measured from a fixed reference point. The drop in the water level in sixty (60) minutes or the time it takes until four inches (4") of water has percolated into the soil shall be measured. This information shall be used to calculate the percolation rate for each individual hole in minutes per inch.

(d) **Identification of acceptable absorption field.** The following explain how to identify an acceptable absorption field:

(1) If each of the three (3) test holes exhibits a rate faster than or equal to sixty (60) minutes per inch,

then the applicant has identified an acceptable absorption field site.

(2) If any of the three (3) test holes exhibits a rate slower than sixty (60) minutes per inch, the applicant has identified an unacceptable absorption field site. However, the applicant may conduct additional testing, using uniformly positioned holes, until three (3) holes are located which will define an acceptable absorption field.

(3) An absorption field shall not contain test holes that failed to percolate or in which groundwater was encountered.

(f) **Information to be reported.** The location (identified from a fixed reference point), depth and percolation rate for all test holes and the results of the percolation test, with all results rounded to the nearest whole number, shall be reported to the DEQ.

252:641-3-3.　Linear feet requirements
All subsurface sewage disposal systems must meet the minimum linear feet requirements as set forth in Appendix G.

252:641-3-4.　Soil profile descriptions
The DEQ may approve the use of a soil profile description in lieu of a percolation test to identify an acceptable absorption field area.

SUBCHAPTER 5. BUILDING SEWER AND OTHER SOLID PIPE

Section
252:641-5-1.　General provisions
252:641-5-2.　Installation

252:641-5-1.　General provisions
The applicant shall comply with the pipe specifications as set forth in Appendix C.

252:641-5-2.　Installation
(a) **Minimum fall.** The following minimum fall requirements shall be met:

(1) Pipe which delivers sewage to a septic tank or aerobic treatment unit shall be installed with a minimum fall of one- eighth inch (1/8") per foot.

(2) The fall from the outlet of the septic tank to the highest perforated pipe must be a minimum of six inches (6"), except when a lift pump is used.

(3) If a retention structure is installed anywhere in the absorption field, the fall from the septic tank to the highest perforated pipe must be at least ten inches (10"), except when a lift pump is used.

(b) **Cleanouts.** A two-way sanitary tee cleanout shall be installed upstream of the septic tank.

SUBCHAPTER 7. SEPTIC TANKS

Section
252:641-7-1.　General provisions

252:641-7-2.　Types of tanks
252:641-7-3.　Design
252:641-7-4.　Liquid capacity

252:641-7-1.　General provisions
(a) Once installed, the tops of septic tanks shall be level.
(b) Septic tanks shall be installed in accordance with Appendix I.

252:641-7-2.　Types of tanks
(a) **Concrete tanks.** Concrete tanks shall be constructed of a mix which demonstrates a 28-day compressive strength of three thousand pounds per square inch (3,000 psi). They may be poured in place or precast, but, in either case, shall be monolithically poured and mechanically vibrated.

(b) **Fiberglass and plastic tanks.** Fiberglass and plastic tanks shall be approved by the DEQ prior to installation and shall be installed according to the manufacturer's recommendations.

252:641-7-3.　Design
(a) **Compartments.** A septic tank may consist of one (1) or two (2) compartments. All septic tanks shall have removable lids or a manhole opening of at least twenty-four inches (24") over each compartment. All lids and manholes shall be sealed to prevent leakage.

(b) **Two-compartment tanks.** The passage in the common wall of two- compartment tanks shall be located below the liquid level between twenty percent (20%) to forty percent (40%) of the liquid depth. There shall be a vent through the common wall.

(c) **Inlets and outlets.** Inlets and outlets shall be constructed and located as follows:

(1) **Construction.** Baffles shall be used on all inlet and outlet lines. Cleanout openings shall be located directly above the inlet and outlet baffles. Inlets and outlets shall have a watertight seal.

(2) **Location.** All baffles shall extend to within two inches (2") of the top of the septic tank.

(A) **Inlet.** Inlet baffles shall extend at least six inches　(6") below the liquid depth of the septic tank.

(B) **Outlet.** Outlet baffles shall extend below the liquid　level by twenty percent (20%) to forty percent (40%) of the　liquid depth.

(d) **Precast concrete tanks.** Precast concrete tanks shall have a minimum:

(1) wall thickness of two and one-half inches (2-1/2");

(2) bottom thickness of three inches (3"); and

(3) cover thickness of three and one-half inches (3-1/2").

(e) Poured-in-place concrete tanks. Poured in place concrete tanks shall have a minimum:

(1) wall thickness of six inches (6");

(2) bottom thickness of three inches (3"); and

(3) cover thickness of four inches (4").

then the applicant has identified an acceptable absorption field site.

(2) If any of the three (3) test holes exhibits a rate slower than sixty (60) minutes per inch, the applicant has identified an unacceptable absorption field site. However, the applicant may conduct additional testing, using uniformly positioned holes, until three (3) holes are located which will define an acceptable absorption field.

(3) An absorption field shall not contain test holes that failed to percolate or in which groundwater was encountered.

(f) **Information to be reported.** The location (identified from a fixed reference point), depth and percolation rate for all test holes and the results of the percolation test, with all results rounded to the nearest whole number, shall be reported to the DEQ.

252:641-3-3.   Linear feet requirements

All subsurface sewage disposal systems must meet the minimum linear feet requirements as set forth in Appendix G.

252:641-3-4.   Soil profile descriptions

The DEQ may approve the use of a soil profile description in lieu of a percolation test to identify an acceptable absorption field area.

SUBCHAPTER 5. BUILDING SEWER AND OTHER SOLID PIPE

Section
252:641-5-1.   General provisions
252:641-5-2.   Installation

252:641-5-1.   General provisions

The applicant shall comply with the pipe specifications as set forth in Appendix C.

252:641-5-2.   Installation

(a) **Minimum fall.** The following minimum fall requirements shall be met:

(1) Pipe which delivers sewage to a septic tank or aerobic treatment unit shall be installed with a minimum fall of one- eighth inch (1/8") per foot.

(2) The fall from the outlet of the septic tank to the highest perforated pipe must be a minimum of six inches (6"), except when a lift pump is used.

(3) If a retention structure is installed anywhere in the absorption field, the fall from the septic tank to the highest perforated pipe must be at least ten inches (10"), except when a lift pump is used.

(b) **Cleanouts.** A two-way sanitary tee cleanout shall be installed upstream of the septic tank.

SUBCHAPTER 7. SEPTIC TANKS

Section
252:641-7-1.   General provisions

252:641-7-2.   Types of tanks
252:641-7-3.   Design
252:641-7-4.   Liquid capacity

252:641-7-1.   General provisions

(a) Once installed, the tops of septic tanks shall be level.
(b) Septic tanks shall be installed in accordance with Appendix I.

252:641-7-2.   Types of tanks

(a) **Concrete tanks.** Concrete tanks shall be constructed of a mix which demonstrates a 28-day compressive strength of three thousand pounds per square inch (3,000 psi). They may be poured in place or precast, but, in either case, shall be monolithically poured and mechanically vibrated.

(b) **Fiberglass and plastic tanks.** Fiberglass and plastic tanks shall be approved by the DEQ prior to installation and shall be installed according to the manufacturer's recommendations.

252:641-7-3.   Design

(a) **Compartments.** A septic tank may consist of one (1) or two (2) compartments. All septic tanks shall have removable lids or a manhole opening of at least twenty-four inches (24") over each compartment. All lids and manholes shall be sealed to prevent leakage.

(b) **Two-compartment tanks.** The passage in the common wall of two- compartment tanks shall be located below the liquid level between twenty percent (20%) to forty percent (40%) of the liquid depth. There shall be a vent through the common wall.

(c) **Inlets and outlets.** Inlets and outlets shall be constructed and located as follows:

(1) **Construction.** Baffles shall be used on all inlet and outlet lines. Cleanout openings shall be located directly above the inlet and outlet baffles. Inlets and outlets shall have a watertight seal.

(2) **Location.** All baffles shall extend to within two inches (2") of the top of the septic tank.

(A) **Inlet.** Inlet baffles shall extend at least six inches (6") below the liquid depth of the septic tank.

(B) **Outlet.** Outlet baffles shall extend below the liquid level by twenty percent (20%) to forty percent (40%) of the liquid depth.

(d) **Precast concrete tanks.** Precast concrete tanks shall have a minimum:

(1) wall thickness of two and one-half inches (2-1/2");
(2) bottom thickness of three inches (3"); and
(3) cover thickness of three and one-half inches (3-1/2").

(e) **Poured-in-place concrete tanks.** Poured in place concrete tanks shall have a minimum:

(1) wall thickness of six inches (6");
(2) bottom thickness of three inches (3"); and
(3) cover thickness of four inches (4").

252:640-7-4.   Liquid capacity

(a) **Individual system.**   A septic tank used in an individual sewage disposal system for a residential unit with four (4) or less bedrooms shall have a liquid capacity of at least one thousand (1,000) gallons. Two hundred and fifty (250) gallons of capacity must be added for each additional bedroom.

(b) **Small public system.** The liquid capacity for a septic tank used in a small public sewage disposal system shall be the daily flow plus fifty percent (50%) with a one thousand (1,000) gallon minimum.

(c) **Two-compartment tanks.**   The capacity of the influent compartment of a two-compartment tank shall not be less than one-half (1/2) nor more than two-thirds (2/3) of the total required liquid capacity of the tank.

(d) **All septic tanks.**   All septic tanks shall have a liquid depth of not less than three feet (3') nor more than six and one-half feet (6-1/2') and an air space of eight inches (8") or more inside the tank.

SUBCHAPTER 9. LIFT STATIONS

Section
252:641-9-1.   General provisions
252:641-9-2.   Design
252:641-9-3.   Installation

252:641-9-1.   General provisions

(a) **Septic tank.** All sewage entering a lift station must first pass through a septic tank.

(b) **Type of tank.** The type of tank used must meet the requirements of 252:641-7-2.

(c) **Pump discharges.** Pump discharges shall flow through a structure that provides an air gap.

252:641-9-2.   Design

Lift stations shall be designed as follows:

(1) Pumps shall be designed to pump sewage or other liquid containing fine particles/suspended solids.

(2) The pump chamber shall have a manhole opening of at least twenty-four inches (24").

(3) An alarm to alert the owner or operator of a system failure shall be installed. The alarm shall be set to activate if the pump tank becomes more than one-half (1/2) full.

(4) The pump compartment shall have a minimum storage capacity of one thousand (1000) gallons.

252:641-9-3.   Installation

Lift stations shall be installed in accordance with Appendix J. The lift station shall be installed so that the pump can be removed without workmen entering the pump chamber.

(1) A threaded union shall be installed in the discharge line, located within eighteen inches (18") of the manhole entry to the wet well.

(2) A check valve shall be installed in the discharge line after the threaded union. The check valve shall be the same diameter as the discharge line.

(3) The manhole opening shall extend a minimum of two inches (2") above ground elevation.

SUBCHAPTER 11. ABSORPTION FIELDS

Section
252:641-11-1.   General provisions
252:641-11-2.   Absorption trenches
252:641-11-3.   Retention and distribution structures
252:641-11-4.   Exceptions

252:641-11-1.   General provisions

(a) **Septic tank.** All sewage entering an absorption field must first pass through a septic tank.

(b) **Location.** No perforated pipe or chamber shall be installed within five feet (5') of a septic tank or within a major earth fill area.

(c) **Limitation.** Systems shall be constructed so that no sewage flows through more than one hundred fifty feet (150') of perforated pipe in any given path.

(d) **Surface water.**   Surface water shall be diverted around or away from the absorption field.

(e) **Layout examples.** Refer to Appendix K, Figures 1-5.

252:641-11-2.   Absorption trenches

(a) **Width.**   Trenches shall be twenty-four inches (24") wide.

(b) **Depth.** The depth of the trenches shall be within six inches (6") of the percolation test hole depth, at least eighteen inches (18") deep, but no deeper than thirty inches (30").

(c) **Surface contours.** Each trench shall be constructed to follow the surface contours and to maintain a uniform depth throughout the length of the trench.

(d) **Spacing.** The trenches shall be spaced at least eight feet (8') apart, center to center.

(e) **Absorption media.** Where perforated pipe is used, absorption trenches shall contain at least ten inches (10") of clean, screened rock, gravel or tire chips or any combination of the three.   At least two inches (2") of material shall be installed above and below the perforated pipe. The size of these materials shall range from one-half to two and one-half inches (1/2"-2-1/2") with no more than 10% by weight passing through a one-half inch (1/2") screen. Refer to Appendix M, Figure 1.

(f) **Backfill.** The depth of the backfill shall be consistent, shall not vary more than four inches (4"), and shall consist of at least eight inches (8") of topsoil.

(g) **Level.**   For purposes of this subsection, "level" is considered to be the same elevation, within a four inch (4") range.

(1) The top of each absorption trench must be level.

(2) The top of the absorption media must be level.

(3) If absorption trenches are not separated by a retention structure, all parts of the absorption trenches must be level.

(h) **Retention structure.** In an absorption field where it is not possible to keep the chamber or top of the absorption media level and the backfill a consistent depth, a retention structure shall be used.

252:641-11-3. Retention and distribution structures
(a) Retention and distribution boxes shall be constructed in accordance with Appendix L, Figure 1.

(b) Tees and ells may be used to construct retention or distribution structures.

(c) Distribution and retention boxes shall be sealed.

(d) The top of the outlet pipe of a retention structure shall be seven inches (7") above the top of the perforated pipe. The line from the outlet of a retention structure shall be constructed of solid pipe.

(e) A compacted earthen dam, the entire width of the trench, shall be constructed on the downstream side of each retention structure to reduce any seepage that may bypass the retention structure.

(f) If perforated pipe is used between distribution structures and installed in accordance with this Subchapter, it may be counted as part of the overall required length of absorption trenches.

252:641-11-4. Exceptions
(a) Evapotranspiration/absorption (ET/A) systems. If ET/A systems are installed:

(1) The trenches shall be backfilled with clean sand to within two inches (2") of the surface; the sand shall be separated from the gravel by material which allows the flow of water but prevents the flow of sand. Refer to Appendix M, Figure 2;

(2) After a trench is backfilled with sand, two to four inches (2"-4") of sandy loam soil shall be mounded over the trench;

(3) The trench depth shall not exceed twenty-four inches (24"); and

(4) The length of the trenches shall be determined according to Appendix H, Figure 2.

(b) Chamber systems. When using chamber systems, the following exceptions apply:

(1) The top of the chamber shall be below the outlet of the septic tank.

(2) The trenches do not need to contain gravel;

(3) The trenches shall be backfilled only with native soil or sandy loam; and

(4) The top of the chamber outlet pipe shall be thirteen inches (13") above the trench bottom. (Refer to Appendix N.)

SUBCHAPTER 13. AEROBIC SYSTEMS

Section
252:641-13-1.   General provisions
252:641-13-2.   Applications
252:641-13-3.   Acceptable application surfaces
252:641-13-4.   Surface application

252:641-13-1. General provisions
Aerobic systems shall be comprised of the following:

(1) A septic tank, ranging from a minimum of three hundred (300) gallons to one thousand (1,000) gallons, shall be used as an equalization tank;

(2) An NSF Standard 40, ANSI approved, aerobic treatment unit;

(3) At a minimum, a seven hundred (700) gallon pump tank;

(A) A sampling port shall be provided in the treated sewage   line near the pump tank;and

(B) The float in the pump tank shall be set so that the pump   tank is never more than half full.

(4) A method to disinfect the treated sewage before surface application;

(5) A method of applying properly treated sewage onto the surface of the ground, such as spray or drip application; and

(6) An alarm to alert the owner/operator of a system failure.

252:641-13-2. Applications
The applicant shall submit a completed and signed DEQ Form #641-581 or a form approved by the DEQ and the following information to the local DEQ office:

(1) Site drawing. A site drawing shall show the location of all existing and proposed buildings, the application disposal area, buffer zones, and water wells. The drawing shall be to scale or shall include dimensions from substantial landmarks, structures, and property lines. (Refer to the separation distance requirements in Appendix E.)

(2) Maintenance contract. A copy of a signed maintenance contract provided by the manufacturer of the aerobic treatment unit or a designated maintenance company shall be attached.   The maintenance contract shall be maintained for the life of the sewage disposal system.

252:641-13-3. Acceptable application surfaces
The surface application area shall be landscaped and/or terraced to prevent runoff.

252:641-13-4. Surface application
(a) Application area. The applicant must comply with the size requirements of Appendix H, Figure 3.

(b) Uniform application. Distribution pipes, sprinklers, and other application devices which are designed to provide uniform distribution of treated effluent shall be used.

(1) Sprinkler design. When sprinklers are used as the application method, they must function at the design radius. The spray must cover the proper area without misting. Nozzles must have a thirteen degree (13°) or less trajectory to keep the spray stream low to the ground surface.

(2) Timing. Surface application shall be controlled by a timing device and shall take place daily between 1:00 a.m. and 6:00 a.m., not to exceed three (3) hours per day.

(3) Circular spray patterns. The total spray area must meet the design criteria. Overlapped areas may only be counted once toward meeting the total application area requirement.

(c) **Disinfection.** Treated sewage shall be disinfected prior to surface application.

(1) Approved disinffection methods shall include but not be limited to chlorination, ozonation, or ultraviolet irradiation. Fecal coliform bacteria must be effectively reduced to less than (<) 200MPN/1000 ml. If chlorination is used, a free chlorine residual of one miligram per liter (1 mg/l) must be maintained. Properly encapsulated and/or stabilized calcium hypochlorite shall be used in chlorinators that employ tablets or other dry forms such as granules.

(2) The efficiency of the disinfection procedure shall be established through monitoring of the fecal coliform count or the free chlorine residual. Sampling frequency and testing requirements are listed in the table provided in Appendix D. Samples shall be collected following treatment and disinfection. The results shall be submitted to the local DEQ within thirty (30) days of sampling.

(d) **Application rate.** The application rate shall be adjusted and maintained in a manner which will not allow runoff.

SUBCHAPTER 15. LAGOONS

Section
252:641-15-1. General provisions
252:641-15-2. Lagoon design
252:641-15-3. Bottom construction
252:641-15-4. Dikes
252:641-15-5. Lagoon inlet and septic tank outlet lines
252:641-15-6. Fence

252:641-15-1. General provisions

(a) **Application.** The applicant shall submit a completed and signed "Report for On-Site Sewage Disposal", DEQ Form #641-581, or a form approved by the DEQ to the local DEQ office and obtain approval from the DEQ before beginning construction.

(b) **Septic tank.** All sewage entering a lagoon must first pass through a septic tank.

(c) **Total retention.** All lagoons shall be total retention.

(d) **Location.** Applicants shall not locate lagoons where vegetation, timber, or terrain could interfere with prevailing wind action or shade the lagoon during daylight hours. The applicant must comply with separation distance requirements in Appendix E.

(e) **Minimum lot size exception.** Minimum lot size requirements for the installation of a lagoon may be waived without going through the alternative system process for an existing residence having a failing absorption field on a lot smaller than two and one-half (2-1/2) acres when additional lateral lines cannot be installed or will not be effective.

(f) **Prohibitions.** The owner/operator shall not dispose or store wastes or contaminants other than sewage in the lagoon. The owner/operator shall not discharge or dispose of sludge prior to obtaining a discharge permit or approval of a sludge management plan by the DEQ under 252:605,

252:520 or 252:655.

(g) **Closure.** The DEQ may require the owner/operator to properly close a lagoon when it is no longer in use.

(h) **Examples.** Refer to Appendix O, "Examples of Minimum Design Criteria for Lagoon Installation".

252:641-15-2. Lagoon design

(a) **Sizing.** The lagoon shall be designed according to the Residential Lagoon Size Chart in Appendix H, Figure 1, or the Small Public Lagoon Size Chart in Appendix H, Figure 4.

(b) **Uniform shape.** The shape of all cells shall be uniform, essentially square and reasonably level, with no islands or peninsulas.

(c) **Total Depth.** The total depth of the lagoon shall be at least seven feet (7').

252:641-15-3. Bottom construction

(a) **Level bottom.** The bottom of the lagoon shall not vary more than three inches (3") in elevation.

(b) **Compacted clay.** The bottom shall be constructed of homogeneous clay soil and shall be compacted thoroughly.

(c) **Leakage test required.**

(1) During the final inspection, a leakage test shall be conducted on the lagoon.

(2) The leakage test shall be performed in a manner approved by the DEQ or by digging one (1) hole in the bottom of the lagoon no deeper than six inches (6") and filling the hole with water.

(3) The leakage rate shall not exceed one inch (1") in sixty (60) minutes.

(d) **Failing leakage test.** If the leakage rate exceeds one inch (1") in sixty (60) minutes, the lagoon shall be lined with bentonite, twelve inches (12") of compacted clay, or a synthetic liner in accordance with 252:655. The lagoon bottom shall be retested after installation of a clay or bentonite liner.

252:641-15-4. Dikes

(a) **Topsoil.** Before construction, all vegetation and topsoil shall be removed in the area of the dikes.

(b) **Lifts.** The dikes shall be constructed of homogenous clay in six to nine inch (6"-9") compacted lifts.

(c) **Slope.** Dikes shall be constructed with a slope of no more than one foot (1') vertical rise per three feet (3') horizontal run (1:3) with a minimum top width of four feet (4'). The top of dikes shall be uniformly graded with no depressions or mounds that would hinder maintenance.

(d) **Gravity flow systems.** For gravity flow systems, the top of the dike shall be at least six inches (6") below the lowest floor elevation of any building served.

(e) **Surface runoff.** The top of the dikes shall be at least one foot (1') above the surrounding terrain to divert surface runoff.

252:641-15-5. Lagoon inlet and septic tank outlet lines

(a) **Lagoon inlet line.** The lagoon inlet line shall

terminate in the center of the lagoon and shall discharge onto a concrete structure. The inlet line shall be anchored and supported.

(b) **Septic tank outlet line.** For gravity flow systems, the outlet of the septic tank shall be at least one foot (1') above the designed five foot (5') maximum liquid depth of the lagoon.

252:641-15-6. Fence

(a) **Fence required.** The lagoon area shall be surrounded with a fence unless the entire property is fenced and access is controlled. A gate shall be provided for access for mowing equipment and maintenance needs. In order to protect public health and safety, the DEQ may require more strict fencing requirements, even when the entire property is fenced.

(b) **Specifications.** At a minimum, the fence shall be four feet (4') high and provide protection equivalent to the protection afforded by a chain link or equally-spaced five (5) wire fence. Lagoons serving more than one residential unit shall be surrounded by a six-foot (6') chain link fence or equivalent. No fence shall interfere with wind action to the lagoon's surface or shade the lagoon.

SUBCHAPTER 17. ALTERNATIVE SYSTEMS

Section
252:641-17-1.   General provisions
252:641-17-2.   Applications

252:641-17-1.   General provisions

(a) The DEQ may approve alternative on-site sewage treatment and disposal systems if:

(1) The applicant provides reasonable assurance that the system will work properly;

(2) The DEQ approves the design of the system before installation;

(3) There is no discharge to the waters of the state;

(4) Waste is treated and disposed properly to protect the public health and the environment;

(5) The applicant complies with all local codes and ordinances.

(b) The DEQ shall consider alternative systems on a case-by-case basis, with site specific conditions weighing heavily in the approval process.

252:641-17-2.   Applications

The applicant shall submit a completed and signed DEQ Form #641-581 or a form approved by the DEQ to the local DEQ office for approval before beginning construction.

SUBCHAPTER 19. [RESERVED]

SUBCHAPTER 21. VOLUNTARY CERTIFICATION FOR INDIVIDUAL SEWAGE DISPOSAL SYSTEM INSTALLERS

Section

252:641-21-1.   General provisions
252:641-21-2.   Prerequisites
252:641-21-3.   Filing times and deadlines
252:641-21-4.   Approved training courses
252:641-21-5.   Examinations
252:641-21-6.   Record-keeping
252:641-21-7.   Identification credentials
252:641-21-8.   Classifications
252:641-21-9.   Class C requirements
252:641-21-10.   Class B requirements
252:641-21-11.   Class A requirements
252:641-21-12.   Installer duties and responsibilities
252:641-21-13.   Certification suspension and revocation
252:642-21-14.   Reciprocity

252:641-21-1.   General provisions

(a) **Purpose.** Persons may become DEQ certified installers of individual sewage disposal systems.

(b) **Inspections.** Certified installers can inspect systems they install, depending on their classification. However, self-inspection may be prohibited by municipal or county ordinances.

(c) **Compliance.** Certified installers shall comply with all the rules in this Chapter.

(d) **Examinations.** Requests to take an examination for any classification of certified installer certification may be made to the local DEQ office or to the central DEQ office in Oklahoma City.

252:641-21-2.   Prerequisites

(a) **General.** An applicant must be eighteen (18) years of age or older, owe no outstanding fees or fines to the DEQ, and be in compliance with all final DEQ orders.

(b) **Experience.** The applicant shall provide verification of having installed at least ten (10) individual sewage disposal systems in Oklahoma which meet or exceed the rules in this Chapter.

(c) **Competence.** The applicant shall demonstrate competence by having at least ninety percent (90%) of systems he/she installed within the last year approved upon initial inspection, with any disapproved systems only requiring minor changes.

(d) **Training.** The applicant shall provide verification of training in individual sewage disposal system installation and inspection.

(e) **Application.** An applicant shall submit an initial application on a form provided by the DEQ and fulfill all certification requirements within one hundred eighty (180) days of submitting the application to the DEQ.

(f) **Bonding.** The applicant shall provide a copy of a surety bond guaranteeing payment or performance in an amount required by the individual sewage disposal system installer classification to cover costs resulting from the faulty or improper installation of an individual sewage disposal system. The bond must be effective before the certification is granted by the DEQ. Under the terms of the bond, the surety will become liable on the bond obligation when the certified installer fails to perform as guaranteed by the bond. Payments made under the terms of the bond will be made by the surety directly to the DEQ. The DEQ will establish an account with these funds from which the DEQ will draw to pay its response and oversight costs. The certified installer must maintain a surety bond while certified.

252:641-21-3. Filing times and deadlines
(a) **Initial certification.** An application for initial certification may be filed with the DEQ at any time.
(b) **Renewal.** An unexpired certification may be renewed as follows.
    (1) **Continuing education.** A certified installer must successfully complete four (4) or more hours of approved training per certificate year.
    (2) **Filing deadlines.** The renewal application shall be completed and submitted to the DEQ with all applicable fees by 4:30 p.m. on or before June 30.
    (3) **Grace period.** There is a thirty-one (31) day grace period.
    (4) **Late fees.** There is a Ten Dollar ($10.00) late fee for renewal applications received by the DEQ after July 31.
    (5) **Failure to renew.** Renewal applications will not be accepted by the DEQ after two (2) years following the certificate's date of expiration.
(c) **Specified dates.** If any date specified in this Section falls on a weekend or holiday, the date of the following working day shall be the effective date.

252:641-21-4. Approved training courses
Training credit will be granted only for courses or workshops listed as approved by the DEQ or for courses, workshops or alternative activities which have been approved in writing by the DEQ in advance.

252:641-21-5. Examinations
(a) **Scheduling and administration.** Certification training and examinations shall be administered by the DEQ at such times and places as determined by the DEQ.
(b) **Confidentiality.** Examinations, answer sheets and test scores are confidential and are not subject to disclosure, except that a person's test score may be disclosed to that person at his/her request.
(c) **Prohibitions.** Any applicant found cheating on an examination shall be deemed to have failed the examination and shall be prohibited from applying for certification for a period of twelve (12) months.

252:641-21-6. Record-keeping
Each person is responsible for keeping his/her own records of training and experience. When applying for initial certification or renewal, each person must present verification of training and experience to the DEQ.

252:641-21-7. Identification credentials
The DEQ will provide identification credentials to certified installers upon initial certification, classification change and/or renewals.

252:641-21-8. Classifications
There are three (3) classifications of individual sewage disposal system installers.
    (1) **Class C.** Class C certified individual sewage disposal system installers are only allowed to self-inspect lift stations and subsurface absorption systems excluding ET/A systems.
    (2) **Class B.** Class B certified individual sewage disposal system installers may self-inspect subsurface absorption systems, ET/A systems, lagoons and lift stations.
    (3) **Class A.** Class A certified individual sewage disposal system installers may self-inspect subsurface absorption systems, ET/A systems, lagoons, lift stations and aerobic systems.

252:641-21-9. Class C requirements
(a) **Training.** The applicant must complete eight (8) hours of DEQ approved classroom training in the basics of individual sewage disposal system installation and inspection, and also conduct at least four (4) joint field inspections with the DEQ.
(b) **Examination.** The applicant must score at least seventy percent (70%) on the Class C examination.
(c) **Bonding.** The applicant must provide a Five Thousand Dollar ($5,000.00) bond.

252:641-21-10. Class B requirements
(a) **Training.** An applicant for Class B certification must complete the training requirement for a Class C certification and an additional four (4) hours of classroom training in the installation of ET/A systems and lagoons.
(b) **Examination.** The applicant must score at least seventy percent (70%) on the Class B examination.
(c) **Bonding.** The applicant must provide a Seven Thousand, Five Hundred Dollar ($7,500.00) bond.

252:641-21-11. Class A requirements
(a) **Training.** An application for Class A certification must complete the training requirement for a Class C certification and an additional eight (8) hours of classroom training in the installation of ET/A systems, lagoons, and aerobic systems.
(b) **Examination.** The applicant must score at least seventy percent (70%) on the Class A examination.
(c) **Bonding.** The applicant must provide a Ten Thousand Dollar ($10,000.00) bond.

252:641-21-12. Installer duties and responsibilities
(a) **Systems installed.** For all systems self-inspected, approved or disapproved, a certified installer shall:
    (1) **Notify DEQ.** The certified installer shall notify the local DEQ office the day construction begins on an individual sewage disposal system. DEQ may inspect a portion of the system to ascertain that the certified installer continues to meet certification requirements;
    (2) **Submittals to DEQ.** Within ten (10) working days after the work has been completed, the certified installer shall submit an accurate, completed Form

#641-576A to the local DEQ office and a Request for Services form to the central DEQ office in Oklahoma City with the required administration fee.

(3) **Maintain records.** The certified installer shall maintain records of all systems installed and make them available for DEQ review.

252:641-21-13. Certification suspension and revocation

(a) Suspension or revocation. After notice and opportunity for hearing, the DEQ may suspend or revoke certification for:

(1) procedural violations such as allowing bond to expire, failing to complete continuing education requirements or other related procedural issues;

(2) gross inefficiency or incompetence;

(3) any violation of the Environmental Quality Code, this Chapter, or the terms of the certificate or any final DEQ order; or

(4) fraud or misrepresentation used to obtain the certification.

(b) **Suspension.** Any person whose certification was suspended by the DEQ for procedural violations may correct the deficiency(ies) and pay a reinstatement fee of Ten Dollars ($10.00). Continuing education requirements must be met.

(c) **Revocation.** Any individual whose certification has been revoked by the DEQ must wait one year from the date of revocation before filing an application for a new certificate.

252:642-21-14. Reciprocity

An applicant may apply for reciprocity by providing proof of a current, valid license or certificate from a municipality or county in Oklahoma.

SUBCHAPTER 23. FEES

Section
252:641-23-1. Fee schedule
252:641-23-2. Certified individual sewage disposal system installer fees

252:641-23-1. Fee schedule

(a) **Applicability.** The following fee schedule applies to services provided by the Environmental Complaints and Local Services Division (ECLS) of the DEQ:

(1) Document search - $15.00

(2) Soil percolation test or soil profile description - $85.00

(3) Final inspection - $85.00

(4) Existing system evaluation report - $85.00

(5) Combinations - $115.00
Soil percolation test & final inspection or existing system   evaluation report

(6) Residential development plat review
(A) 10 lots or less - $115.00
(B) More than 10 lots - $230.00

(b) **Waiver of fees.**

(1) **Individual homeowners.** The DEQ shall waive the fee for document searches for individual homeowners upon the homeowner's request and proper identification.

(2) **Indigents and nonprofit organizations.** The DEQ may waive fees for indigents and nonprofit organizations. Requests for a waiver of fees under this paragraph shall be decided by the Director of Environmental Complaints and Local Services Division of the DEQ.

(3) **Investigation of complaints.** The DEQ may perform a percolation test as a part of an investigation of a system known to be malfunctioning or a system which is the subject of a complaint filed by a third party. No fee shall be charged as a part of this investigation.

252:641-23-2. Certified individual sewage disposal system installer fees

(a) **Certification fees.**

(1) Application filing and examination fee:
(A) Class A - $100.00
(B) Class B - $ 75.00
(C) Class C - $ 50.00

(2) Certification renewal fee - $50.00

(3) Late fee - $10.00

(4) Reinstatement fee - $10.00

(b) **Progression.** Once certified, an installer may move up through the classes at any time by completing the required additional training, taking the appropriate examination and paying the applicable fee, as follows:

(1) Class B to a Class A, fee of $25.00

(2) Class C to a Class B, fee of $25.00

(3) Class C to a Class A, fee of $50.00

(c) **Administration fee.** For each final inspection performed by a certified installer, he/she shall submit Seventeen Dollars ($17.00) to the DEQ.

(d) **Nonrefundable.** Fees are nonrefundable.

APPENDIX O. EXAMPLES OF MINIMUM DESIGN CRITERIA
FOR LAGOON INSTALLATION

Note: Drawings not to scale; slopes are to be 3 horizontal to 1 vertical.

Figure 1.

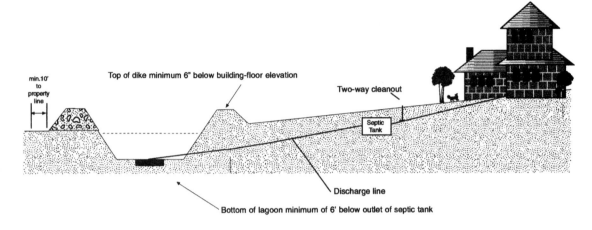

min.10'
to
property
line

Top of dike minimum 6" below building-floor elevation

Two-way cleanout

Septic Tank

Discharge line

Bottom of lagoon minimum of 6' below outlet of septic tank

Figure 2.

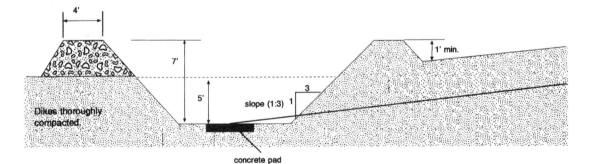

4'

7'

5'

1' min.

3

1

slope (1:3)

Dikes thoroughly compacted

concrete pad

 Compacted soil

Undisturbed soil

The DEQ encourages seeding, sodding or sprigging dikes with perennial, low-growing grasses to prevent erosion.

214

Sources of Information for Building Your Rural Home in Canada

Tragedy in Walkerton: A Case History

During May, 2000, the residents of Walkerton, Ontario, a small rural community about 90 miles west of Toronto, Canada, experienced one of the most deadly water-borne disease outbreaks in recent history. As many as 15 deaths and several hundred hospitalizations in this rural area were attributed to drinking water contaminated with the O157:H7 strain of Coliform bacteria.

This rare, but deadly O157:H7 E. Coli bacteria, once thought to be limited to under-cooked hamburger meat, is now known to be transmitted through a variety of foods and drinking water contaminated with animal manure. Unlike other strains of Coliform bacteria, the O157:H7 E. Coli is able to produce a powerful poison (toxin) that can damage the kidney system. The O157:H7 toxin can be life threatening especially for young children, senior citizens and persons with immune system problems.

The tragedy in Walkerton prompted Ontario Premier, Mike Harris, to advise those visiting rural areas, "If you're concerned about the water, boil it, or take your own drinking water." Ontario's, Environment Minister, Dan Newman warned, "The government is not prepared to directly check the water quality in private wells, at campgrounds, trailer parks or rural gas stations used by the public."

The events in Walkerton actually began several years ago as the region started to experience growth pains similar to those being experienced in many rural areas undergoing rapid development. New homes being built in close proximity to existing farming activities and existing farm operations expanding too near community and private water supplies contributed to the tragedy in this once idyllic community.

Unfortunately, the lessons learned by Dr. John Snow (see Chapter 5) in the 1800s were forgotten or simply neglected, allowing community water wells to become contaminated by runoff from animal feedlots during heavy rains. Even though officials were aware of laboratory reports showing the presence of Coliform bacteria, the public was not advised to boil water prior to drinking. Operators of the community water system did not want to panic local residents unnecessarily or to blame the local farm community for polluting city wells.

No matter in what country you plan to build your country home, the information presented in Chapters 5 and 6 on water and sewage disposal can help you to avoid a Walkerton tragedy of your own. In Canada there are a number of sources of information and assistance when it comes to rural water and sewage disposal. Local and regional health departments have public health professionals who can assist in planning and evaluating on-site water and sewage disposal systems. Information on finding these resources is summarized in this Appendix.

Where To Find Environmental Information in Canada:

Environmental Protection in Canada

Under the Constitution Act of 1867, Canadian provinces are "owners" of water resources and are given wide responsibilities in day-to-day management. In 1970 the federal government passed the Canada Water Act and created the Department of the Environment (Environment Canada) in 1971. Through the efforts of this Department, Canada is now recognized as a leader in the global environmental effort toward sustainable development.

Environment Canada has developed a Web site with information on water quality issues and groundwater protection. This Web site can be found on the Internet at the following address: http://www.ec.gc.ca/water/e_main.html. *Groundwater—Nature's Hidden Treasure* and *WATER—How We Share IT* are two excellent publications that can be downloaded at this site. Both are recommended reading for anyone planning to construct an on-site water or sewage disposal system.

Groundwater—Nature's Hidden Treasure is a must for all rural homeowners wanting to learn more about protecting groundwater from contamination. All phases of the hydrologic cycle are clearly explained. In addition, an introduction to groundwater quality and information on safeguarding groundwater from sources of contamination are provided.

WATER—How We Share IT explains the concept of "watershed management" in easy-to-understand, non-technical language. This publication also discusses the advantages and disadvantages of diverting water from a watershed with little demand to another watershed with a high water demand. The "Chicago Diversion" from Lake Michigan will be of interest to many Canadian readers. Additional information on groundwater resources can be found by exploring the Environment Canada Web site.

Rural Water Supplies

Canada's Prairie Farm Rehabilitation Administration (PFRA) helps to develop drinking water supplies and investigates practical ways of protecting and improving the quality of water in rural areas. With experts in the biological, geological and engineering disciplines, the PFRA works to ensure water quality and treatment of wastewater on the prairies.

The PFRA can provide technical assistance in the planning, investigation and design of water supply projects, including wells, dugouts, springs and water quality enhancement projects. The Administration plans and develops water supply quality improvement projects through the Rural Water Development Program (RWDP). The RWDP establishes partnerships with rural communities and provincial and local governments.

Recognizing that rural homeowners often face unique problems in water quality and quantity, the PFRA has established programs to help rural residents secure reliable and safe water supplies. With increased awareness by rural citizens in Canada regarding water quality, the PFRA is promoting the protection of existing water resources. For example, the Sustainable Water Well Initiative (SWWI) has been developed to improve existing water wells by providing advice on the diagnosis, prevention and rehabilitation of well problems.

The PFRA maintains a Web page at http://www.agr.ca/pfra/pfintroe.htm providing links to information on water chemistry and microbiology; water quality regulations and standards; water quality analysis and interpretation; treatment methods; and sampling to rural clients and local farm groups. The PFRA has established local offices in the following areas:

Location of Local PFRA Offices

Northern Alberta and British Columbia Dawson Creek
- Peace River
- Vegreville
- Westlock

Southern Alberta
- Hanna
- Lethbridge
- Medicine Hat
- Red Deer

Northern Saskatchewan
- North Battleford
- Melfort
- Rosetown
- Watrous

Southern Saskatchewan
- Gravelbourg
- Maple Creek
- Melville
- Moose Jaw
- Swift Current
- Weyburn

Manitoba
- Beausejour
- Brandon
- Dauphin
- Morden

Institute of Public Health Inspectors

Like their counterparts in the U.S., Canadian health inspectors (sanitarians) working in local health and environmental protection agencies are an excellent source of help in planning on-site water and sewage treatment systems. The Canadian Institute of Public Health (CIPHI) Inspectors promotes professional development and training for local health inspectors throughout Canada.

The British Columbia Branch of the CIPHI is promoting an excellent groundwater protection video. Produced in cooperation with the British Columbia Groundwater Protection Association, the video is intended as an educational tool to raise awareness of the general public about the problems of protecting groundwater supplies. Copies of the video can be purchased for about $15.00. Contact the BC Groundwater Association, 1708 - 197A Street, Langley, BC V2Z 1K2, for information on ordering.

Standards for On-site Water and Sewage

In Canada, local agencies will have significant influence on construction standards and regulations for on-site water and sewage disposal systems. Standards can be expected to differ from region to region. Inspection and enforcement of standards will also vary. Just because your water well may not need to be inspected is not an excuse to disregard basic standards for protecting your water supply.

The British Columbia Ministry of Environment, Lands and Parks has published *Guidelines for Minimum Standards in Water Well Construction* and *Code of Practice for Construction, Testing, Maintenance, Alteration and Closure of Wells*. Both of these publications could serve as model standards for constructing water wells in any country. These publications can be downloaded at the Ministry's Web site at http://www.gov.bc.ca/elp/. For additional information write to: The Water Management Branch, Environment and Lands Headquarters Division, Ministry of Environment Lands and Parks, Province of British Columbia, PO BOX 9340, STN PROV GOVT, VICTORIA, BC V8W 9M1.

The Ministry of the Environment in Nova Scotia has enacted model regulations for on-site sewage disposal systems. The Nova Scotia regulations are similar to many state and local standards found in the U.S. The Ministry has also published *Tips for Testing Your Well Water*, a how-to guide for sampling your water well. Information on obtaining copies of these materials can be requested from the Nova Scotia Ministry of the Environment, PO Box 2107, Halifax, NS B3J 3B7. These publications can also be viewed on the Internet at http://www.gov.ns.ca/envi/.

Helping the World Find Safe Water

Lifewater Canada is a federally incorporated, non-profit organization providing training and information on developing drinking water systems worldwide. While the organization's main focus is on training people in underdeveloped countries, anyone can obtain information on the proper construction of on-site water supplies. Lifewater maintains a Web site with a unique on-line tutorial and other groundwater educational resources. The Web site found on the Internet at http://www.lifewater.ca/ is recommended for anyone wanting to learn more about the process of developing on-site water supplies and how to protect drilled wells from contamination. The organization can also be contacted by writing to: Lifewater Canada, PO Box 44, Kakabeka Falls, ON P0T 1W0.

Canadian Drinking Water Quality Publication

Since first beginning in 1973, the British Columbia Water & Waste Association (BCWWA) has evolved into an organization supporting over 3,000 water and wastewater professionals in BC and the Yukon. The main goal of the BCWWA is to provide operators of public water and wastewater treatment systems with training and educational opportunities.

The BCWWA office has copies of *Guidelines for Canadian Drinking Water Quality - Sixth Edition.* This publication provides a wealth of information on drinking water quality throughout Canada. Instructions on ordering can be obtained from the BCWWA by writing to: British Columbia Water & Waste Association, 342 - 17 Fawcett Road, Coquitlam, BC V3K 6V2, Phone: (604) 540-0111, Fax: (604) 540-4077. The organization also maintains a Web page at http://www.bcwwa.org.

ASK-A-GEOLOGIST

The Geological Survey of Canada (GSC) is Canada's premier agency for geoscientific information and research, with world-class expertise focusing on geoscience surveys, sustainable development of Canada's resources, technology innovation and groundwater protection. The GSC has extensive capability in interpreting and managing geoscience information related to groundwater quality. This expertise is applied to assessments for developing energy and mineral resources, planning for natural hazards, and exploring environmental and policy issues. The GSC provides a unique "ASK-A-GEOLOGIST" service at their Web site http://www.nrcan.gc.ca/ess/esic/cgi-bin/askageol_e.cgi. To contact the GSC write to: Geological Survey of Canada, Natural Resources Canada, 601 Booth Street, Ottawa, Ontario K1A 0E8.

Water Research

The National Water Research Institute (NWRI) carries out research concerning ground and surface water quality in Canada. As a major element of Environment Canada, the NWRI conducts a diverse program of research and development related to groundwater quality, surface water contamination and the aquatic sciences. Here are a few examples of recent technical and scientific reports related to groundwater quality that have been published by the NWRI staff:

Al-Abed, N., H.Y.F. Ng, C.S. Tan, C.F. Drury, J.D. Gaynor, M. Soultani and T.W. Welacky. 1997. *Modelling nitrate in a tile-drained field using RZWQM.* Environment Canada, National Water Research Institute, Burlington, Ontario, NWRI Contribution No. 97-187.

Booty, W.G., A.S. Crowe, A. Piggott, R. deLoe, G.S. Bowen, S. Holysh, T. Svensson, B. Beatty and G. Kauffman (ed.). 1998. *Proceedings of the Groundwater in a Watershed Context Symposium,* Canada Centre for Inland Waters, Burlington, Ontario, December 2-4, 1998, Canadian Water Resources Association.

Brown, A., P. Lapcevic, K. Novakowski, S. Lesage, S. Brown, K. Millar, J. Voralek and L. Zanini. 1997. *Characterization of trichloroethylene contamination in the fractured bedrock at the Smithville site.* Environment Canada, National Water Research Institute, Burlington, Ontario, NWRI Contribution No. 97-140.

Cessna, A.J., K.B. Best, R. Grover and W. Nicholaichuk. 1997. *Potential for contamination of the South Saskatchewan River with herbicides applied in an irrigation district.* Can. Water Resour. J. 22: 237-248.

Lapcevic, P.A., K.S. Novakowski and E.A. Sudicky. 1998. *Groundwater flow and solute transport in fractured media,* p. 17-1 - 17-39. In J. Delleur (ed.), Groundwater Engineering, CRC Press, Boca Raton, FL.

Piggott, A.R. 1998. *Regional groundwater assessment of the Grand River watershed,* vol. 2, p. 537-541. Proceedings of the 51st Canadian Geotechnical Conference, Canadian Geotechnical Society, Edmonton, Alberta.

Schellenberg, S.L. and A.R. Piggott. 1998. *An assessment of groundwater usage in thirteen counties in southern Ontario,* p. 195-202. Proceedings of Groundwater in a Watershed Context, Canadian Water Resources Association, Canada.

Zanini, L., K.S. Novakowski, P. Lapcevic, G.S. Bickerton, J. Voralek and C. Talbot. 1998. *Groundwater flow in a fractured carbonate aquifer inferred from combined hydrogeological and geochemical measurements.* Environment Canada, National Water Research Institute, Burlington, Saskatoon, NWRI Contribution No. 98-249.

Additional research articles can be found on the NWRI's Web page at http://www.cciw.ca/nwri/nwri.html.

An Ounce of Planning—
Better Than a Pound of Cure

No matter in what country you plan to build that rural dream home, your best source of environmental information will be local environmental and public health offices. The professional staff at these local agencies are often over worked and under paid, but will be willing to share their expertise and vast knowledge on the construction of on-site water and sewage systems. Most of these professionals will agree that the best advice for rural homeowners is, "An ounce of planning and prevention is worth a lot more than a pound of cure."

GLOSSARY

acid rain: Rain with a pH of less than 5.6; results from sulfur and nitrogen oxides emitted from burning fossil fuels or from volcanic activity; may cause damage to buildings, monuments, car finishes, crops, forests, wildlife habitats and aquatic life.

activated carbon: Granules of carbon commonly used in home water treatment units. These granules have a high capacity to remove certain trace and soluble materials from water.

aeration: Process of adding air by electrical mixers or blowers.

aerobic bacteria: Bacteria that require oxygen to survive when feeding on sewage and other matter. Normally some type of aeration unit must be used to provide enough oxygen to meet the oxygen demand.

aerobic treatment unit (ATU): An on-site sewage treatment process which uses aerobic microbes to decompose organic compounds. A blower, mixer or other mechanical device is used to provide oxygen. The size of the ATU is based on the expected biochemical oxygen demand (BOD) loading. If the unit fails to provide sufficient oxygen, aerobic bacteria will die and be replaced by anaerobic microbes, producing typical septic tank odors.

algae: Large group of aquatic plants that contain chlorophylll; many are single cell or form filaments, includes the larger seaweeds and related freshwater and land plants.

algal bloom: A heavy growth of algae in and on a body of water; usually results from high nitrate and phosphate concentrations entering water bodies from farm fertilizers and detergents; phosphates also occur naturally under certain conditions.

alternative or non-conventional on-site system: On-site sewage disposal systems other than the common septic tank and underground drain lines. When soils or other site factors prohibit the installation of a standard septic tank system an alternative on-site system might do the job. Common alternative systems include ATUs, wetlands, sandfilters and mound systems.

anaerobic bacteria: Bacteria that do not require the presence of oxygen to survive. Anaerobic bacteria readily survive in the typical septic tank, breaking down sewage and producing noxious-smelling sewer gases.

aquatic life: Plants, animals and microorganisms that spend all or part of their lives in water.

aqueduct: A conduit designed to transport water from a remote source, usually by gravity.

aquifer: An underground layer of rock or soil that is saturated with usable amounts of water (a zone of saturation).

Army Corps of Engineers: Branch of the U.S. Army; responsible for maintaining and regulating inland waterways.

artesian well: A well in which the water comes from a confined aquifer and is under pressure. One type of artesian well is a free-flowing artesian well where water just flows or bubbles out of the ground without being pumped.

bacteria: Single-cell microbes that grow in nearly every environment on Earth. A few, known as pathogens, are able to cause disease. Useful bacteria produce antibiotics, ferment foods and make chemical solvents, among other things.

biodegradable: Capable of being decomposed (broken down) by natural biological processes.

biosolids: Solid materials resulting from wastewater treatment that meet government criteria for beneficial use, such as for fertilizer.

blackwater: Domestic wastewater containing human wastes.

blue baby syndrome: A medical condition, known as methemoglobinemia, in which blood's capacity for oxygen transport is reduced, resulting in bluish skin discoloration in infants. Caused by drinking water contaminated with nitrates.

Biochemical Oxygen Demand (BOD): A measure of the organic strength of sewage. Represents the amount of oxygen required to break down organic materials present in the waste. When high BOD waste enters a stream, all available oxygen may be depleted causing fish kills and other problems.

brine: Water saturated with or containing large amounts of a salt, especially sodium chloride.

carcinogenic: A substance found to produce cancer.

cesspool: A covered hole or pit for receiving untreated sewage.

channelization: The process of channeling or carving a route.

chlorination: Water disinfection by chlorine gas or hypochlorite.

chlorine: A chemical element, symbol Cl, atomic number 17, atomic weight 35.453; used as a disinfectant in drinking and wastewater treatment processes.

cholera: An acute, often fatal, infectious epidemic disease caused by the microorganism Vibrio comma, that is characterized by watery diarrhea, vomiting, cramps, suppression of urine and collapse.

Clean Water Act (CWA): Water pollution control laws based upon the Federal Water Pollution Control Act of 1972 with amendments passed in 1977, 1981 and 1987; main objective is to restore and maintain the "chemical, physical and biological integrity of the Nation's waters."

coliforms: Bacteria found in the intestinal tract of warm-blooded animals; used as indicators of fecal contamination in water.

compost: An aerobic mixture of decaying organic matter, such as leaves and manure, used as fertilizer.

The Comprehensive Environmental Response, Compensation, and Liability Act (CERCLA or Superfund): Legislation passed in 1980 and amended in 1986 by the Superfund Amendments and Reauthorization Act (SARA); provides for short-term actions, called removal actions, in response to accidents and improper handling of hazardous materials which pose an immediate threat to human health and safety. It also provides for long-term actions called remedial actions for cleanups of other sites, which pose no immediate threat to public safety.

condensation: The act or process of reducing a gas or vapor to a liquid or solid state.

cone of depression: A cone-shaped area formed when the spaces in the rock or soil are emptied as water is withdrawn from a well. The cone of depression from a neighbor's well could lower the water level in your well.

confined aquifer (artesian aquifer): An aquifer having a dense layer of compacted earth material over it that blocks easy passage of water.

conservation: The practice of using water and other resources only when needed for the purpose of reducing waste or loss.

constructed wetlands: Wetlands that are designed and built similar to natural wetlands; some are used to treat wastewater. Constructed wetlands for wastewater treatment consist of one or more shallow depressions or cells built into the ground with level bottoms so that the flow of water can be controlled within the cells and from cell to cell. Roots and stems of the wetland plants form a dense mat where biological and physical processes occur to treat the wastewater.

contaminant: An impurity, that causes air, soil or water to be harmful to human health or the environment.

decomposition: The process of breaking down complex organic materials in sewage into simple inorganic elements which can be returned to the atmosphere and soil.

desalination: Removing dissolved salts in salt water and brines.

digestion: Decomposition of organic waste materials by the action of microbes; the process of sewage treatment by the decomposition of organic matter.

discharged: Released into a water body.

disinfect (disinfected): To destroy or inactivate harmful microorganisms.

dissolved oxygen (DO): Oxygen dissolved in water to sustain the fish and other aquatic organisms.

dissolved solids: Materials that enter a water body in a solid phase and dissolve in water.

distillation: The process of heating a liquid or solid until it sends off a gas or vapor and then cooling the gas or vapor until it becomes a liquid.

distribution box: A place where one pipe or line enters and exits through several pipes or lines; they are used in municipal drinking water systems to distribute water to homes, in municipal wastewater systems to retrieve wastewater, and by electric companies to distribute power.

divining rod: A forked branch or stick used in an attempt to locate subterranean water or minerals; it is said to bend downward when held over a source.

domestic sewage: Waste produced through the functioning of a household.

drainfield: The part of a septic system where the wastewater is released into the soil for absorption and filtration.

drought: A lack of rain or water; a long period of dry weather.

duck stamp: Required, for a fee, of all duck hunters over age 16 by the U.S. Fish and Wildlife Service; a conservation program aimed at preserving wetlands.

ecology: A branch of science concerned with the interrelationship of organisms and their environments; the totality or pattern of relations between organisms and their environment.

ecosystem: An ecological community together with its physical environment, considered as a unit.

effluent: Wastewater discharged from a point source, such as a pipe.

endangered animal species: A species of animal identified by official federal and/or state agencies as being faced with the danger of extinction.

environment: The sum of all external conditions and influences affecting the development and life of organisms.

Environmental Protection Agency (EPA): The U.S. agency responsible for efforts to control air and water pollution, radiation and pesticide hazards, ecological research and solid waste disposal.

epidemic diseases: Diseases that spread rapidly and extensively by infection among many individuals in an area.

eutrophic: Pertaining to a lake containing a high concentration of dissolved nutrients; often shallow, with periods of oxygen deficiency.

evapotranspiration: Combination of evaporation and transpiration of water into the atmosphere from living plants and soil.

filtration: The process of passing a liquid or gas through a porous article or mass (paper, membrane, sand, etc.) to separate out matter in suspension.

fish kill: The sudden death of fish due to the introduction of pollutants or the reduction of the dissolved oxygen concentration in a water body.

flocculation: The process of forming aggregated or compound masses of particles, such as a cloud or a precipitate.

flood plain: Mostly level land along rivers and streams that may be submerged by flood water. A 100-year flood plain is an area that can be expected to flood once in every 100 years.

food chain: A succession of organisms in a community that constitutes a feeding order.

fresh water: Water containing an insignificant amount of salts, such as in inland rivers and lakes.

grey water: Domestic wastewater that does not contain human wastes such as tub, shower or washing machine water.

groundwater: Water that infiltrates into the earth and is stored in usable amounts in the soil and rock below the earth's surface; water within the zone of saturation.

groundwater recharge: The addition of water to an aquifer.

hardness: The amount of calcium carbonate dissolved in water.

hazardous chemicals: Chemical compounds that are dangerous to human health and/or the environment.

hazardous waste: Waste containing chemical compounds that are dangerous to human health and/or the environment.

heavy metals: Metallic elements (Example: cadmium, chromium, copper, lead, mercury, nickel and zinc) which are used to manufacture products; they are present in some industrial, municipal and urban runoff.

hydrogen sulfide gas: A flammable, toxic, colorless gas with an offensive odor (similar to rotten eggs) produced during the anaerobic decomposition of sewage.

hydrologic (water) cycle: The cycle of the earth's water supply from the atmosphere to the earth and back which includes precipitation, transpiration, evaporation, runoff, infiltration and storage in water bodies and groundwater.

infiltration: The gradual downward flow of water from the surface of the earth into the soil.

inorganic material: Material derived from nonorganic, or nonliving, sources.

ion exchange: A chemical reaction between a solid (ion exchanger) and a fluid (usually a water solution) in which ions may be interchanged from one substance to another. Ion exchange treatment is a common water softening method.

karst: A topography formed over limestone, dolomite or gypsum and characterized by sinkholes, caves and underground drainage.

lagoon: As a wastewater treatment method, an animal waste treatment method which uses a deep pond to treat manure and other runoff from a livestock operation; may be aerobic or anaerobic (both use bacteria to break down wastes).

landfill: A large, outdoor area for waste disposal; landfills where waste is exposed to the atmosphere (open dumps) are now illegal; in "sanitary" landfills, waste is layered and covered with soil.

landscaping: Improving the natural beauty of a piece of land by planting or altering the contours of the ground.

maximum contaminant levels (MCL): The highest content levels of certain substances allowable by law for a water source to be considered safe.

microbe: See definition of microorganism.

microorganisms: Organisms too small to be seen with the unaided eye, including bacteria, protozoans, yeasts, viruses and algae.

milligrams/litre (mg/l): A measure of concentration used in the measurement of fluids; mg/l is the most common way to present a concentration in water and is roughly equivalent to parts per million.

National Pollutant Discharge Elimination System (NPDES):
Part of the Clean Water Act requiring municipal and industrial waste-water treatment facilities to obtain permits which specify the types and amounts of pollutants that may be discharged into water bodies.

nitrates: Used generically for materials containing this ion group made of nitrogen and oxygen; sources include animal wastes and some fertilizers; can seep into groundwater; linked to human health problems, including "blue baby" syndrome (methemoglobinemia).

non-point-source pollution (NPS): Pollution that cannot be traced to a single point (Example: outlet or pipe) because it comes from many individual places or a widespread area (typically urban, rural and agricultural runoff).

nutrient: An element or compound, such as nitrogen, phosphorus and potassium, that is necessary for plant growth.

oxygen depletion: The reduction of the dissolved oxygen level in a water body.

package plants: A small, semi-portable prefabricated wastewater treatment system that services a new housing development, apart-ment complex, trailer park, camp or self-contained business that is not connected to a city sewer system and is not on a site appropriate for a septic system. Homeowners may become responsible for opera-tion and maintenance of these systems.

parts per billion (ppb): One ppb is comparable to one kernel of corn in a filled, 45-foot silo, 16 feet in diameter.

parts per million (ppm): One ppm is comparable to one drop of gasoline in a tank full of gas (full-size car).

parts per trillion (ppt): One ppt is comparable to one drop in a swimming pool covering the area of a football field 43 feet deep.

pathogen: Microorganisms that can cause disease in humans, ani-mals and plants. Certain bacteria, viruses or parasites found in sewage and in runoff from farms may contain a number of pathogens.

percolate: The downward flow or filtering of water through pores or spaces in rock or soil. The soil percolation rate is a major factor used to determine the type of on-site sewage treatment.

permeable: Passable; allowing fluid to penetrate or pass through it.

pH: A measure of the concentration of hydrogen ions in a solution; the pH scale ranges from 0 to 14, where 7 is neutral and values less than 7 are acidic and values greater than 7 are basic or alkaline; pH is an inverted logarithmic scale so that every unit decrease in pH means a 10-fold increase in hydrogen ion concentration. Thus, a pH of 3 is 10 times as acidic as a pH of 4 and 100 times as acidic as a pH of 5.

phosphate: Used generically for materials containing a phosphate group; sources include some fertilizers and detergents; when wastewater containing phosphates is discharged into surface waters, these chemicals act as nutrient pollutants (causing overgrowth of aquatic plants).

plankton: Minute animal and plant life in a body of water.

point-source pollution: Pollution that can be traced to a single point source, such as a pipe or culvert (Example: industrial and wastewater treatment plant, and certain storm water discharges).

pollutant: An impurity (contaminant) that causes an undesirable change in the physical, chemical or biological characteristics of the air, water or land that may be harmful to or affect the health, survival or activities of humans or other living organisms.

pollution: Contaminants in the air, water or soil that cause harm to human health or the environment.

polychlorinated biphenyls (PCBs): A group of toxic, persistent chemicals used in electrical transformers and capacitors for insulating purposes, and in gas pipeline systems as a lubricant. The sale and new use of PCBs were banned by law in 1979.

potable water: Water that is considered safe to drink.

precipitation: Water droplets or ice particles condensed from atmospheric water vapor and sufficiently massive to fall to the earth's surface, such as rain or snow.

primary treatment: The first process in wastewater treatment which removes settled or floating solids.

pristine: Describes a landscape and/or a water body remaining in a pure state.

privy: An outhouse; a latrine.

protozoans: Small single-cell microbes; frequently observed as actively moving organisms when impure water is viewed under a microscope; cause a number of widespread human illnesses, such as malaria, and thus can present a threat to public health.

radon: A colorless, radioactive, inert gaseous element (atomic number 86) formed by the radioactive decay of radium; exposure to high levels causes cancer.

recharge: Replenish a water body or an aquifer with water.

recharge areas: An area where water flows into the earth to resupply a water body or an aquifer.

reverse osmosis (RO): A process where water is cleaned by forcing water through an ultra-fine semi-permeable membrane which allows only the water to pass though and retains the contaminants. These filters are sometimes used in tertiary treatment and to pretreat water in chemical laboratories.

riparian area: The area along a waterway.

runoff: Water (originating as precipitation) that flows across surfaces rather than soaking in; eventually enters a water body; may pick up and carry a variety of pollutants.

Safe Drinking Water Act: A regulatory program passed by the U.S. Congress in 1974 to help ensure safe drinking water in the United States; sets maximum contaminant levels for a variety of chemicals, metals and bacteria in public water supplies.

saline intrusion: The saltwater infiltration of freshwater aquifers in coastal areas, when groundwater is withdrawn faster than it is being recharged.

salinity: An indication of the amount of salt dissolved in water.

sand filtration: Process of filtering wastewater through sand. As wastewater trickles over the bed of sand, bacteria decompose the wastes. Filtered water flows out through drains in the bottom of the bed.

saturated zone: Underground layer in which every available space is filled with water.

saturation: The state of being infused with so much of a substance (Example: water) that no more can be absorbed, dissolved or retained.

secondary treatment: Wastewater process where bacteria are used to reduce organic matter in the wastewater. Requires more care and maintenance than primary treatment.

septic system: A domestic wastewater treatment system (consisting of a septic tank and a soil absorption system) into which wastes are piped directly from the home; bacteria decompose the waste, sludge settles to the bottom of the tank, and the treated effluent flows out into the ground through drainage pipes.

septage: Solid matter that settles to the bottom of septic tanks. Homeowners must have a licensed pumper remove septage at regular intervals of 3-4 years to prevent solids from entering and clogging drainlines.

sinkhole: A natural depression in a land surface connected to a sub-terranean passage, generally occurring in limestone regions and formed by solution or by collapse of a cavern roof; makes it easy for pollutants to reach aquifers and contaminate groundwater.

slope: To take a slanting direction, such as a bank sloping down to a river; a piece of slanting ground, such as a hillside; the upward or downward slant, such as that of a roof.

sludge: Wastewater treatment plant sedimentation normally treated by bacterial digestion or other methods and then pumped for land disposal or incineration.

surface water: Precipitation that does not soak into the ground or return to the atmosphere by evaporation or transpiration. It is stored in streams, lakes, rivers, ponds, wetlands, oceans and reservoirs.

teratogen: A substance capable of causing birth defects.

tertiary treatment: An enhancement of normal sewage treatment to provide water of nearly potable quality using further chemical and physical treatment.

topographic map: A map showing the relief features or surface configuration of an area, usually by means of contour lines.

topography: The detailed mapping or description of the features of a relatively small area, district or locality; the relief features or surface configuration of an area.

total dissolved solids (TDS): The quantity of dissolved material in a given volume of water.

toxic chemical: A chemical with the potential of causing death or damage to humans, animals or plants; poison.

toxin: Any of various poisonous substances produced by certain plant and animal cells, including bacterial toxins, phytotoxins and zootoxins.

transpiration: Direct transfer of water from the leaves of living plants or the skins of animals into the atmosphere.

turbidity: The cloudy or muddy appearance of a naturally clear liquid caused by the suspension of particulate matter.

typhoid (fever): An acute, highly infectious disease caused by the typhoid bacillus, Salmonella typhosa, transmitted by contaminated food or water and characterized by rashes, high fever, bronchitis and intestinal hemorrhaging.

ultraviolet light: Similar to light produced by the sun; produced by special lamps. As organisms are exposed to this light, they are damaged or killed.

unconfined aquifer: An aquifer without a confining layer above it; the top surface of water in an unconfined aquifer is the water table.

unsaturated zone: An area underground between the ground surface and the water table where the pore spaces are not filled with water, also know as the zone of aeration.

wastewater: Water that has been used for domestic or industrial purposes.

wastewater treatment: Physical, chemical and biological processes used to remove pollutants from wastewater before discharging it into a water body.

waterborne disease: A disease spread by contaminated water.

water table: The upper surface of the zone of saturation of ground-water.

zone of saturation: The layer beneath the surface of the land in which all soil openings are filled with water. Represents the top of the water table.

About the Author

Homer C. Emery holds a Ph.D. in Environmental Science from the University of Oklahoma and is a Diplomate of the American Academy of Sanitarians and a Registered Sanitarian in Texas, Oklahoma and Maryland.

The author, a public health sanitarian, is shown checking nitrate levels in water sample collected from a rural homeowner's new well. See Chapter 5 for more information on nitrate and other pollutants of concern in rural groundwater supplies.

Mr. Emery is a Senior Environmental Scientist with a major water utility and a public health consultant in southwestern Texas. With over 30 years of experience as an environmental and public health professional in local, state and federal agencies, he has penned more than 50 articles on environmental health, rural water supply and on-site sewage disposal systems in industry and consumer publications.

Mr. Emery resides in San Antonio, Texas.